Applied Sociology

NEIL THOMPSON

 Routledge
Taylor & Francis Group

NEW YORK AND LONDON

First published 2018
by Routledge
711 Third Avenue, New York, NY 10017

and by Routledge
2 Park Square, Milton Park, Abingdon, Oxon, OX14 4RN

Routledge is an imprint of the Taylor & Francis Group, an Informa business

Library of Congress Cataloging-in-Publication Data
A catalog record for this book has been requested

ISBN: 978-1-138-62969-1 (hbk)
ISBN: 978-1-138-62970-7 (pbk)
ISBN: 978-1-315-21026-1 (ebk)

Typeset in Avenir and Dante
by Apex CoVantage, LLC

Printed in the United Kingdom
by Henry Ling Limited

Applied Sociology

Sociology offers fascinating insights into social life that tell us so much about people and society. But what can we do with those insights? How can we put them to good use? That is exactly what this book is all about. It explores the *practical* value of sociology, how sociological understanding can be of help in a variety of settings.

Neil Thompson's wealth of experience in using sociology in practice comes shining through in this clearly written and accessible text that succeeds in conveying complex ideas without oversimplifying them. Key concepts are explained and clear links are drawn with how the ideas can be used to inform professional practice and cast light on a wide range of situations across all sectors of working life, and in our personal lives too.

So, whether you are involved in the helping professions or any other occupation where success depends on having a good understanding of people; a student of sociology wanting to put your learning into practice; or simply interested in how sociology can help address social issues, this book offers a solid foundation of understanding. It is an ideal text for anyone seeking to use sociological ideas to make a positive difference.

Neil Thompson PhD, DLitt, is an independent writer and educator with over 40 years' experience in the people professions. He is a sought-after consultant and international conference speaker, and is currently involved in developing a range of online learning resources and surveys. His website and blog are at www.neilthompson.info.

For Jason

Contents

Preface

"Sociology is just common sense made difficult" is a refrain I have heard many times over the years. It highlights the significant gap between common (mis)perceptions of sociology and the actual reality. Part of the reason for this gap is that we are constantly immersed in society and have developed an understanding of it from an early age. Unless they already have a background in nuclear physics, anyone picking up a book on that subject is likely to be starting largely from scratch, with few preconceptions. However, anyone coming to sociology for the first time will already have some well-established understandings—implicitly at least—of what society is all about and how it operates.

This has a tendency to create (at least) two sets of problems:

- *Inaccuracy* The understandings developed will often be inaccurate. For example, it is commonly assumed that women talk more than men. However, as we shall see in Chapter 7, the reality is far more complex than this. Such inaccuracies are not just technical matters of minor significance; they can affect how we relate to one another and decisions we make about the circumstances we find ourselves in.
- *Overgeneralization* Something that may be perfectly true and accurate in one context may not apply in other contexts. If, however, that "truth" is overextended to apply across the board, difficulties may arise. For example, what is considered "good manners" varies from culture to culture. What is deemed acceptable in one culture may be regarded as offensive in another. Mistakenly seeing someone else's culture as "deficient", rather than just different, can therefore be a recipe for (unnecessary) conflict and strife.

Sociology, then, is not "common sense made difficult," but it does involve questioning what counts as common sense in order to highlight the power and impact of taken-for-granted assumptions. That can be difficult at times, as it involves an element of "unlearning" parts of what we have been taught through our upbringing, but the rewards are certainly worth it. This is because sociology helps us to see society in a new light, to appreciate the complex processes and interactions that are going on all around us that normally fade into the background, like the wallpaper.

Seeing society in a new light can be not only fascinating and exciting, but also very useful—helping us to develop a much fuller and broader understanding of people; the social contexts in which people live and work, struggle and thrive; the problems we face and the potential solutions; and the opportunities to make a positive difference to society and to human well-being. It is no exaggeration to say that sociology can profoundly change our outlook on life. This is because we grow up with a range of filters—we are taught to notice certain things and pay them attention, while disregarding other things that are made to seem of little or no importance. For example, we are generally encouraged to see life and society in individualistic terms, to conceive of society as a collection of individuals. However, sociology teaches us that individuals are important, but they are just one part of the story. There are also groups, collectivities, structures, processes and a myriad other things that are highly important elements of our experience.

Sociology allows us to put those filters to one side while we examine society more closely. Of course, we cannot keep those filters to one side, as we are part of society, but by being aware that they are there and "suspending" their use temporarily, we can become aware of some fascinating and very important insights that open up new vistas. This is particularly significant when we focus on *applied* sociology, as these insights and these vistas mean that we can have a much fuller picture of the situations we are dealing with.

Another key element of sociology is its role in *questioning* aspects of society and social life. It is a process of *critical* questioning—that is, looking critically at whatever aspect of society we are focusing on. But this is where another common misconception of sociology can arise. There is a significant difference between *critique* (questioning taken-for-granted assumptions) and *criticism* (adopting a negative attitude, attacking). Adopting a critically questioning approach is a key part of how sociology manages to open up new vistas. But that is far removed from the much narrower idea of "criticizing" society.

Sociological study will often highlight aspects of society that are problematic in one or more ways, and different theorists may come up with different explanations of what is involved. So, there will be times when sociology is critical in the everyday sense of criticizing, but we need to be aware that this is not what is meant when we talk about *critical* sociology, *critical* analysis or *critical* practices. The emphasis needs to be on questioning, on not taking things at face value, and that is what can make sociology as an *applied* undertaking so valuable and worthwhile.

Socrates, it is claimed, argued that the unexamined life is not worth living. While that may be something of an exaggeration, it is certainly the case that sociology can enrich our understanding (and our potential for benefiting practically from that understanding). Sociology sets about examining life and, more specifically, the social elements of life so that we can be better informed to rise to the challenges we face—individually and collectively—in the modern world.

In this sense, sociology has much to offer everyone. However, where it really comes into its own is for those people whose profession involves them in working with people and their problems, whether that be in a health care context, in addressing social problems, tackling organizational and workplace problems or whatever. If your work (or the line of work you intend to pursue) involves the three Ps (people, problems and potential—to be discussed further in the Introduction), sociological understanding can help to equip you to support those people, address those problems and realize that potential. Sociology does not offer magic answers, but what it can provide is a strong foundation of understanding and a critically questioning approach that can be put to very good use in addressing a wide variety of human problems and challenges.

Once we put our filters to one side we start to see a fascinating, amazing world of complex processes, structures, interactions, institutions and so much more, we become alive to the possibilities sociology offers—not only as an intellectual pursuit, but also as basis for informed practice in a variety of work settings. Without those filters we see a dynamic, constantly changing and evolving world and recognize the possibilities for acting upon that world, for building on the advantages it offers and addressing its problems and challenges. That is the beauty of applied sociology.

Acknowledgments

Many people play a part in the production of a book, and this is my opportunity to express my thanks to the main people who have contributed to this one. I am grateful to Dean Birkenkamp and Amanda Yee at Routledge for their support and enthusiasm for this project. I am also grateful to their colleague, Anna Moore, for putting me in touch with Dean in the first place.

I have been fortunate to receive practical support from two very capable young women, Anna Thompson and Gem Jones. In addition, as with all my work, I am deeply indebted to Dr. Sue Thompson who makes such a positive difference in so many ways.

About the Author

Neil Thompson, PhD, DLitt, teaches on the online MSc Advanced Practice in the Human Services at Wrexham Glyndŵr University in north Wales. He is also an independent writer and consultant, having previously held full or honorary professorships at four UK universities. He has over 40 years' experience in the helping professions as a practitioner, manager, educator, consultant and author.

He has 39 books to his name. These include:

Power and Empowerment (Russell House Publishing, 2007)
The Palgrave Social Work Companion (with Sue Thompson, 2nd edn., 2016)
People Management (Palgrave Macmillan, 2013)
People Skills (Palgrave, 4th edn., 2015)
Understanding Social Work (Palgrave, 4th edn., 2015)
The Authentic Leader (Palgrave, 2016)
Anti-discriminatory Practice (Palgrave, 6th edn., 2016)
Social Problems and Social Justice (Palgrave, 2017)
Theorizing Practice (Palgrave, 2nd edn., 2017)
Handbook of the Sociology of Death, Grief, and Bereavement (co-editor with Gerry Cox, Routledge, 2017)
Promoting Equality: Working with Diversity and Difference (Palgrave, 4th edn., 2018)
The Critically Reflective Practitioner (with Sue Thompson, Palgrave, 2nd edn., 2018)
Effective Communication (Palgrave, *3rd edn., 2018*)

He is a Fellow of the Chartered Institute of Personnel and Development and the Higher Education Academy and a Life Fellow of the Royal Society of Arts and the Institute of Welsh Affairs.

Neil is a sought-after conference speaker who has presented in the United Kingdom, the United States, Ireland, Italy, Spain, Greece, Norway, the Netherlands, the Czech Republic, Turkey, India, Hong Kong, Canada and Australia. In 2011 he was presented with a Lifetime Achievement Award by BASW Cymru (the Wales branch of the British Association of Social Workers). In 2014 he was presented with the Dr. Robert Fulton Award for excellence in the field of Death, Dying and Bereavement from the Center for Death Education and Bioethics at the University of Wisconsin-La Crosse.

He has qualifications in social work, training and development, mediation and alternative dispute resolution and management (MBA), as well as a first-class honors degree, a doctorate (PhD) and a higher doctorate (DLitt). His website and blog are at www.neilthompson.info, where you can also connect with him on social media.

Introduction

This book has been developed to offer a foundation in sociological thought, outlining many of the various concepts and themes that have developed through social research and theoretical analysis. It emphasizes the significance of making use of a sociological perspective as a basis for professional practice in a wide range of occupational settings. It covers some of the early thought that established sociology as an academic discipline, while also addressing a number of contemporary issues and debates. As the emphasis is on *applied* sociology, this material is presented in a clear and accessible style, with numerous practice illustrations, self-test questions and exercises designed to bring the ideas to life.

My intention in writing the book was to offer a helpful text that:

- Clarifies what sociology is and why it is important.
- Discusses key concepts, themes and issues in classical and contemporary sociological thinking.
- Makes links between the theory and the practice implications associated with sociological thinking.
- Identifies the dangers of narrow, individualistic approaches to practice that do not take account of the often vitally important role of wider social factors.
- Encourages you to adopt a sociological approach to your professional practice and/or helps you to consider a career where sociological insights can be used.

I present sociological thought as an essential underpinning of professional practice, but I also emphasize that the insights it offers need to be understood as additions to those offered by other disciplines (psychology, law, social policy and so on), rather than as replacements for them—complementary, rather than competing.

Who Is the Book For?

This book should be of interest to two broad groups of people. First, for students undertaking a degree in sociology, social science or applied social studies, it should provide a picture of: (i) a range of occupational settings where sociological understanding can be of significant value; and (ii) a wealth of food for thought to serve as the basis of a broader and more holistic grasp of the key issues in those work settings. As such, it should be of value for present studies and future career development. Second, students, practitioners and managers involved in a number of work roles where success depends on *people* will find considerable evidence of how a sociological approach is necessary for an adequate understanding of the complexities involved when it comes to working with people and their problems. So, whether it is the caring professions (health care; social work; counseling and so on); public protection; education and training; management and human resources; or any other aspect of commerce, industry or public service, if having a good understanding of *people* and being able to interact effectively with them is a requirement of the job, sociology can be of great value.

The Three Ps: People, Problems and Potential

A major theme throughout my career has been problem solving. One of the things I have learned is that problems are *normal*, in the sense that they are part and parcel of everyday life. They can range from relatively minor to life changing or even life threatening. It is not realistic to imagine a world or a life without problems, of course—hence the idea that, wherever there are people, there will be problems. However, what I have also learned is that, wherever there are problems, there is potential. That is, people experiencing problems can:

- Find new solutions and extend their repertoire of coping methods;
- Learn from the experience;
- Develop their confidence in problem solving;

- Change their attitude and/or approach;
- Attract helpful support; and
- Be better equipped for any future occurrences of that problem or similar ones.

From this we get the idea of the 3P model: where there are **p**eople, there will be **p**roblems, but there will also be **p**otential. But, you may be thinking, how does this relate to sociology? The answer is that sociology can cast light on a wide range of human problems. Unfortunately, there is a very strong tendency to individualize people's problems—that is, to assume that the problem lies within the individual. For example, stress is often assumed to be the sign of someone who is "not coping," someone who is perhaps weak or even inadequate. The focus tends to be on *psychological* factors (Thompson, 2015a). However, while psychological factors no doubt have a role to play, it is a mistake to assume that they are the only aspects of the situation that need to be considered. In reality, there will also be *sociological* factors to take into account. To continue with the example of stress, the following sociological issues could be very relevant:

- The organizational culture—Does it help or does it hinder? For example, is there a culture of low morale, negativity and cynicism that feeds stress?
- Power relations—Is there any bullying or harassment going on? Are people in positions of power abusing or misusing that power?
- Leadership—Are employees made to feel safe, valued and supported or does poor or nonexistent leadership add to the existing pressures and leave people feeling vulnerable and insecure?
- Are there gender- or ethnicity-related tensions that are adding to the pressures?
- Are some staff under additional pressure because they are being asked to undertake tasks that run counter to their religion, moral beliefs or social expectations?
- Are problems arising or being exacerbated because of poor communication systems?

Focusing narrowly or exclusively on individual factors is therefore likely to: (i) not provide a complete picture of the situation and therefore block off potential routes to solutions or at least an alleviation of the situation; and (ii) "blame the victim"—that is, unfairly regard people as the architects of their own distress or difficulties (Ryan, 1988). Both of these possibilities (especially in combination) can contribute to a worsening of the situation, which means that efforts to help can prove counterproductive (see the discussion of "counterfinality" in Thompson, 2017a).

In my writings over the years I have frequently used the term "psychosocial" to emphasize that, in order to understand human behavior, reactions and interactions, we need to incorporate psychological *and* sociological factors. This book has been written to counterbalance the common tendency to focus mainly, if not exclusively, on individualistic, psychological factors and thereby miss or distort the immense significance of the social context. Here I have used stress as an example, as it lends itself well to a psychosocial analysis. However, as we shall see throughout the book, sociology can offer useful insights into human problems in general—stress is just one example.

Where there are **p**eople, there will be sociological issues to consider, as human beings are "social animals". Where there are **p**roblems, sociology can help us explore wider solutions and prevent the problem of "blaming the victim." But, what is also important to recognize is that sociology can also help to realize **p**otential—that is, it can open up new vistas that a narrow, individualistic focus can conceal. For example, people with low self-esteem as a result of being downtrodden by poverty can be helped, through a sociological analysis, to understand that poverty is a wider sociopolitical matter and not simply a sign that they are inadequate or unworthy. Similarly, managers can be helped to think holistically by adopting a sociological perspective, so that they are better placed to understand wider organizational dynamics and not have to rely on a distorted individualistic perspective.

Theory and Practice

There is a major emphasis on linking theory to practice in many quarters. A fundamental principle on which it is based is that theory without practice is useless, while practice without theory is dangerous (Langan and Lee, 1989). Sociology provides an important basis of understanding for the complex web of factors that can so often have a significant bearing on the circumstances we encounter in working with people and their problems. Without that theoretical understanding we are placing ourselves in what could be highly complex and demanding situations with only a very limited grasp of key issues, such as power dynamics, patterns of conflict, communication (helps and hindrances), cultural norms and so on. This book is therefore firmly premised on a recognition of the importance of theory as an underpinning of practice.

In an earlier work (Thompson, 2017b), I emphasized the importance of "theorizing practice." The traditional approach to the relationship between theory and practice is characterized by the notion of "applying theory to practice." This is based on the idea that we should begin with theory and then explore how it can be used to fit the practice situations we encounter. The "theorizing practice" approach challenges this and argues that it is wiser and more effective to begin with practice and draw on our professional knowledge base (theory) as and when required—we tailor the knowledge we need to draw upon to suit the specific circumstances. This latter approach is what informs this book. I do not expect you to learn a great deal of theory and then feel stuck when it comes to "applying theory to practice." Rather, I want to encourage you to start with a concrete, real-life practice situation and then reflect carefully on how sociological themes, issues and concepts can cast light on aspects of that situation. To help you with this I will, from time to time, provide a "practice focus" illustration—that is, a short cameo of practice to help you to see links between theory and practice.

This focus on theorizing practice is particularly important in relation to the *applied* emphasis of the book. Very many people will study sociology, whether formally via an academic institution or informally under their own steam, and find the subject matter enjoyable and stimulating, but not feel able to do anything with the knowledge gained. They file their study experience under the heading of "interesting," but not under the heading of "useful." Returning to the idea mentioned above that theory without practice is useless, what I am trying to do in this book is highlight how sociological ideas and frameworks are not just interesting background information; they are also useful insights that can be of great value in the real world of business, public service and everyday social life. The aim, then, is to be able to file sociological understanding under the heading of "interesting *and* useful."

Should Sociology Be an Applied Discipline?

Obviously, in a book with the title, *Applied Sociology*, my answer is going to be yes. However, we should note that not all sociologists would accept that as an answer. Some would see sociology as a value-free science that should not get involved in social policy, politics or real-life social challenges. Many others may not have given the matter much thought, preferring to press on in their own particular niche of theory and/or research without paying more than cursory attention to how sociological insights can be used in pragmatic ways.

In 2005, the president of the American Sociological Association raised the important question of whether sociology should have more of a "public" face—that is, should be more fully engaged in helping to make positive differences in society through the use of sociological understanding (Buroway, 2005). His emphasis on the need for a "public" sociology was well received, but was not without its critics. Similarly, some sociologists have sought to develop a "clinical" sociology to explore how sociological insights can be of value in the helping professions (Jaeckel, 1991). And, indeed, social work has been drawing on sociological insights for many years, as have other professional disciplines.

So, it is by no means unanimous that sociology should be used in an applied way, but as the chapters that make up this book should readily testify, there is certainly a strong case for promoting more and better use of sociology in a wide range of settings. Steele, Scarisbrick-Hauser and Hauser share my enthusiasm for sociology as a tool for informed social action, rather than just as a tool of understanding for its own case:

> Today, applied sociology crosses a number of dimensions. It is a way of taking many of the areas of the sociological endeavor and giving them real-world applications. Through its involvement with a wide range of community, business and governmental audiences, applied sociology provides the discipline with opportunities for further growth and development. It is also a way for students to view and better understand the foundations of the discipline and its practical uses in their own unique social environments.
>
> *(1999, pp. xi–xii)*

Structure of the Book

The book is divided into three parts. Part One sets the scene by clarifying what sociology is and, in particular, the role and importance of what is known as "the sociological imagination." The two chapters in Part One therefore provide a firm foundation of understanding on which to build.

Part Two is much larger, with six chapters in total. Part Two is organized around the "SPIDER" framework (to reflect the "web" of society that sociology is concerned with). Chapters 3 to 8 therefore cover, in turn, social:

- Structures
- Processes
- Institutions
- Discourses
- Expectations
- Relations

Each of these elements reflects a key component or dimension of social life. The respective chapters identify central concepts relating to the area concerned and explain how these ideas can be used to make sense of practice (that is, as an aid to "theorizing" practice).

Part Three focuses on different areas of working life that sociology can cast light upon. Chapter 9 concentrates on examining individuals in their social context. It warns of the dangers of focusing too narrowly on individual factors and thereby not paying sufficient attention to the wider cultural and structural contexts in which those individual factors operate.

Chapter 10 examines the range of organizational factors that affect the workplace across various settings. "Organizational psychology" is a popular and helpful field of study, but this can usefully be supplemented by a *sociological* analysis of organizational life. The organizational context can—and generally does—have a major influence on working practices.

Chapter 11 is entitled "Holistic Practice," by which I mean forms of practice that look at the "big picture," approaches to professional practice that cannot be criticized for being too narrowly focused or too partial in their compass. This final chapter in effect pulls together important messages from the earlier discussions and thereby serves as a useful guide to how you can make the most of what applied sociology offers in whatever career path you choose to pursue.

It is to be hoped that each of these chapters, and indeed the book as a whole, will offer you a foundation for developing a fuller understanding of how sociology offers an important—indeed, a vital—component of the professional knowledge base needed by anyone whose work involves working with people; seeking to address their problems; and attempting to maximize their potential.

PART ONE

Making Sense of Sociology

Introduction to Part One

Part One comprises two chapters. In the first I address the question of "What is sociology?" This is to make sure that we are on the same wavelength when it comes to discussing applied sociology—that is, that we are clear what it is that we are applying. This will include a brief historical overview and a consideration of how sociology can be useful in an applied sense. Finally, the chapter explores some of the groups of people who are likely to find sociological insights of value.

Chapter 2 builds on the discussion in Chapter 1, with the theme of "the sociological imagination," the distinctive way of seeing the world through a critical and holistic sociological lens. This includes a discussion of the key concept of "social construction," which then leads into a discussion of ideology, discourse and "common sense." This in turn leads into a discussion of "praxis," the fusion of theory and practice as a basis for applied sociology.

Together these two chapters provide a foundation for Part Two, where we focus on six specific aspects of the "web" of society.

What Is Sociology? 1

Introduction

In this chapter our focus is on establishing a firm baseline of understanding by clarifying precisely what we mean by sociology and establishing why it is important to use sociology as an underpinning of our work across a wide range of occupational settings. We also look at sociology, albeit in broad outline only, from a sociological perspective in order to appreciate how sociological thought has developed to reach the current point where it offers excellent potential for casting very helpful light on so many different aspects of human experience.

In order to demonstrate the value of *applied* sociology, we will also look at who uses sociology, who are the people in their respective work settings who can benefit from thinking sociologically about the circumstances they find themselves in and the challenges they face.

Defining Sociology

Definitions can be problematic because they often involve trying to fit a great deal of information into just a few lines of text. For complex concepts like sociology, that can generate more confusion than clarity. I am therefore going to "explore" a definition, rather than just present one. I will begin with a very common definition of sociology as: "The scientific study of society." Superficially, that sounds straightforward enough, but, in reality, apart from "of," each word in this definition needs to be carefully considered:

- *The* This implies that there is just one, definitive version of sociology, a neat consensus. In actual fact, sociology comprises a diverse range of ideas and approaches. It is a vibrant multiplicity of perspectives, although there is also much common ground, of course. None the less, it would be a mistake to assume that sociology is uniform or standardized or speaks with one voice. Also, it is important to acknowledge that sociology is not the only social science—there is also anthropology, economics, political science and so on.

- *Scientific* Early versions of sociology tried to mimic the natural sciences and their methods—what came to be known as a "positivist" approach. However, this approach has proven to be unsuitable, because the subject matter covered by sociology (people) does not work the same way as the subject matter of the natural sciences (nature) does. The natural sciences base their work on the objective study of natural, relatively regular processes. With sociology (and the other social sciences), it is much more complex: there are subjective factors, such as patterns of meaning (as we shall see), that play a significant part; social processes interact with choices made ("agency," to use the technical term) to produce less predictable outcomes; and various other complicating factors. We need to recognize, therefore, that, in the social sciences, we use the term "scientific" in a slightly different sense from the natural sciences. Some people prefer to avoid confusion by not using the term "scientific" at all and use the term "systematic" instead.

- *Study* Sociologists do indeed engage in study—for example, through various forms of empirical research. However—and this is particularly significant for our present purposes—it is important to be fully aware that sociology is also an *applied* discipline. It is not simply a matter of studying society for its own sake. There is also an important role for sociology to inform efforts to address problems and contribute to social amelioration (tackle social problems; improve working life; reduce conflict and so on). We shall return to this point below.

- *Society* Sociology does, of course, involve studying "society," but we need to recognize that the term "society" is a shorthand. We have to be careful not to assume that "society" is a single, monolithic entity. "Society" is a convenient shorthand for, among other things: social structures, processes, institutions, discourses, expectations and relations (hence the SPIDER model). This helps us to realize just how complex and multidimensional "society" is. So, there is no problem with using the term "society," provided that we do not allow it to seduce us into thinking that what we are dealing with is simple and straightforward.

A basic premise of sociology is that all human activity takes place within a social context. A basic premise of *applied* sociology is that failing to consider that social context at best gives us only a partial picture of what we are dealing with and, at worst, significantly exacerbates the problems we are seeking to address and/or introduces new problems.

Practice Focus 1.1

Nia was a human resources adviser in a large retail organization. She was asked to interview Karen, one of the sales assistants about her poor and deteriorating attendance record. Karen had taken much more sick leave than anyone else in the company and had been late for work on a number of occasions too. Nia's manager told her that she would need to impress upon Karen that this level of absence and poor punctuality would not be tolerated any more. With this in mind, Nia began the interview with a clear focus on "laying down the law"—in a polite and friendly way, but none the less quite firmly. However, things did not go according to plan. Once Nia started to broach the issues, Karen became quite tearful and was shortly in floods of tears. Karen started to explain that she had been experiencing extensive domestic violence—both physical and emotional abuse. There had been times when she was so emotionally drained by the experience that she could not face coming into work. In particular, the thought that she would have to be friendly and smiling to all and sundry when inside her heart was broken and she was feeling extremely vulnerable and fragile was just too much. Nia was so shocked by what she heard that she decided to look up domestic violence as a subject. She was amazed to find out just how common the problem is and how much harm it could do. She was particularly interested in what she read about "emotional labor," the expectation that certain people need to display particular emotions as part of their job, even if that does not fit with their actual emotional state. She recognized that this was exactly what Karen had been struggling with.

The Role of Meaning

One of the things that separates sociology from the natural sciences is that a key element of what sociology is concerned with is *meaning*. As human beings, we do not simply act according to the objective circumstances we encounter. We act according to how we *interpret* those circumstances—what they mean to us. Although meaning is often conceived of as an individual, psychological matter, it is, in fact doubly sociological, in the sense that:

(i) social interactions rest on meanings—for example, conflict often arises as a result of differing interpretations of an action or attitude; and

(ii) meanings themselves arise from social sources—for example, language is necessarily social in nature; similarly, symbols and gestures and other "markers" of meaning are culture specific and therefore social.

The role of meanings—how they arise and how they affect people ("social actors," to use the technical term)—is therefore something that we will return to at various points in the book.

The study of meaning is known as "hermeneutics." Renowned sociologist, Zygmunt Bauman, writes about "sociological hermeneutics." As he explains:

> It consists in the interpretation of human choices as manifestations of strategies constructed in response to the challenges of the socially shaped situation and where one has been placed in it. Human choices are not more determined—though no less either—than the moves of card players are determined by the cards in their hand. A placing in a situation manipulates the distribution of possibilities. It sets apart moves that are feasible from those that are not, and the more probable from the less probable. But it never eliminates choice altogether.
>
> *(2014, pp. 50–51)*

This passage highlights one of the important principles of sociology (the need to take account of the role of the social context), but also recognizes the significance of choice (human agency). A common misunderstanding of sociology is that it is based on the idea that people have no control over their lives, that they are just "puppets" of their circumstances. While a minority of sociologists have put forward deterministic ideas that leave little or no room for agency, it is now widely recognized that sociology needs to account for both the social context and our response to it—see the discussion of structuration theory in Chapter 3.

Bauman goes on to clarify the concept further:

> The postulate of '*sociological* hermeneutics' demands that whenever we pursue the meaning of human thoughts or actions we ought to look into the socially shaped conditions of people whose thoughts or actions we intend to

understand/explain. In other words, the hermeneutics of human conduct is primarily a sociological, not a semantic or philological operation.

(2014, p. 52)

Although meanings are personal in many ways, we should not lose sight of the fact that they are also sociological—that is, they can best be understood as *psychosocial*. When it comes to applied sociology, then, we will need to make sure that we do not lose sight of the central role of (social) meanings.

The "Social Animal"

The idea that we are "social animals" is well established, but so very often the emphasis is on the animal element of the phrase, and once again the social element is relegated to simply a matter of background. Sociology can be defined, in part, as a process of drawing out the implications of being a *social* animal. It does not detract from the fact that we are animals—mammals, to be more specific—but animals *in a social context*; and that social context is much more than just a backdrop for our primarily animal behavior. The social context is important because:

- It brings a set of highly powerful influences and constraints—for example, sexual attraction is a biological phenomenon, but it is: (i) influenced by social factors (cultural variations on who or what is considered attractive; sexual stimulus through pornography; and so on); and (ii) constrained by social factors (manners; courting etiquette; laws against rape and other forms of sexual abuse; and so on).
- Sexuality is filtered through social norms and expectations—consider, for example, how, in some societies or cultures, sex before marriage is frowned upon; adultery may lead to being stoned to death; and same-sex relationships are considered as manifestation of illness.
- Attitudes to sexuality change over time, as society changes—consider, for example, how, in Victorian times, sexuality was seen as a taboo subject, but is now spoken and written about much more freely.

Similar points could be made about various other aspects of what are perceived as reflections of our "animal nature." For example, the need to curb and penalize "natural" aggressive tendencies is widely accepted in peace time, but there is a different attitude towards human aggression in times of war. So, animals we may be, but focusing primarily or exclusively on the animal aspects once again gives a very incomplete and misleading picture of the situation.

While being "social" is a common feature of the animal world, we need to acknowledge that, in human terms, the social elements are far more complex, far more significant, and potentially far more problematic. Contrast, for example, the relative simplicity of the "social" nature of worker ants who collaborate in achieving various tasks with the hugely complex nature of modern society, with its multiplicity of cultures, ideologies, political systems; its globalized economic systems; its international music and arts scene; an international network of sporting competitions; its extensive use of social media and other forms of technological communications; and so on. In many ways, it is these complexities that distinguish humanity from the other animals.

Harari argues that the highly evolved social nature of human existence has enabled huge advances, leading to very important achievements:

> If you tried to bunch together thousands of chimpanzees into Tiananmen Square, Wall Street, the Vatican or the headquarters of the United Nations, the result would be pandemonium. By contrast, [Homo] Sapiens regularly gather by the thousands in such places. Together, they create orderly patterns—such as trade networks, mass celebrations and political institutions—that they could never have created in isolation. The real difference between us and chimpanzees is the mythical glue that binds together large numbers of individuals, families and groups. This glue has made us the masters of creation.
>
> *(2011, p. 42)*

That glue is, of course, an important feature of social functioning and thus of sociology.

Voice of Experience 1.1

When I did my professional training it was hammered home to us that I needed to be sensitive to what the tutor called "the space between people." What he meant by that was the subtle and complex ways in which people interact and influence each other. I could see that the idea was applicable across the board as far as people were concerned, but I could also see how it especially related to the young people I was working with. I could see just how important peer pressure was at that time when they were trying to let go of their childhood, but weren't quite adults yet. I also saw how devastating it was when some of the young people were rejected by their peers. How people relate to one another can be incredibly positive and helpful, but at times, it can also be so destructive.

Jay, a youth worker

Harari also points out that it is this social glue that has also helped us to survive—for example, to work together to develop food production systems; housing; health care systems; educational facilities; and so on. It is also true, of course, that this glue has enabled us to work together to kill billions of people through warfare, enslave millions of people against their will after having forcibly uprooted them from their home country; and to do untold damage to our habitat through environmental exploitation for financial gain and the associated power.

So, we are indeed animals and subject to "natural" forces and constraints, but because we are also social beings, we are also able to transcend our animal nature, our biology, and achieve much more than other animals can do—for good or ill. Part of applied sociology is a focus on trying to minimize the ill effects and maximize the positive ones.

Beyond Psychology

Another common misunderstanding of sociology is that it somehow stands in opposition to psychology, as if psychology is some sort of competitor or enemy. It is important that we dispel this myth. Sociology does not seek to deny or invalidate matters of individual psychology. Rather, it is concerned with counterbalancing the individual focus with a concern for the role of the wider social context, with its influences, constraints and "filtering" effect, as discussed above. As we have just noted, sociology does not deny the role of biology in human life, but does seek to counterbalance it with a consideration of the key role of social factors, and thereby go beyond, or transcend, biology. Similarly, it does not set out to deny or invalidate psychological insights, but, rather, seeks to transcend these too.

The technical term for focusing on individual matters and neglecting the wider social picture is "atomism." It is a philosophical term that refers to approaches that have a narrow individualistic focus and pay little or no attention to contextual factors. An atomistic approach is the opposite of a holistic one. "Holism" refers to approaches that seek to see the big picture, to look widely rather than narrowly on human affairs.

A good example of atomism is identity. Traditionally we have tended to think in terms of personality as a relatively fixed entity, implying that our sense of self is stable and consistent. However, sociology helps us to appreciate that this is an oversimplification of a much more complex set of social processes. Identity can be understood to be:

- Interactive—emerging from our interactions with others (from birth and throughout our lives);
- Rooted in social processes, discourses and structures—for example, relating to gender and ethnicity (to be discussed in later chapters);
- Dynamic, constantly evolving over time—while there may well be considerable continuity, there are always elements of change also; as individuals we grow and develop over time;
- Subject to outside social forces—for example, through stigma; and
- Different in different circumstances—this reflects the idea of "managed identity," the various ways in which we adapt and adjust our sense of self depending on the circumstances we find ourselves in.

Even something as personal and unique as our identity, our sense of self, is also sociological, rooted in the wider social context and, in effect, inextricable from it. These are such important issues that Chapter 9 focuses on their significance in some detail. But for now what I want to emphasize is that these issues are extremely important when it comes to applied sociology. For example, if we assume that people are not capable of change, that they just "are who they are," then opportunities for positive change, empowerment and learning will be sealed off. The recognition of the fluid, social nature of identity is therefore a central plank of applied sociology.

Critical Thinking

One further aspect of sociology that we need to be aware of is its use of critical thinking. The term "critical" can be used in three main senses:

(i) Related to a crisis, a turning point—for example, when someone is critically ill;

(ii) Negative towards, as in "Chris was critical of Sam's approach"; and

(iii) Questioning, not taking things at face value.

It is in this third sense that it is used in sociology and, indeed in the social sciences more broadly. Sociology helps us to look beneath the surface, to cut through stereotypes and ideology (see Chapter 6). Power is exercised through, among other things, the use of language, and so, in order not to be "taken in" by power plays, we need to look critically at what is said and done—that is, we need to adopt a questioning approach. A critical approach is also part of being holistic, of looking at the big picture, rather than focusing narrowly on certain areas that may give us a distorted perception.

Thompson and Thompson (2008) write about "critical breadth" and "critical depth." By critical breadth, they mean the need to look broadly at situations, to take account of the social context and the significant role it generally plays. By critical depth, they mean the ability to look beneath the surface and look at the underlying dynamics, processes that can be very significant—for example: discrimination, marginalization or stigmatization (see Chapter 4).

Sociology, as a critical endeavor, can therefore be characterized as an approach to human experience that involves questioning hidden processes and locating these and other factors in their wider social context. In this regard, it is an antidote to "atomism," the constant tendency to reduce complex, multilevel situations to a narrow range of individual factors.

Historical Overview

In trying to make sense of sociology it can be helpful to think of it from a historical perspective. Although philosophers had studied various aspects of social life back to the ancient Greeks and even beyond, society was generally not a major focus and, significantly, social life was not studied systematically (or what we might today call "scientifically"). As you would expect of philosophers, the focus was on reflection and contemplation, rather than necessarily on building theories that could be tested empirically through research. The contribution of Auguste Comte (1798–1857) was therefore very significant, because he wanted to found a *scientific* study *of society*. He wanted to establish sociology alongside the natural sciences as a prestigious and credible discipline, because it would be *rigorous*, it would follow the established scientific method. He valued to some extent what social philosophy could offer, but he felt that more than this was needed.

Historically, the reception of Comte's contribution has been mixed. On the one hand, his influence in establishing sociology in the first place has been immense. He is generally regarded as one of the "founding fathers" of sociology (although it is ironic that sociology, as a discipline that questions unhelpful social orthodoxies, should use the gender-specific term, founding *fathers*, thereby contributing to women's scholarship in this area being marginalized—see Allan, 2017). Despite his beneficial influence, however, we also need to consider how his *positivist* emphasis was not so positive. His view that the methods of the natural sciences could also be applied equally well to the social sciences has proven to be highly problematic. We now have a much clearer view that, while rigorous, systematic investigation and empirical research have an invaluable role to play, we have to move away from the idea that we can simply transfer natural science methods into the social sciences (Gergen, 2009). We now have various *social* scientific methods that are of value, but which are not used in the natural sciences: qualitative methods; phenomenological methods, life story approaches, ethnography, autoethnography and so on—see the *Guide to Further Learning* at the end of the book for further discussion of social science research methods. These methods are part of what can make sociology useful as an applied discipline. For example, sociological research can be used in a variety of work settings to inform policy development on important issues to allow decision makers to be operating on a more informed basis.

We cannot really discuss the history of sociology without including reference to Émile Durkheim (1858–1917). For many people Durkheim is synonymous with sociology, such has been the influence of his work on the development of sociology as a discipline. He made many major contributions, but I am going to focus briefly on just three of them here. Durkheim helped us to understand that:

- Suicide is a *social* phenomenon. Even something as personal and intimate as taking one's own life could be understood as a sociological matter. For example, he identified that there was a lower rate of suicides among Catholics than Protestants, which he attributed to the greater focus on discipline and control characteristic of the former group compared with the latter.
- Anomie is an important concept. It refers to a sense of "normlessness" that arises at times of rapid social change. As we shall see in Chapter 10, this is a concept that can be useful in making sense of reactions to change initiatives in organizations.
- "Social facts" have an important part to play in understanding social issues. The term refers to entities that exist above and beyond individuals (structures, norms and values, for example). These "supraindividual" entities may not exist in a direct concrete way, but they are none the less very real—they are "socially constructed" facts, but facts none the less, in the sense that they have very real, concrete consequences (we shall discuss "social construction" in Chapter 2). This reflects Durkheim's conception of society as "sui generis"—that is, something that exists in its own right. A society is not just the amalgamation of all the individuals

within it, it is something that, in a very real sense, has a life of its own (and we shall see how and why in later chapters).

Practice Focus 1.2

Andy was a team leader in a large office. He was pleased with the positive feedback he received at his annual appraisal. He even found the one note of criticism helpful. He was told that he was very good at relating to each individual staff member, but still had some development work to do in relation to how he managed the team as a whole. His manager recommended that he should go on a leadership course and learn more about influencing team culture. He didn't understand at first as he had just been praised for how well he interacted with each team member. However, his manager helped him by explaining: "Yes, you can relate well to individuals, but that's not the same as relating to the team as a whole. Have you heard of a Gestalt?" she said: "You know, the idea that the whole is greater than the sum of its parts. Leading a team involves different skills from supervising individuals," she added. Now it was starting to make sense. Andy was beginning to appreciate that a team is not just a collection of individuals—it is an entity in its own right and needs to be managed as such. Although his manager did not say so in so many words, she was helping Andy to understand that a team is a social fact in Durkheim's sense, as is leadership.

Both Comte and Durkheim helped establish sociology as a social science and earn it some degree of credibility and influence. They were not unaware of the potential applications of sociological understanding, but their primary focus was on science and theory development. It took the advent of Karl Marx in the sociological world for there to be a strong emphasis on sociology as an *applied* discipline, a discipline that could make a significant impact outside the world of science and academia.

Karl Marx (1818–1883) made important contributions to economics, political thought and sociology. In politics his thought had a major impact, although largely in a distorted form far removed from what he actually intended. So, in a sense, it was the distortions of his ideas that shaped the development of communism, rather than his actual ideas (Thompson, 2017c). Despite the very real problems associated with the distortions of his ideas that led to the development of oppressive totalitarian systems, his influence on sociology has been much more positive, in particular his emphasis on the role of social class in shaping social relations. But, what is of especial interest to us for present purposes is that he saw sociology as something that could have a positive impact on society. As he famously put it: "Philosophers have only interpreted the world, in various ways; the point, however, is to change it" (Marx, 1845, reprinted in Marx and Engels, 1968, p. 30). Writing in a time of severe poverty and major social problems, appalling working conditions, gross inequality and injustice and little or nothing by way of a governmental safety net, he was impassioned to bring about positive social change. For Marx, the role of sociology was not just social understanding, but also social amelioration. Marx and his ideas were therefore an important part of the historical picture in the development of applied sociology, although it has to be acknowledged that many sociologists reject Marx's theoretical ideas *and* his conception of sociology as a practical activity. However, there is now a growing recognition of the potential for sociology to step away from the idea of a value-free science and make a commitment to social change and improvement (Gergen, 2009). We shall return to this point below.

Another important figure in the development of sociology was Max Weber (1864–1920). He introduced some important concepts that have been very influential over time, and thereby played an important role in establishing sociology as a legitimate intellectual discipline. He shared an interest with Marx in the significance of socioeconomic class, but widened his analysis of class to incorporate such issues as status alongside income and financial capital. He became famous for drawing links between religious beliefs and expectations on the one hand (especially Protestantism) and economic structures and systems on the other (especially capitalism). However, what could arguably be seen as his most important contribution was his emphasis on social *action*. Action was seen as distinct from behavior, in the sense that behavior simply describes what people do—it can be directly observed and viewed objectively. Action, by contrast, is behavior plus meaning—that is, action seeks to go beneath the surface manifestations and try to understand the meanings associated with the behavior. For example, "Lee left the room" could be a straightforward description of Lee's behavior, witnessed objectively. To understand the behavior as action, by contrast, requires a focus on the meanings associated with the behavior. Put simply, behavior is about what Lee did, action is about what was happening *socially* in terms of what Lee did. When Lee walked out, was this:

- A storming out in disgust because of an offensive comment made by someone else?
- Lee needing to leave for a more pressing engagement?
- Going out for a short comfort break, with a view to returning shortly?

- Lee feeling unwell and needing to go home?
- A meeting where Lee was no longer needed as the agenda items concerning Lee had now been discussed?

In each of these cases the observable behavior may be objectively identical, but, when it comes to action and the meanings involved, we encounter a much more complex picture and one in which we have to take account of both subjective and objective factors.

I deliberately use the term meanings in the plural because it is quite likely that there will be different meanings attached to the behavior, different perceptions on the part of different people. Indeed, this is generally how misunderstandings and conflicts arise. Weber therefore laid down the foundations for sociology to focus on the meanings that connect individuals to their social context, the linking threads that shape in large part how we make sense of the social situations we find ourselves in.

These four "giants" stand out in the history of sociology, although they are by no means the only ones—other people played an important role too, but this brief overview should be sufficient to clarify some of the key strands of how sociology evolved into the discipline that it is today.

Before leaving the historical picture, however, we should also acknowledge a significant irony here, in so far as the people who played such a key role in developing our understanding of society and developing a critical approach to its workings are, as I mentioned earlier, generally referred to as the "founding fathers." Modern sociology has a strong emphasis on gender and the need to question "masculinist" assumptions (that is, assumptions that both reflect and reinforce damaging and limiting gender stereotypes and role expectations). Despite this, the role of women in developing sociology is generally largely omitted from the picture, as also mentioned above. We could be forgiven for assuming that women played no role in sociology's development until more recent times. However, it would be a false assumption, as there were various women thinkers whose ideas were important, but which have largely been written out of history. For example, Jane Addams (1860–1935); Anna Julia Cooper (1858–1964); Charlotte Perkins Gilman (1860–1935); Ibn Khaldun (1332–1406); Harriet Martineau (1802–1876); and Ida Wells-Barnett (1862–1931) all played an important part. For an important analysis of this issue see Allan (2017).

The Sociological Imagination

It would be a serious omission to try to clarify "what is sociology?" without discussing the sociological imagination. The idea comes from the work of

C. Wright Mills who produced a book of that title (Mills, 1959) that has turned out to be a classic, one of the most widely cited texts on sociology ever published. The key message of the book was that we tend to think in individualistic terms ("atomism," to use the technical term), even though everything we say, do, think and feel happens in a social context. It is as if the social milieu becomes invisible to us and we see the individual(s), but not the other side of the coin, the social factors that are such a significant set of influences and constraints on such individuals. Mills's plea, therefore, was for us to think sociologically, to look holistically at the big picture and not oversimplify the complexities involved by focusing narrowly on individual factors.

Consider the following contrast:

Atomistic view Ronald is very wealthy because he worked hard and made something of his life.

Sociological view Ronald inherited a large fortune from his father. He had had a privileged upbringing and the most expensive education money can buy. He developed important connections with other wealthy, privileged families that would later enable him to build up his business empire. His businesses benefited from significant corporate tax breaks that enabled him to invest in a portfolio of businesses. That portfolio enabled him to enjoy further tax benefits because he could transfer losses and profits around his portfolio to ensure that he paid the minimum of tax.

In a nutshell, putting the sociological imagination into practice is a matter of moving away from atomism and taking into consideration the full range of social factors that will be at work in any given situation. Thinking in atomistic terms is so ingrained in modern western cultures that thinking sociologically can be difficult at first. However, once we develop the knack of doing so, it opens up new doors of understanding, new vistas that can be not only fascinating and exciting, but also *useful* and pragmatic—in other words, a firm basis for *applied* sociology. As Ulrich Beck has put it: "Marcel Proust was right: the true voyage of discovery is not to visit new countries but to see reality with new eyes" (p. 120).

Another important sociologist, Zygmunt Bauman explains:

> It is the job of the sociological imagination to help people "understand the meaning of their epoch for their own lives", and it is the ambition or the sociological imagination, according to Mills, to "make a difference in the quality of human life in our time".
>
> *(2014, p. 4)*

Such is the importance of the sociological imagination, especially in relation to *applied* sociology, that the whole of Chapter 2 is devoted to a much fuller consideration of its significance.

How Is It Useful?

Perhaps the most significant use of sociology is to encourage holistic, critical thinking in order to move away from the distortions of atomism. Whatever line of work we may be in, it is likely that people will be a key feature of it. Psychology can teach us much about people, of course, and it is a popular topic of study for that reason. However, an individualistic focus gives us only part of the story. To get a much fuller story, we need to draw on sociology; we need to make use of the sociological imagination in order to get a much clearer picture of the overall situation.

Focusing on individual factors oversimplifies a complex picture. It prevents us from seeing the "web" of interconnections that are so influential, and which form the basic subject matter of sociology. This need to appreciate complexity is echoed by Hames when he comments that: "Complexity teaches us that nothing happens in isolation and that most phenomena and events are interconnected in some form or other" (2007, p. 90).

Sociology can help us "tune in" to this complexity. It can do so at two main levels, micro and macro. The micro level focuses on interpersonal interactions and shows us how these are socially significant. For example, classic work by Erving Goffman highlighted how selfhood is part of a "performance," part of a social drama in which we present ourselves to the world (Goffman, 1990a). Linked to this, George Herbert Mead was helpful in demonstrating how a "looking-glass self" develops—that is, how we present ourselves to the world, receive feedback from others through their reactions to us and then amend our subsequent presentation of self accordingly (Mead, 1967). For example, if I present myself confidently in a particular situation, the reaction of others can either reinforce that confidence or undermine it, thereby affecting how I present myself subsequently. In this way, we can see that "being me" is not a simple, straightforward matter; it is part of a much wider, much more complex whole. Sociology gives us conceptual tools for engaging with that complexity.

At a macro level, sociology helps us to understand how we are part of much bigger systems and structures. For example, there will be "social divisions," wider structures, such as class, race and gender that will play a significant part in so many different ways. Once again, if we neglect consideration of these, we may be omitting highly important aspects of the situation. For example, we may miss significant links between depression in women and oppression, related to patriarchal systems that encourage women to "swallow" negative emotions (Appignanesi, 2008; Ussher, 1991). Being aware of this link can make us much better informed in any circumstances where we are called upon to work with a woman who is depressed. A key use of sociology, therefore, is its ability to help us look more holistically at situations and not get sidetracked by adopting a partial view that neglects important elements of the circumstances.

Voice of Experience 1.2

I had been a serving police officer for quite some time before I was given the chance to study for a degree. Some of what we covered on the degree was not new to me, as I had picked up a lot of learning along the way. But what really opened my eyes was the sociology module. It taught me a whole new way of thinking. At times I would laugh to myself, as I would start seeing things that had been there right in front of me all along, but I had never noticed them before. I had known all along that the people we dealt with were generally from deprived areas. But I suppose I had just put that down to the way things work, just the way things are. But when we studied cycles of poverty and how people can get trapped in them, I understood more about why so many people chose crime as a way out. It didn't make crime any more acceptable, of course, but it did make it more understandable. It made me feel better informed.

Kelly, a police sergeant

This is particularly important because it opens doors to new possibilities, to new potential solutions. Mathewman and West-Newman recognize this when they point out that: "Sociology shows us that there are alternatives: it can be otherwise" (2013, p. 1). This is in direct opposition to the "TINA approach" to social policy adopted by certain groups committed to a political philosophy known as neoliberalism. TINA refers to the idea that: "There Is No Alternative"—that is, the assumption that neoliberalism, with its emphasis on relying on free markets and the reduction in public services is the only viable way forward (Piketty, 2014; Thompson, 2017a). The philosophy underpinning sociology is therefore one of hope. Sociology enables us to question the idea that the way things are is because that is the "natural order" of things. It is more a case of recognizing that: (i) what is generally presented as the natural order is, more often than not, a reflection of the *social* order; and (ii) the social order was created through human actions and interactions and so—crucially—it can be changed through human action and interaction. This is clearly a message of hope, but it is a cautious message, This is because there are major social forces at work in sustaining the existing social order (with all its power hierarchies of dominance and subordination and the array of privileges associated with them), and so bringing about social change is a complex business. Indeed, one of the benefits of being able to use sociology is that it gives us a range of analytical tools and insights that can help us to approach social change and amelioration in a much more informed way.

Bauman talks about encouraging "sociologists to identify themselves as the active subjects of a way of addressing the world rather than the value-free technicians of an alleged science" (2014, p. vii). This reflects two things: (i) the positive potential of sociology to make a difference in terms of addressing social problems, promoting well-being, improving working life and so on; and (ii) the tension between seeing sociology as an "objective," value-free science that simply seeks to understand society and a committed discipline that seeks to be of social value and bring about positive changes. We shall return to this latter point in Chapter 11, but for now, I want to emphasize the former point, the potential for sociology to be a major force for good in a variety of ways and in a variety of settings. This brings us nicely to the question of "Who uses sociology?"

Who Uses Sociology?

Perhaps really the question should be: Who could use sociology? I say this because part of the rationale for writing this book was my recognition that sociology is so often underused, its value so infrequently recognized. So, in terms of the groups and settings I shall list below, it should be remembered that I am talking about *potential* use, as actual use will vary considerably from group to group and from setting to setting.

The short answer to the question of who could use sociology is anyone where effectiveness in their work relies on having a good understanding of *people*. In reality, then, there will be relatively few work settings where sociology will not have something to contribute.

The reason I emphasize the importance of understanding people is that it has long been recognized that organizational success depends on people (Thompson, 2013)—that is, if you do not get your people issues right, you are going to really struggle to have a successful organization, and you will certainly not be achieving optimal results. Even organizations that spend huge fortunes on cutting-edge technology will struggle if they do not have the right people to: (i) use that technology; and (ii) market and sell the products or services facilitated by the technology.

How people behave, how efficient and effective they are, how motivated and committed they are will all depend on a number of *social* factors. For example, leadership is not simply a matter of a range of personality traits; it hinges on how effective managers (and others) are at influencing the social environment, in particular organizational culture (Thompson, 2016a). Leadership can be the difference between employees being motivated and engaged, productive and happy, on the one hand and, on the other, being disengaged, disaffected, alienated and potentially troublesome, experiencing stress, burnout, energy-sapping low morale and higher levels of tension and conflict (we shall return to these issues in Chapter 10). Seeing leadership simply in terms of individual personality characteristics leaves much of the story untold and leaves us severely weakened in any efforts to improve the quality of leadership and working life.

Practice Focus 1.3

Mal was a newly promoted manager in a large public sector organization. His new team were very friendly and made him feel very welcome. However, he did not feel very comfortable. This was because members of the team kept coming to him and asking him to make decisions on their behalf. At first he went along with this because he wanted to fit in and to be helpful. But, before too long, he realized he would have to do something about it, that this wasn't right. He realized they weren't taking responsibility for their work, there was no sense of ownership. He thought long and hard about this. At first, he put it down to being a characteristic of the team members, but he then decided it would be too much of a coincidence for so many people to share that characteristic. So, he decided to think more holistically. He remembered his leadership training and the emphasis on leaders achieving success by influencing the organizational culture in a positive direction. Yes, he thought, that's the way forward: not to think about individual behaviors, but, rather, to focus more sociologically on the organizational behavior that was feeding that behavior.

So, when it comes to who can benefit from using sociology, the range of people is very broad indeed. To help clarify just who stands to benefit, the following groups or categories should provide a useful overview:

- *The caring professions* Health care; social services work; counseling and psychotherapy; advice work; and so on.
- *Public protection* Police work; probation and prison service work; child protective services; security services and so on.

- *Management and organizational development* Management; leadership; supervisory work; human resources management; trade union work; and so on.
- *Public policy* Policy development and implementation; research and evaluation; and so on.
- *Commercial services* Sales and marketing; copywriting; negotiation; publishing; and so on.
- *Education and training* Tutors; professors; mentors; coaches; training and development professionals; and so on.

This is by no means a comprehensive list, but it should give you a clear picture of just how wide a range of people can be helped by drawing on sociological insights. We shall revisit the theme of who can use sociology in Chapter 11.

The basic point is this: people operate within a social context; if your work setting means that you need to have a good understanding of people, then you need to make sure that you incorporate the powerful role of the social context into that understanding. Sociology helps us understand people, which makes it easier for us to address the people aspects of our work, whatever they may be within our specific setting.

Conclusion

One very common myth is that psychology is about people, but sociology is just about the context, the backdrop, as it were, and not about the people. The reality is, of course, that psychology and sociology are both about people, but looking at the subject matter from different perspectives, psychology focusing mainly on the individual level and sociology on the much wider social level. We are social animals, and that means that we are *psychosocial* beings, strongly influenced by both psychological and social factors, and indeed the interactions between them. This should become clearer in the chapters that follow, but for now, we need to note that sociology is a *human* science, in the sense that it is concerned with *people*. We study the social context not just for its own sake, but because that social context is part of who we are, what we do, how we live and how we make sense of it all.

Another common and misleading myth is that psychology is a (largely biological) science, but sociology is not. Sociology is a *social* science, and so it plays by different rules, as we noted earlier. Despite the fact that it is not appropriate to treat human issues the same way natural scientists treat inert matter, sociology can still offer a rigorous and systematic study of social life, and as such it has a wealth of insights to offer us that can be used in so many different occupations and, indeed, in our private lives also.

We have seen that, where there are people there will be problems, but there will also be potential. We have also seen that sociology can help us to understand people and their problems and therefore give us a firmer foundation for realizing that potential. As Bauman has so neatly put it: "sociology is a conversation with lived experience" (2014, p. 63). In a similar vein, Back (2007) describes sociology as "a listening art": "We live in dark times but sociology— as a listening art—can provide resources to help us live through them, while pointing to the possibility of a different kind of future" (2007, p. 167).

Sociology is also a "seeing art," in the sense that it enables us to see past the distortions and illusions that are part and parcel of social life. By adopting a holistic and critical perspective, we are able to be part of our society, while also taking a step back and being able to develop a fuller understanding of what is going on—and, from an *applied* sociology perspective, to understand better what is going wrong and how the problems can be addressed. That is both the promise and the challenge of applied sociology.

Points to Ponder

1. Why do you think it is important to understand people *in their social context*? What problems might arise if we do not consider the wider context?
2. Which aspects of sociology do you feel most comfortable with? In what ways might you be able to use them in an applied way?
3. Why do you think that some people may object to sociology being used in an applied way, rather than as a "pure" science?

Exercise 1

Search through some newspapers or magazines for an article that describes a social problem. Think carefully about the problem concerned. How might what you know about sociology so far cast some light on the problem in question? How might sociology offer the basis for some potential solutions?

The Sociological Imagination

2

Introduction

In Chapter 1 I introduced the notion of the "sociological imagination," but in that brief discussion, we just about managed to scratch the surface. So, in this chapter, we shall look into what it means in much greater detail. I will begin by revisiting the notion of "thinking sociologically" before exploring the central concept of "social construction." This is an idea that some people find very difficult to understand at first, because it is so different from what they have come to know as "common sense." Indeed, common sense is something we shall also explore in this chapter and, in so doing, I shall link it to two other central sociological concepts, ideology and discourse. As I mentioned in the Preface, the common jibe that sociology is just common sense made difficult is far from the truth, but there is an important relationship with common sense, in so far as sociology questions, and even challenges, the role of common sense in social life.

Before concluding the chapter I will outline how sociological thinking (the sociological imagination) can be of practical value in tackling a wide range of social issues and concerns. This will reinforce the book's core message that sociology is not just an academic discipline that "lives" in the academic world; it can also inhabit, with great positive impact, the world of real-life problems and challenges wherever a good understanding of people, their problems and their potential is needed.

Thinking Sociologically Revisited

In his classic work on the role of sociology, Mills (1959) drew a distinction between private troubles and public issues. He went on to draw links between the two, to show how private troubles are generally a reflection of wider public issues. For example, someone's asthma can be understood as a "private trouble," a personal health concern, linked to how their particular body functions. However, from a sociological point of view, this is only one part of the story. This person's asthma may also be linked to:

- Atmospheric pollutants linked to industrialization and advanced capitalist production systems that generate toxic substances;
- Poor-quality housing that is damp and overcrowded due to social policies that have failed to address the shortage of good-quality housing; and
- Stress caused by pressures of modern living—for example, having to cope with unemployment or insecure employment.

This is not to say simplistically that asthma is "caused" by wider social factors. Rather, it is a case of needing to think holistically. Instead of focusing just on individual factors (Sal has asthma), we need to see the big picture: Sal has asthma that is linked to atmospheric pollutants, poor housing and stress, all of which are, in turn, linked to wider social factors. It is for this reason that there is now a strong emphasis on *public* health as well as individual health support, in recognition that the personal trouble of ill-health is linked to the public issues of industrialization, social policy and the economy (Davidson, 2014; Nettleton, 2013).

Standing Back

One of the reasons Mills used the term "imagination" was that it requires us to see the situation, not from the narrow perspective of our own personal experience, but from a *social* perspective—that is, one that considers individual factors, but also recognizes, and takes account of, social factors, such as:

- *Social structures* This refers to the various ways in which people are subject to "social divisions," such as class, race and gender. Society is not a level playing field. In accordance with a range of factors, people will be assigned to different categories, and those categories will be either *dominant* (men in a patriarchal society) or *subordinate* (women and children). Social structures are therefore imbued with power. This is partly how atomistic explanations can be misleading—by neglecting power relations. Atomism, by not addressing power dynamics and the inequalities involved, implies that society is a level playing field, when clearly it is not.
- *Social processes* Society is not static; there are processes going on all the time. For example, some individuals and groups are systematically excluded

from mainstream society (prisoners, for instance). Exclusion is seen as a process, rather than just a static state of affairs because it is changing all the time—it is dynamic. We do not have to look very far before we see social exclusion operating. Newspapers readily give us such examples.

- *Social institutions* The law, the family, the education system—these are all social institutions that will generally have a highly significant impact on our lives, but will normally fade into the background and become taken for granted. They become the social "wallpaper" that is plain for all to see, but generally becomes part of the background relatively unnoticed.
- *Social discourses* Discourses, as we shall see below, are frameworks of meaning. We tend to think of meaning as a personal matter—for example, what my life means to me is personal and unique to me. However, our individual meanings reflect wider frameworks of meaning, such as cultural norms and expectations. Cultures, and the discourses they encompass, are immensely powerful because: (i) we are exposed to them at an early age, so they become part of our sense of identity; and (ii) they are "policed" in various ways (consider the range of "sanctions" that can be brought to bear if people deviate from their cultural norms).
- *Social expectations* We do not live in a social vacuum. We are constantly surrounded by "messages" setting expectations for us—for example, though the media, including, these days, social media. Women who are at a healthy weight may feel pressure to lose weight to fit in with unrealistic images in the media of "attractive" women. Similarly, children may experience problems at school because their parents cannot afford the latest designer labels that their peers expect them to have in order to be accepted. These expectations can be extremely powerful in certain circumstances and can lead to significant pressures and problems.
- *Social relations* We are constantly engaging with other people, whether face to face, by telephone, via social media or, in a virtual sense, by watching television programs, movies, DVDs and so on. Such relations will generally comprise a mixture of harmony and conflict. The nature and extent of such harmony and such conflicts will be important factors in shaping our experience. Our quality of life can very much depend on the quality of our social relations.

These six areas are precisely the six areas we shall focus on in Part Two of the book, spelling out, as they do, the SPIDER model that I shall be using to explain these six important areas of the "web" of social life.

To use the sociological imagination what we need to do, therefore, is to be able to stand back from our own personal perspective and adopt the broader view. Of course, we are rooted to our personal perspective, it is our window on the world, and so we cannot completely detach ourselves from it. However, what we can do is *imagine* whatever situation we are in by taking account of the wider issues. We can use our knowledge of the various aspects of society to develop a fuller, more informative picture—although such matters are so complex and variable that we will never have the full picture.

This notion of "standing back" fits well with the idea of critically reflective practice (Thompson and Thompson, 2008) which involves standing back from what we are dealing with, drawing on our professional knowledge base and thinking carefully, critically and holistically about it.

Practice Focus 2.1

Michael had studied sociology as part of his multidisciplinary social sciences degree and had found various aspects of the subject useful in his work after graduation. When his manager asked him to attend a reflective practice course he wasn't sure what to expect. So, he approached the course with some degree of trepidation. However, his anxiety was to be short-lived, as he soon settled into the course and ended up finding it a very worthwhile professional development experience. He was able to see clear links between the trainer's plea that participants should "stand back" from their work, from time to time, review it and think carefully about how best to proceed, rather than just pressing on with the work in an unthinking, unquestioning way due to workload pressures. This was very similar indeed to what he had been taught at university about the sociological imagination—standing back and looking holistically and critically at what he was engaged in. He realized that, although that was what he had been taught, he hadn't actually put it into practice—he had not connected theory and practice. But, now, that was going to change. He left the course determined to make sure that he did put it into practice in future, as he could see what he had been missing out on.

Beyond Atomism

Mills's notion of private troubles has proven very influential, not only in relation to the public health emphasis I mentioned above, but also in relation to community-based approaches to social work; outreach approaches in youth work; workplace well-being approaches to human resources issues; and crime prevention initiatives. This is not to say that a sociological approach is used universally. Atomistic approaches are still very much to the fore in many areas, with scant attention paid to the wider social context. In terms of applied sociology we still have a long way to go. Indeed, the dominance of neoliberalism as a political and economic philosophy can be seen to be pushing us firmly in the direction of increased individualism.

Bauman captures well the continuing dominance of atomism when he argues that: "In this new world, humans are expected to seek private solutions to socially generated troubles, instead of looking for socially generated solutions to private troubles" (2010, pp. 24–25). An example of this would be in the context of workplace bullying and harassment (Thompson, 2015b). In my consultancy work I have come across many examples of individuals who have been bullied and subsequently offered confidential counseling to help them "get over" their negative experience, but little or nothing has been done at an organizational level to address the culture of bullying and disrespect that led to the difficulties in the first place. This is not to devalue the role of counseling, but if counseling is seen as the appropriate response to such problems, it leaves the wider organizational factors intact—in fact, in some ways, it could be seen to reinforce them by giving a message to perpetrators of bullying or harassment that their behavior "went a little too far" this time, rather than a strong message that depriving people of their dignity through bullying or harassment will not be tolerated.

Similarly, we can see that problems associated with discrimination and oppression produce "personal troubles" for those on the receiving end of such discrimination, but need to be understood as "social issues." For example, seeing discriminatory behavior as simply a reflection of personal bigotry fails to take account of the wider cultural and structural factors that contribute to such behavior (Thompson, 2018). It presents experiences of discrimination as "unfortunate incidents," rather than reflections of discriminatory assumptions, processes and structures. These wider, highly problematic issues can remain untouched if our focus is a narrow, atomistic one on "personal prejudice." This is not to say that personal prejudice is not an issue, but, rather, that it needs to be understood holistically as part of a wider social milieu, and not in isolation. For example, a human resources officer being faced with a complaint of discrimination would do well to consider not only any prejudicial attitudes on the part of the perpetrator, but also the possibility of an organizational culture that feeds such attitudes.

Bauman and May, in their important text on thinking sociologically, point out that:

To think sociologically can render us more sensitive and tolerant of diversity. It can sharpen our senses and open our eyes to new horizons beyond our immediate experiences in order that we can explore human conditions which, hitherto, have remained relatively invisible. Once we understand better how the apparently natural, inevitable, immutable, eternal aspects of our lives have been brought into being through the exercise of human power and resources, we shall find it much harder to accept that they are immune and impenetrable to subsequent actions, including our own. Sociological thinking, as an antifixating power, is therefore a power in its own right. It renders flexible what may have been the oppressive fixity of social relations and in doing so opens up a world of possibilities. The art of sociological thinking is to widen the scope and the practical effectiveness of freedom. When more of it has been learnt, the individual may well become just a little less subject to manipulation and more resilient to oppression and control. They are also likely to be more effective as social actors, for they can see the connections between their actions and social conditions and how those things which, by their fixity, claim to be irresistible to change, are open to transformation.

(2001, p. 11)

This is an important passage in a number of ways:

1. It affirms that thinking sociologically is helpful in promoting equality and diversity.
2. It reflects the role of sociology in opening doors, creating new opportunities.
3. It highlights the role of sociological thought in generating hope, as I mentioned at the end of Chapter 1.
4. It refers to how sociology can be empowering by giving people the awareness to resist manipulation and oppressive processes.

It should be clear, then, that thinking sociologically has much to offer.

Continuity and Change

An important theme of sociological thought is that of continuity and change. Sociologists have long recognized that:

(i) Society is dynamic—that is, it is constantly changing and evolving. Society is, in a very real sense, history in the making. Social change is a constant feature of social life. Although many changes may be happening slowly and imperceptibly, this does not mean that they are not taking place.

(ii) Within a context of constant change there is also continuity. This is because of the process of "autopoiesis" (Maturana and Varela, 1980). The term originates from biology and refers to how cells reproduce themselves in their own image, so that continuity is maintained. Ironically, then, autopoiesis is a process of change that succeeds in maintaining continuity. We can also use the terms sociologically to see how certain aspects of society (social institutions, for example) continue to exist even in a constantly changing social milieu because there are autopoietic processes at work that constantly reproduce those institutions. For example, one such institution would be marriage. The traditional Western institution of marriage has changed significantly over the years in terms of, first of all, divorce legislation, and, more recently, the introduction of same-sex marriages. However, despite these significant changes, marriage remains as popular as ever.

Consequently, we should not be thinking in terms of continuity vs. change, but rather, considering what elements of change and what elements of continuity are present. Change and continuity are not opposites. They are, rather, two sides of the same coin, two ever-present dimensions of human experience. This insight too is part of the sociological imagination: we need to bear in mind that whatever we are trying to understand will be subject to change, while elements of continuity will also be present. The balance between forces for changes and forces for continuity will often be a key factor in shaping how a situation evolves, and thus how problems and concerns are addressed.

One conceptual tool that can help us understand continuity and change is the "progressive-regressive method" which stems from the existentialist social theory of Jean-Paul Sartre (Sartre, 2004). This is a complex idea, but basically it involves trying to understand the present, the current social situation we find ourselves in, by reference to both the future (the progressive element) and the past (the regressive element) and how they constantly interrelate (the dialectical element). What is happening now will owe much to future plans and aspirations (people's behavior will be strongly affected by what they are trying to achieve or where they are trying to get to) and to past experiences (lessons learned, views formed and so on will also influence current behavior, of course). In addition, we need to recognize that: (i) our future aspirations and plans will in large part have been shaped by our past experiences; and (ii) we will interpret our past experiences in light of future aspirations and current circumstances. These three temporal elements (present, past and future) are therefore constantly interacting and influencing one another. For example, if I were trying to form a friendship with someone (future aspiration) who tells me they are very interested in sport (present situation), then I am likely to choose to focus on my own experiences of having played and followed various sports (past experience). Similarly, part of the reason I want to make friends with this person may well be that my own long-standing interest in sport (past experience) forms much of the appeal of wanting to make friends (future).

While this may sound very complex, and perhaps a bit daunting, when you first come across it, it is actually more straightforward than you may originally think. It can be part of our repertoire of applied sociology tools. For example, in managing a situation involving conflict between two colleagues (or groups of colleagues), it can be helpful to try and understand the present situation by considering: (i) How has this conflict arisen? What brought these people into conflict? (past); and (ii) Where are these people trying to get to? Do they have conflicting aims or intentions? (future). This can then open the door to exploring the situation more fully and in a better-informed way.

Voice of Experience 2.1

I studied psychology at university and really enjoyed it. But what I became conscious of was that most of the focus was on the influence of the past on the present. So, psychodynamic thinking, behaviorism, cognitive approaches—all with a heavy emphasis on the past. But, when I became a teacher, I couldn't help but notice that there was so much emphasis on the future: passing exams, pursuing a career and that sort of thing. It made me reconsider what influences us; it isn't just the past, I can see that now.

Manuela, a high school teacher

This is just one example of how the sociological imagination can not only cast interesting light on certain situations, but also give us valuable insights that can inform our practice when we are called upon, for whatever reason, to engage in those circumstances.

Social Construction

There was a great deal of development in sociological thinking in the 1960s, including the publication of what has turned out to be a seminal text, namely *The Social Construction of Reality* (Berger and Luckmann, 1967). Largely, but not exclusively, as a result of that book, the notion of "social construction" has become a mainspring of much sociological work. So, my intention here is to clarify what it means and demonstrate how useful it is as part of the platform needed for developing applied sociology.

Social construction has two main meanings that are separate, but related. First, it refers to how certain things are created by society—they are, to use Durkheim's phrase, social facts. Social institutions are an example of this. For instance, the law is socially constructed, in the sense that, if there were no society, there would be no law (and no need for law). The law in its different forms in different societies, has evolved from within those societies—it was created by them. Similarly, the education system as a social institution is socially constructed, with different educational approaches created by different societies and by different cultures within those societies. In this sense, the term "construction" is being used literally to mean building. Societies "build" certain things, create elements of society that have an important role to play.

Social construction can also be used in a separate but related sense to refer to the process whereby certain social facts are *defined* by society (or, more specifically, through social processes—see Chapter 4). For example, there is a common tendency to see childhood as a distinct phase in human development and therefore to see children as distinct from adults. However, on closer inspection, we can see that childhood is socially constructed—that is, the idea that children are distinct from adults is something that has been defined societally. One way of identifying that something is socially constructed is to see whether its definition (i) has changed over time; and/or (ii) is different in different societies. In terms of (i), we can see that young humans (what we would today call "children") were treated just like adults. They wore adult clothes, they were involved in work and they were largely treated as adults (McNamee, 2016). In terms of (ii), a good example of this would be the legal age of consent for sexual intercourse which can vary from one country to another by several years. The fact that something can be defined differently over time or across social groups shows that its definition is subject to social processes and influences.

Another example would be crime. What counts as a crime has varied over time and continues to differ from country to country or state to state. To stick with the theme of sexuality for a moment, we can note that same-sex relations have been illegal in the past (and still are in some countries). Similarly, in terms of our sexuality theme, prostitution is illegal in some countries and states but not in others. As well as serving as an example of social construction, sexuality is a good example of the need for a sociological perspective. Sexuality is generally thought of as something very private, personal and intimate, but what this discussion has highlighted is that there is very clearly a social—and, indeed, political—dimension to it. There are, for example, various ways in which societies put in place controls over sexuality. Once again, we are seeing how individual matters need to be seen in relation to the wider social context.

But it is not just crimes relating to sexuality that are socially constructed. The very notion of crime as a "transgression" against society illustrates its social roots. There are also social construction issues in relation to how crime is presented in the media (and therefore how it is understood by the general public). Leonard (2015) distinguishes between what she calls "street crime" and "elite crime." The former refers to what is generally thought of (and portrayed in the media) as crime, whereas the latter refers to crimes of the powerful which generally receive far less attention. He points out that the FBI lists seven categories of major crime: murder, assault, rape, robbery, burglary, larceny-theft and auto theft, What are conspicuous by their absence, of course, are corporate crimes. As Leonard puts it:

> These statistics are widely publicized. Most of us would agree that these are significant violations and need to be vigorously addressed, but the exclusion of other offenses from this list is telling. None of the categories, for example, are designed to include the crimes of corporations, yet, surely, the financial crimes of some corporations like insider trading, price-fixing, or the marketing of unsafe products are more serious than the larceny-theft of a bicycle.
>
> *(2015, p. 3)*

It is no coincidence that such crimes receive such a low level of attention. It reflects power hierarchies in society and how they influence the way social issues are perceived. We will return to this point later in this chapter.

Practice Focus 2.2

Lisa was a probation officer serving in a prison. She was well aware through both her training and her work experience that the vast majority of prisoners were from deprived areas characterized by high levels of poverty and social exclusion. For a long time she just took this for granted and accepted that this is the way things are. She was aware that there were also "high-level" crimes, but gave them little thought, because they simply weren't part of her working life. However, that all changed when she had a new colleague who joined the team, a colleague who had studied sociology before becoming a probation officer. Lisa's new colleague brought a different perspective. She was much more "tuned in" to the wider picture and often spoke about how some of the most serious crimes in society got minimal attention, because they were the crimes of the powerful. Lisa found this really interesting and was keen to find out more about the issues involved. She was beginning to get a taste for "the sociological imagination."

Natural or Social?

It is quite common at times for people to distinguish between those things that are "natural" and those that are "social." However, when we look more closely, what we can begin to see is that the very notion of "nature" is itself socially constructed. We have various forces that are considered to be natural (gravity and electromagnetism, for example) plus various natural processes (biosynthesis and autopoiesis, for example), but the tendency to parcel them all up under the one heading of "nature" is a social construction. It is not difficult to imagine a society that does not have a conception of nature. They may well be aware of the forces and processes that are operating, but not necessarily conceive of them as dimensions of this one entity of "nature." Similarly, there are differences of opinion as to what is and what is not "natural"— same-sex relationships, for example. The idea of "nature" varies across cultures and over time, which indicates that it is socially constructed.

This does not mean that nature, as we know it, does not exist. It is a social fact, and social facts are just as real as any other facts. Indeed, a common error that I have come across many times is to assume that because something is socially constructed, therefore it is not real. The law is socially constructed (culturally and historically variable), but it is still very real. Anyone who doubts that social constructions are real need only try throwing a brick at a police officer to find out very forcefully just how real the law is.

As we shall see below, however, the notion of certain things being deemed "natural" is very significant in terms of how ideology works, so we will return to this topic later.

Social Construction: A Worked Example

To conclude our discussion of social construction I want to present a worked example. The focus of this example is loss. Of course, loss and the grief it generates are quite understandably considered to be personal, intimate matters, striking at the very heart of our vulnerability as human beings. They are, of course, intensely and profoundly personal matters. But, they are also social, as this worked example illustrates:

- *Pat is bereft when a close friend dies*

  A widely accepted explanation of grief is that it is a response to the "emotional investment" (cathexis, to use the technical term) we have made in a person, a thing or a relationship that we lose when we lose that person, thing or relationship. In everyday terms, we put our heart into someone or something and we get our heart broken when we lose that person or thing. Or, yet another way of putting it is to invoke the saying that "grief is the price we pay for love." What we need to recognize from a sociological perspective is that the "cathexis," the emotional investment, is based on a social connection—for example, a connection to another person who matters to us. Consequently, Pat's grief, although intensely personal, also has a social component. If there had been no social relationship, there would have been no cathexis and therefore no grief. There is therefore a social basis to grief (Thompson, 2012a; Thompson and Cox, 2017).

- *Pat experiences a wide range of emotions*

  Again, we tend to think of emotions as personal, psychological matters, and, of course, they are. However, what is not so fully recognized is that emotions are also social phenomena. Emotional expression follows social patterns—for example, in relation to gender and ethnicity (Turner, 2011). Expectations around what is an appropriate form of emotional expression are therefore socially constructed.

- *Pat grieves in an "instrumental" way*

  Doka and Martin (2010) describe gender differences in grieving styles. For the most part, men prefer to grieve in an active, instrumental way—through engagement in activities, for example. This type of grieving, whether practiced by the majority of men or a minority of women, as the research found, is traditionally seen as "not grieving properly." It does not fit with the stereotype of the more expressive style of grieving characterized by crying, talking about the loss and so on. What this indicates is that what is considered "healthy" grieving is socially constructed, in this case along gender lines.

- *Pat receives support from family and friends*

  What type of support, in what form and for how long will depend to a certain extent at least on Pat's cultural background. For example, there will be cultural differences in terms of what types of rituals are used to commemorate the loss and bring people together in a spirit of support. Supportive responses to a loss are therefore socially constructed, this time along cultural lines.

• *Pat is part of a faith community*

Which particular faith community Pat is a member of will be significant, as different religions and even different sects within a religion will generally have differing responses to a loss, different ways of acknowledging the loss and supporting the grievers (Thompson, 2017c). The social construction in this case is therefore along religious lines.

• *Pat's workplace is not so supportive*

Workplace responses to bereavement vary considerably. Some offer minimal support in the form of a short period of compassionate leave, while others may have a well-developed policy based on principles of workplace well-being (Thompson, 2009; Thompson and Bevan, 2015). The workplace as a social milieu can therefore also be understood to shape how grief is experienced, adding another social dimension to what is normally seen in individualistic terms.

• *Pat's friend took her own life*

Sociologist, Kenneth Doka, introduced the concept of "disenfranchised grief" to refer to forms of grief that are not socially recognized or sanctioned (Doka, 1989; 2001). Death by suicide is often stigmatized and can lead to grievers not receiving normal levels of support. Social judgments are therefore being made about which types of loss, which types of relationship and which types of griever are worthy of full support.

• *Pat develops problems in the aftermath of the loss*

Loss issues have long been associated with personal problems that can require a therapeutic response (as represented in the literature on "complicated grief"—see, for example, Neimeyer et al., 2011). However, what has received far less attention is how (unresolved) grief can contribute to *social* problems, including problematic alcohol and drug use, crime and homelessness (Thompson, 2012a).

Returning to our discussion in Chapter 1 of the three Ps, people, problems and potential, we should be able to note that loss issues are a common feature. Grief is far more significant in a range of human issues and concerns than is generally recognized, in the sense that, whenever we look at the challenges people face in life, change is usually an issue, and change will very often produce a grief reaction. A sociological understanding of loss and grief is therefore an important basis for applied sociology.

Ideology, Discourse, and Common Sense

Ideology and discourse are concepts that have developed from different theoretical roots, but they have much in common. Indeed, they are quite complementary. Ideology refers to how sets of ideas become used in ways that sustain and serve to justify ("legitimize," to use the technical term) relations of power (dominance and subordination). The idea is closely associated with the work of Marx, particularly his famous dictum that, in any age, the ruling ideas are the ideas of the ruling class (Marx and Engels, 2011). However, Marx's analysis was a narrow one based on socioeconomic class. Over time the term "ideology" has come to be used to refer to ideas that support patterns of dominance in general, where these relate to class, race/ethnicity, gender or any other social division.

An example of ideology would be patriarchy, the set of ideas that reinforces male dominance (Fine, 2011). As with ideologies in general, the way patriarchy works is to present defined gender roles as "natural." It is as if the ideology states, or at least implies, that certain behaviors and attitudes traditionally expected of women (homemaker, caregiver of children and dependent adults and so on) are natural and that, therefore, any deviations from this role are "unnatural," "abnormal," and therefore undesirable. There are, of course, similar "masculine" expectations of men. Going against ideological expectations can come at quite a high price, the sanctions can be quite severe, for men and women. For example, women who show no sign of a (socially constructed) "maternal instinct" can be highly stigmatized and made to feel that they are not "proper" women. Similarly, men who do not live up to stereotypical expectations of a "real man" can be subjected to considerable abuse.

Of course, it is no coincidence that such ideologies exist. They serve only too well to reinforce and thus sustain relations of power. I have used gender as an example, but much the same can be said of other relations of dominance and subordination—for example, the attempt to justify racism through the ideological assumption that white people are "naturally" superior to people of color (the unfounded basis of white supremacism—Dobratz and Shanks-Meile, 2000). An important related concept is that of "hegemony." Literally it means dominance, but it is dominance in a particular way—namely ideological dominance. Groups of people can dominate through force, for example, but social relations of power are usually maintained through ideology, rather than force (but often with force as a "back up"—for example, through military intervention). This type of dominance through ideas is precisely what hegemony means.

Both ideology and hegemony are important terms when it comes to applied sociology. That is because being aware of how these concepts materialize in practice can give us important insights into the operation of power. Psychology can help us understand certain aspects of behavior, but they will not tell the whole story. It can also be helpful to ask ourselves: What is happening here ideologically? How are dominant ideas affecting this situation? How can an awareness of the power relations involved give us ideas about possible positive ways forward—for example, in relation to empowerment?

A similar and equally helpful idea is that of "discourse." As I have explained previously: "A discourse is literally a conversation. However, its usage has been extended to apply to frameworks of meaning that are powerful influences on thoughts, feelings and actions" (Thompson, 2018, p. 254–5). It is generally associated with the work of Foucault (1972; 1975; 1977) who was critical of Marx's emphasis on the role of social structures (see Chapter 3) and presented a different model of power. The details need not concern us here, but what is important to note is that Foucault shared with Marx the view that: (i) power is associated with sets of ideas (ideology in Marx's terms, discourses in Foucault's); and (ii) these ideas influence us without our knowing and thereby serve to sustain relations of dominance. They keep the powerful in positions of power.

An example of a discourse would be "mental illness," the defining of mental health problems as instances of illness. This discourse is a very powerful and highly influential one, despite a growing literature that strongly challenges its basic foundations (Bentall, 2010; Crossley, 2006; Davies, 2013; Tummey and Turner, 2008). No doubt, the fact that the multi-billion dollar pharmaceuticals industry profits immensely from this discourse has played a significant part in its continued dominance (Davies, 2013; Goldacre, 2013). Given the significance of mental health challenges in so many aspects of working life, the ability to think more critically and holistically about what is happening puts us in a much stronger position to make a positive impact than the potentially disempowering effects of applying a psychiatric label and seeking solutions in medication (Tew, 2011). Indeed, an awareness of how certain discourses can paint a misleading and potentially disempowering picture of a situation is an important contribution that applied sociology can make. It can open up new, more positive ways of understanding the situation by questioning dominant (and dominating) assumptions.

There are technical differences between ideology and discourse (for example, ideologies tend to be used at a macro level, discourses at more of a micro level), so the two are not just different terms describing the same thing. However, for present purposes, what we need to be clear about is that both terms share a very important conception of sets of ideas that contribute to keeping power relations intact. We will return to the significance of this in later chapters, particularly in Chapter 6 which is devoted entirely to the concept of discourse and its vitally important role in applied sociology.

Common Sense

If we look closely at common sense we will soon see that it is not always common and it is not always sense. To a large extent common sense can be understood as "cultural wisdom" built up over time, which means that it can vary from culture to culture and over time. And that, of course, means that it is socially constructed, But, what we also need to recognize about common sense is that it is ideological. The "cultural wisdom" it represents bears a striking resemblance to the dominant ideas that maintain hegemony and keep the wheels of power turning.

As Matthewman, West-Newman and Curtis put it:

> Commonsense views offer a simplistic take on the world. Sociology opposes this. We may think in either/or terms in everyday life, but sociologists argue that these binary oppositions are problematic for two reasons. First, in making these distinctions, one side of the supposedly clear divide is routinely privileged over the other, for example, straight over gay, man over woman, and this has profound consequences for the advantaged and the disadvantaged. Second, there might well be more than two options, for example, gay, straight, bisexual, asexual, intersexed. Life is complex and commonsense simplifies by creating boxes in which everyone can be placed and therefore controlled.
>
> *(2013, pp. xi–xii)*

When someone argues that their point of view is "just common sense," they are appealing to ideology, they are basically saying: "This is how I have been brought up to see the world," without necessarily recognizing that their point of view is culture specific. This is an example of "ethnocentrism," whereby people see their own culture as true and correct and any deviations from it as wrong, misguided or defective. It involves confusing cultural diversity with cultural deficiency.

Again we are in the territory of applied sociology. Common sense blocks any form of questioning; a reliance on common sense means taking things for granted, taking things at face value. Sociology, by contrast, with its critical and questioning approach, leads us to challenge these dominant assumptions. In this way, applied sociology can be a very useful tool for cutting through ideological assumptions that are presented as "common sense," as if this means that they are beyond question and thus invulnerable.

Voice of Experience 2.2

> When I was transferred to head office I inherited a team that seemed to have no conception of reflective practice. Work was mainly carried out on a routine, unthinking basis. Whenever I asked anyone what their rationale was for a particular action, all they could come up with was: "Well, it's just common sense, isn't it?" It wasn't so much an explanation as a way of saying that no explanation was needed, as if it were obvious. Well, it wasn't obvious to me and it took me quite a while to get them to see that "common sense" was no substitute for professional accountability.
>
> *Ravi, a team manager in a large corporation*

The Role of Phenomenology

At the heart of the sociological imagination is social construction, and at the heart of social construction is phenomenology. Phenomenology is the study of perception ("phenomenon" means that which is perceived). The reason phenomenology is important for applied sociology is that it teaches us that everything is seen from a particular perspective—we see the world through a set of filters. The German philosopher, Friedrich Nietzsche, wrote of "perspectivism," the acknowledgment that there is always a subjective dimension to our experience (Armstrong, 2013). This is partly psychological, in the sense that our past experience will have shaped how we see the world (for example, someone who has been sexually abused may be more sensitive to the danger of further abuse (such as signs of "grooming") than someone who has never experienced abuse. Likewise, someone who has had a heart attack is more likely to be "tuned in" to issues that can affect heart health). Our experiences shape to a certain extent how we see the world.

However, this is not purely a psychological matter; we also see the world through social "lenses"—through our cultural background, for example. We can also see that ideologies and discourses act as social lenses by influencing how we make sense of the world. They create stories or "narratives" that help provide a thread of meaning to our lives.

Sometimes, those meanings and the narratives that embody them can be problematic. For example, certain groups tend to be stigmatized and marginalized in society and that can feed a narrative of low self-esteem and alienation. Part of applied sociology can, in certain circumstances, therefore, be a challenging of such narratives. Indeed, the idea of "narrative therapy" is rooted in a phenomenological approach that focuses on meaning making and seeks to help people to develop more empowering narratives (Harms, 2018).

But it is not just within the confines of a therapeutic relationship that phenomenology can be helpful. It prompts us to ask questions about what frameworks of meaning (ideologies, discourses, narratives) are shaping our perception of the world in general and our current circumstances in particular. It encourages us to ask: What processes of perception are going on here? What filters or lenses are shaping those perceptions? Are they causing problems? If so, how can we influence them in a positive direction? This logic can apply to any workplace situation where we are engaged in problem-solving activities, and not just in therapeutic work.

I was first introduced to phenomenology and its significance when I attended an evening class in philosophy. The tutor mystified the group by saying that "no-one has ever seen a chair." This seemed a strange thing to say, but it turned out that he was right to say it. That is because he explained that we only ever see part of a chair. We can go round the other side and view it from a different angle, but we are still seeing only one side. He was using this point as an example of the fact that perception is *active*. That is, we do not simply "see" a chair in a direct way, we see part of a chair and, based on our previous experience and understanding, we "construct" a model of a chair in our mind. But it is not just physical objects that we construct in this way. We also develop our own constructions of abstract things like love, anger, intelligence, and society. But these constructions do not arise in a social vacuum—they are influenced by our social circumstances (our "social location," to use the technical term). So, in this sense, they are also socially constructed. There are social filters in place, and this is why I earlier referred to sociology as a "seeing art," as it allows us to examine what these filters are and how they are affecting us. They also give us the opportunity, where we identify that some of these filters are oppressive, for example, to explore means of changing those filters.

In short, everyone sees the world through their own unique eyes, but there will inevitably be social filters that influence and constrain that perception and the meanings we develop based on those perceptions. That is what phenomenology is all about. It is a key part of how social construction works, and it is a key reason why we need a sociological imagination, by which I mean the ability to look critically and holistically at the big picture (based on what we know of social structures, processes and so on, as we shall explore in Part Two) and thereby question the role and value of the filters that are in place.

Sociology in Action: Praxis

"Praxis" is a technical term that refers to a fusion of theory and practice. It fits well with the notion of "theorizing practice" discussed in the Introduction. It is based on the idea that we should not see theory and practice as two distinct entities. In a sense, this is what applied sociology is all about: not developing theoretical understanding just for the sake of it, but using the knowledge gained as a basis for making a practical difference in the world.

Sociology is well placed to do this because the sociological imagination gives us the tools to see past ideologies and discourses, to recognize problematic and disempowering narratives and to tune in to how power dynamics can help or hinder in tackling problems and challenges. It offers no easy answers, but it does provide a platform for developing our understanding further and putting that understanding to good use. I have given some examples of how this can be done and there will be more such examples in the chapters that follow, but for now, the point I want to emphasize is that individualistic understandings can take us only so far, and so the critical and holistic perspective offered by the sociological imagination can complement well the insights offered by other disciplines.

In particular, what we have to bear in mind is that sociology does not simply offer an understanding of the background to human behavior. The social context is a key factor (or set of factors) in shaping human action. This challenges the traditional view that places most if not all of the emphasis on the individual, a view that fails to recognize that it is artificial and misleading to separate out individuals from their social context (see Chapter 9). As I have explained in an earlier work:

> Sartre (1969) described human experience in terms of a mixing of coffee and cream, in the sense that, once the coffee and cream are combined, they become a new entity in their own right and cannot be separated out. This

analogy applies to individuals in society: personal and social factors merge together and cannot then be distinguished. The two sets of factors, unique personal ones and contextual social ones, become two sides of the same coin, in the sense that they are both aspects of the same reality. Unfortunately, much of the theoretical work about the individual in society has conceived of the individual in society in terms, not so much of coffee and cream, but rather of soup and bowl (Elkjaer, 2005). That is, a common oversimplification of human existence is to see the individual contained within society in the same way that soup is contained within a bowl, but the bowl does not become part of the soup and the soup does not shape the bowl.

(Thompson, 2017b, p. 68)

Human beings are not autonomous beings who just happen to operate in a social context (soup and bowl). We are *psychosocial* beings—that is, our actions stem from both psychological and social sources *and* the interaction between them. Understanding people from this more holistic perspective gives us a much better basis for making a positive difference—for *praxis*.

Practice Focus 2.3

Bobbi was a community development worker in a large city. She had originally studied for a degree in psychology and really found it interesting and helpful. She found the social psychology module particularly interesting and this motivated her to want to find out more about social issues and their impact. This was what led her to a career in community development work. Her professional training in that field got her really excited about looking at situations sociologically. She was keen to develop good working relationships with community members and to respect their individuality, but she also knew that she needed to look more broadly at social issues like poverty and deprivation, racism, social exclusion, and drug-related problems. She felt that her psychological understanding fitted well with what sociology had taught her and gave her a good basis for understanding community issues.

Conclusion

The sociological imagination sensitizes us to key issues, like power dynamics, that might otherwise be camouflaged by ideology and hegemonic discourses.

This does not in itself present us with solutions, but it opens doors to a fuller understanding and a basis for critically reflective practice.

Linguist and political commentator, Noam Chomsky has made the important point that: "It's costly to oppose power" (2012, p. 69). Indeed, it would be naive to think that people in positions of power will welcome challenges to their vested interests. A sophisticated understanding of the issues is therefore needed. This chapter has laid the foundations for that fuller understanding and Part Two contains six chapters that will build on that understanding. Power will remain a theme, but in each of the six chapters we will start to appreciate the complexities involved, while also exploring how the sociological insights offered can be put to good use.

The sociological imagination will, of course underpin those chapters, and indeed the three chapters in Part Three. We shall not be losing sight of the sociological imagination, for, as Bauman has pointed out:

> Sociology bereft of the sociological imagination can only provide information, and, as Mills saw, the world already has more information than it can deal with. The world has grown thin in stories, not information, and where stories are thin so too is the ability of men and women to make sense of their lives in its broader historical context.
>
> *(2014, p. 3)*

Points to Ponder

1. How can you create opportunities for the "standing back" that is necessary for both the sociological imagination and critically reflective practice?
2. What does it mean to say that crime is socially constructed?
3. What problems could arise if we just took "common sense" for granted and did not question it or look at it critically?

Exercise 2

Think about an aspect of your work (or the work you are intending or considering engaging in) and try to identify how the sociological imagination could help you to think holistically and critically. Try to think of specific tasks or aspects of the work, rather than just at a generalized level.

PART TWO

Making Sense of Society

Introduction to Part Two: The Web of Society

In Part Two we build on the foundations laid down in Part One. We shall be focusing on a range of sociological concerns, key aspects of the knowledge base we need to underpin our applied sociology endeavors. The SPIDER approach will be used, reflecting the nature of society as a *web* of interconnections. SPIDER refers to social:

Structures
Processes
Institutions
Discourses
Expectations
Relations

These are not the only dimensions of the web of society, so what is offered in Part Two is by no means a comprehensive or exhaustive review. However, the six areas we will be focusing on combine to give a very helpful basis of understanding. Each one is an important aspect of society in its own right, but what should emerge as you make your way through this part of the book is that the six areas also interconnect. We shall be examining them separately for the sake of clarity and ease of understanding, but we should not allow the fact that we are addressing each aspect in a separate chapter to fool us into thinking that they are not parts of the same whole. This is why I am using the "web" analogy, to emphasize the interconnections. Indeed, it would run totally counter to the sociological imagination to assume that these different areas are somehow operating in isolation from each other.

Figure 3.1 SPIDER in the Web of Society

Each chapter ends with a set of "points to ponder" and an exercise to aid understanding. You may be tempted to skip over these, but I would urge you to resist that temptation. This is because sociology is a complex subject matter and paying attention to how its insights can be used in practice adds an extra layer of complexity. So, there is much to be gained by thinking carefully about what has been covered in one chapter before moving on to the next one, which is precisely why the points to ponder and exercises are there. These do not have to be tackled alone. If you have the opportunity to discuss the issues with colleagues or friends, then feel free to do so, as this can add extra benefit.

Social Structures

3

What Are Structures?

Broadly speaking, a structure is a set of enduring connections that give a sense of a whole (that is, not just any random set of connections). They can be quite concrete and tangible or more abstract. Buildings would be examples of physical, tangible structures. Architecture, in its literal sense, can be thought of as the study of structures. For example, an architect designing a building would be drawing on their expertise relating to: (i) matters of safety (Will the building stay standing?); (ii) facilities (Will it serve the purpose for which it is being built?); and (iii) aesthetics (Will it look good? Will it be an attractive place for people to work or live in or visit?). However, the term "architecture" can also be used in a more metaphorical sense to refer to an understanding of structures more abstractly. We could say, then, that this chapter is about "social architecture," how society has within it certain enduring structures that play an important role in shaping social life.

The notion of structures is also used in other disciplines, of course, such as chemistry, physics, biology, geology and linguistics. The basic idea should therefore be familiar. What makes social structures more complex, though, is that ideology and related discourses serve to camouflage those structures. For example, in some quarters at some times (courtesy of some politicians, for example) there has been much discussion about the idea that we have now reached a "classless society," even though evidence of class disparities are plain to see if you know where to look, or, perhaps more significantly, if you know "how" to look, if you are able to use the sociological imagination to look beyond ideology and discourse and the power interests they serve. This is partly why atomism is so dangerous and applied sociology is so important. By looking at individuals in isolation, we can work with them as if we are on a level playing field. Looking at the situation more holistically, we can see that, due to the significance of social structures, the playing field is far from level—some people located in one part of a structure can find themselves severely disadvantaged compared with others in more privileged sectors of the structure—see the discussion of social structures below.

Practice Focus 3.1

Kofi was a law student following in his father's footsteps. He had grown up in a household with a strong commitment to justice. He felt quite comfortable, therefore, in the Law Department at university. However, what made him feel quite uncomfortable at first was that one of his fellow students was constantly raising the issue of *social* justice, arguing that the legal system is based on individual justice, but is also open to criticism for not doing enough to challenge social injustices, to make wider society a much fairer place. Gradually, Kofi came round to this idea and started joining his colleague in wanting to see a recognition that it wasn't just about winning individual cases, it was also about addressing structural inequalities. This change of focus in his thinking gave him the impetus to decide that he would be a campaigning lawyer, adopting a much broader sense of justice than case law alone would allow.

Class

Perhaps the one social structure that has traditionally attracted most attention is that of class, or "socioeconomic class," to give it its full title. The distribution of income and wealth is, of course not uniform. We have a spectrum ranging from people living in dire poverty at one extreme, through to people with immense wealth at the other. There have been varying theories over time about the nature and significance of class (as per the discussion of Marx and Weber in Chapter 1), but what is clear is that class differences, however they may be conceptualized and measured, make a huge difference to the life chances people have. For example, there is a significant and growing literature on the impact of health. Where you are on the socioeconomic scale will have a strong bearing on not only your life expectancy, but also the quality of your health across your lifespan (Dorling, 2013). These disparities reflect significant inequalities that have their roots in the class-based distribution of wealth and income.

The impact of class differentials on health is just one example of the significance of class structure. There is also evidence to show class-related differences in educational attainment (Smith, 2012), criminal justice (Leonard, 2015) and various other issues. This is a further example of the importance of thinking sociologically. For example, it is not difficult to imagine a child from a poverty-stricken environment growing up in a family with no books or other learning resources and no family history of educational achievement finding it much harder to do well at school, regardless of their intelligence level, compared with a child from an affluent background, with educational resources aplenty, supportive parents and high expectations. Of course, those high expectations can also be problematic for some children, but the difference in starting points on the educational journey due to differing class positions is enormous.

Sticking with the educational theme, there is also the potential for class-based discrimination—for example, children from certain class groups being "written off" at times by people who adopt prejudicial attitudes towards them, thereby stymieing the fulfillment of their educational potential (Smith, 2012). Such structural disadvantages can then, in an atomistic society that focuses so heavily on individualistic factors and often neglects the wider social contexts, be interpreted as personal inadequacy. Due to the structural constraints, a highly intelligent child from a disadvantaged background may achieve less educationally than a child of average ability from a more privileged background and then ironically be seen as lacking intelligence. Sadly, intelligence (educational potential) is often confused with educational attainment. The result can be that an intelligent child who, for structural reasons, does not do well in the educational stakes is wrongly perceived as lacking in ability (which can then reinforce the stereotypical view that can contribute to children from poor families being written off).

Beyond Class

For a very long time the primary focus in sociology on social structure related to class. However, in no small part due to the rise of the women's movement and the civil rights movement, the focus was extended to incorporate gender and race/ethnicity. This was in recognition of the fact that there are structured inequalities (patterns of domination and subordination) that relate to gender (giving rise to sexism) and to race/ethnicity (giving rise to racism). We now therefore have a significant literature base relating to these areas (for example, Back and Solomos, 2009; Connell and Pearse, 2015). Even today, after decades of a more multidimensional approach to social structure (or "stratification," to use the technical term), it is still often the case that certain people focus primarily, if not, exclusively on class.

Voice of Experience 3.1

When I first came into this type of work all the emphasis was on class issues—getting better pay deals for low-paid workers, promoting workers' rights and so on. To begin with issues to do with gender equality were very much a side issue, and anti-racism barely got a mention. But, thankfully, it's all changed now. Class issues are still seen as important, of course, but we now have a much broader, more inclusive approach to equality issues and worker rights.

Frankie, a trade union official

But, we can also go beyond gender and race / ethnicity, as we are now increasingly aware of a much wider range of social structures that are characterized by: (i) power relations of dominance and subordination leading to significant inequalities; and (ii) the tendency for such structures to be masked by ideology—that is, for their significance to be played down or rendered "invisible." These structures include:

- *Age* Membership in an age group is socially significant, in the sense that there are age structures that can have a significant effect on how we are treated and what opportunities and restrictions we face. For example, older people can be subject to the myriad disadvantages of ageism (Cann and Dean, 2009), while children and young people can also face forms of social exclusion at times. In reality, the way age structures operate in society is highly complex and multifaceted. So, the idea that "age is just a number" does not fit with the sociological reality. Sue Thompson (2013) provides an interesting and telling example of this in discussing the significance of "reciprocity" in old age. In our younger lives we benefit from giving as well as receiving. We gain self-esteem from being helpful and useful; it can even be an important source of spiritual fulfillment and thus identity. However, as her research showed, it is often the case that older people will be denied the opportunity to reciprocate. The focus will be on their receiving support as they age, with the idea that they can also give, help, support, contribute and be useful fading into the background. The negative impact of this for so many older people will be quite profound and far reaching.
- *Disability* The conventional view of disability is that it is a matter of personal misfortune. However, a more sociologically informed view recognizes that

disability can be understood as a social process, in the sense that it is not the physical impairment *per se* that disables the person concerned, but social attitudes and expectations. For example, a wheelchair user is not disabled by the fact that they use a wheelchair; they are disabled by the failure of appropriate access aids to be provided (ramps, elevators and so on), on a consistent and systematic basis (Swain et al., 2014). This "social model" of disability, as it has come to be known is a good example of the sociological imagination in action, in that it challenges misleading and disempowering common sense conceptions of disability and replaces them with a much more positive and empowering perspective. This is another example of a potential role for applied sociology, to assist disabled people in moving away from medicalized, disempowering discourses towards a discourse of rights, independence and empowerment.

- *Religion* In these days of Islamophobia in the context of heightened fears of terrorism (Kennedy-Pipe et al., 2015), it is quite clear that, while religion can bring people together, it can also drive people apart, often with highly worrying consequences. There are also significant structural divisions that can be recognized within specific religions. Consider, for example, the sectarian problems associated with the "Troubles" in Northern Ireland (McKittrick and McVea, 2012) and the Sunni/Shia spilt in Islam (Cockburn, 2015). Social structure is therefore a significant part of religion, and religion is an important part of how society is structured,
- *Sexuality* While attitudes towards same-sex relationships have changed drastically in the last decade or two, sexual orientation remains a dimension of social structure, in the sense that belonging to a minor group in terms of sexuality (gay, lesbian, bisexual, transgender, intersex) can bring significant social disadvantages in terms of discrimination, marginalization, stigmatization and so on. Despite the progress made in terms of equality and diversity in relation to sexual identity, it would be naive not to recognize that there remain significant structural inequalities.
- *Language group* Sometimes language differences are part of racial or ethnic differences, but language group membership can also be a feature of stratification in its own right. Speakers of minority languages can be marginalized and stigmatized, even within their own community. Language can be a strong feature of identity, and so having one's linguistic standing disrespected can be oppressive and undermining (Mooney and Evans, 2015).

For quite some time, these various forms of stratification were largely addressed separately—for example, feminist scholars addressing gender-related structures, anti-racist scholars addressing structures of race and ethnicity and so on. However, what we have seen develop since those early days is an emphasis on "intersectionality." This was initially used by anti-racist feminists to refer to how issues of sexism and racism "intersect"—that is, how they relate to one another and produce complex social and interpersonal dynamics (May, 2015). However, it is now being used to encompass the various social structures more holistically, rather than be limited to race and gender issues. For example, in my own work (Thompson, 2016b; 2018), I have referred to the importance of understanding social structures and the associated power relations and discrimination as "dimensions of existence," by which I mean that we should not be artificially separating out the effects of different social structures. People will be experiencing the effects of more than one social structure and, in addition, they will experience the effects of the interactions of the other structures. For example, to be black and old is to experience the consequences of not simply being part of these two separate structures, but also how those structures work in tandem—how they influence each other.

This is an important consideration when it comes to applied sociology. This is for two reasons:

(i) It avoids people focusing too narrowly on one social structure to the exclusion of others—for example, a black woman may be part of a supportive black culture that helps her to cope with any racism she encounters, but that same black culture may not offer her the same level of support in relation to sexism. Anyone focusing on experiences of racism may therefore miss vitally important aspects of the situation.

(ii) It highlights the significance of how different social structures interact. It is not simply a matter of adding them together. Multiplication would be a better analogy than addition. For example, being white and affluent does not just give two sets of privileges. The combination of the two can intensify the advantages given. Similarly, different structures can counteract each other—a rich black person is likely to be able to shelter him- or herself from the worst effects of racism in ways that a poor black person would not be able to do.

Practice Focus 3.2

Soroya worked in the policy development department of a large nonprofit organization. She was involved in a project that included a demographic analysis—that is, she was called upon to draw up a picture of the different groups within their catchment area in terms of age groups, ethnicity, socioeconomic grouping and so on. She was delighted about this, as this was real progress. She had been with the organization for two years and during that time she had been constantly raising the issue that they focused (quite rightly) on poverty, deprivation and class issues, but did not complement this with a focus on other social structures and patterns of inequality. She had felt that their approach was too one sided. This new project was clearly a step in the right direction. It would give them a basis of information that could inform their future policy development in more sophisticated ways to reflect the complications involved. At last, she would be able to apply her sociological knowledge more fully.

Social Divisions and Inequality

One important point to emphasize about social structures is that they are highly significant in relation to inequality. This is because they create "social divisions," separate groups or categories, some who are advantaged by their position within the hierarchy (or "social location") and some who are disadvantaged. This reflects the operation of power that, when it functions at a structural level, creates relations of dominance and subordination, those who benefit and those who lose out.

Again this is important in relation to applied sociology, as it helps us to think in terms of social location—that is, in working with an individual, family, group or community, we can consider to what extent and in what ways these structural factors and power relations are affecting the situation. Similarly, it can sensitize us to the need to bear inequality in mind.

In an earlier work (Thompson, 2018), I described two types of inequality. There is: (i) economic inequality, which is basically the gap between the richest and the poorest in society; and (ii) sociopolitical inequality, which is the basis of discrimination—that is, when differences between groups of people are used as a means of disadvantaging minorities or other stigmatized groups. As Witcher (2015) points out, equality should not be interpreted to mean "sameness." In a very real sense, equality can be seen as being free from discrimination, free from being treated less favorably because of being different from the majority group in some way(s).

Both types of inequality can be seen to be highly detrimental in terms of the negative effects they have on people (Dorling, 2011; 2013; 2014; Stiglitz, 2013; Thompson, 2017a; Wilkinson and Pickett, 2009). As Dorling comments:

"Growing income and wealth inequality is recognised as the greatest social threat of our times" (2014, p. 1).

He reinforces this point in an earlier work:

> Recent scientific evidence of many kinds makes it increasingly clear that great inequality in modern societies is damaging: damaging to human abilities, performance and happiness. We can now see that most of the differences in outcomes between rich and poor, whether in measures of IQ, health, violence or educational attainment, which are so often used to justify elitism, hierarchy and social exclusion, are in fact caused by social status differentiation itself. That is why more hierarchical socie-ties with bigger income differences between rich and poor have so many more of almost all the health and social problems which tend to be more common lower down the social ladder.
>
> *(2011, p. xvi)*

This is a theme to which we will return from time to time, as the significance of this is something that the sociological imagination can continuously alert us to.

Voice of Experience 3.2

> I came into nursing because I knew how illness and disease can make people's lives a misery and I wanted to do my bit to make a difference. But what I hadn't realized until I worked in a clinic in a deprived area was how much of a difference inequality made. It was such a different world from the comfortable middle-class family I had grown up in. I had read about health disparities when I was at uni-versity, but all that stuff hadn't really registered with me that much. Now, it was staring me in the face. It really made me rethink my whole attitude towards health and illness. The whole thing is much more complex than I had naively thought at first.
>
> *Meg, a general nurse*

Structuration Theory and Beyond

Anthony Giddens has made a major contribution to our sociological knowl-edge in a number of ways, in particular through his work on "structura-tion theory" (Giddens, 1979; Stones, 2005). His work is worth mentioning here because it emphasized the need to understand structure in relation to agency—that is, in relation to people's ability to exercise choice and make decisions. Prior to this there had been many representations of structural factors in deterministic terms—that is, as aspects of society that governed people's lives in ways that left them with no choices, as if they were simply "social puppets" pushed here and there by structural forces. Much of this determinism came from distorted and oversimplified versions of Marx's approach to social stratification that did not do justice to the complexities of his thought that did indeed include a role for agency. Dennis Wrong presented a classic critique of this form of determinism when he coined the phrase of "the oversocialized conception of [wo]man" (Wrong, 1961).

Giddens took this critique further by explicitly theorizing a dialectical (that is, two-way, interactive) relationship between agency (human action) and structure (the structural context in which that action takes place). Structure constrains and channels agency (but does not determine it), while agency contributes to maintaining and/or changing structure. Human actions will largely reinforce the structure, but they can also, at times, play a part in how those structures evolve.

This has proved to be a useful outlook and a welcome extension of our understanding. However, in my view, it is incomplete. This is because it offers a model based on a direct relationship between structure and agency. In my own work (Thompson, 2016b; 2018) I have developed a conceptual framework that introduces an intermediate level of culture. This framework goes by the name of PCS analysis because it involves analyzing social interactions in terms of three levels:

Personal: individual actions, attitudes and approaches, at times incorporating some degree of prejudice. This therefore includes agency.
Culture: the level of shared meanings, taken-for-granted assumptions, unwritten rules and stereotypes. This dovetails well with the notion of discourse that we shall explore in more detail in Chapter 6.
Structural: the various social structures and stratification systems we have been discussing in this chapter.

Atomism encourages us to think in narrow, individualistic terms (the **P** level). **P** level issues are important, but—as sociology teaches us—we need to see them in their wider social context. Giddens conceptualized that context in structural terms. However, in my approach, the **C** level comes next. That is, we need to understand the **P** level by reference to the frameworks of meaning at the **C** level. Our actions, attitudes and approaches will be largely influenced by the cultural context, by our upbringing and the values and norms to which we were exposed and by the cultural context in which we are now operating (which will be the same context for many people, but also quite different for others—for example, people who have moved to a different country, culture, religious group or whatever). In turn the **C** level will both reflect and reinforce the wider structures at the **S** level. For example, someone may have sexist attitudes (**P** level) that reflect their upbringing and cultural background (**C** level), and it will be no coincidence that such attitudes are part of the culture if that culture is part of a wider, male-dominated patriarchal structure (**S** level).

One way of understanding this is that the **P** level is embedded within the **C** level, which in turn is embedded within the **S** level, as illustrated in Figure 3.2.

Giddens presented the relationship between structure and agency as dialectical. The same logic can be applied to PCS analysis, but this time we need to think of it as a "double dialectic." As I have explained this previously:

> PCS analysis is premised on the interaction of three levels, personal, cultural and structural. These three elements form part of a double dialectic, in the sense that the personal and cultural levels influence each other (cultural frameworks of meaning influence thoughts, feelings and actions at the personal level, while these very thoughts, feelings and actions will also play a part in reinforcing or undermining the culture). In turn the cultural and structural levels influence each other: cultural frameworks of meaning are shaped in large part by wider structures, while also contributing to sustaining and/or changing those structures over time.
>
> *(Thompson, 2018, p. 255).*

Figure 3.2 PCS Analysis

Source: Thompson, 2016b

This notion of a double dialectic shows us what a complex picture we are dealing with and moves us quite some distance from a simplistic atomism that focuses narrowly on the **P** level. PCS analysis, understood in terms of this complexity, gives us a useful analytical tool for understanding various aspects of social life, not least issues relating to equality, diversity and social justice (Thompson, 2016b).

One further benefit of this framework is that it is *dynamic*, it is based on a constantly changing, constantly evolving picture of social life. So, while both cultures and structures are very powerful mechanisms that can be highly resistant to change, the fact that they are both, by their very nature, evolving phenomena within a dynamic interplay shows that change is possible—difficult, yes, but possible.

Structures and Power

You may have noticed that a recurring theme throughout this chapter has been power. There are different types and manifestations of power (Thompson, 2007), as we shall see in later chapters, but for now what we can note is that *structural* power operates by assigning people, individually and collectively, to a place within a set of hierarchies, and those hierarchies create relations of dominance and subordination. Discourses at the cultural level, as we shall see in more detail in Chapter 6, serve to camouflage these relations and present a misleading picture of a level playing field, a misleading picture that is itself part of the discourse that keeps the powerful in positions of power and the not so powerful in a position of subordination. We shall fill out more details of this important story in later chapters.

Practice Focus 3.3

Ravi was a social worker specializing in child protection work. He was used to working in low-income areas where there were a lot of social problems associated with poverty and social exclusion. He could have been forgiven for thinking that child abuse was a working-class phenomenon. However, all this changed when he was asked to handle a case of a 14-year-old girl who claimed that her step-father had sexually abused her. In his normal, day-to-day work, he sometimes met a degree of hostility, but he could usually use his skills to calm people down and keep things under control. But what he encountered in his new case was something really quite different. The step-father spoke to him quite calmly and politely when in the presence of the girl's mother. The situation was different, though, when the step-father walked down the drive with him back to his car. When out of his wife's earshot, the step-father stated quite plainly that Ravi had better drop the case or his life would not be worth living. He told Ravi he had friends in high places and that his "cards would be marked." He later told his manager about this, but he just played it down and said it was all just "bluster" and to take no notice of it. However, the following day he received a telephone call from a legal firm that the step-father had engaged. The caller wanted to know about Ravi's qualifications and experience. He refused to say, put the phone down and immediately went to see his manager, hoping he would get a more supportive response this time. This whole incident made him think very carefully about power.

Implications for Practice

The focus of the whole book is on practice, on the ways in which sociological understandings (through the process of "theorizing practice," as discussed in the Introduction) can be drawn upon to inform practice, whatever that practice may be across the wide range of work settings where "people issues" are to the fore. But, in this section, I want to just comment briefly on the practice implications of having a greater awareness of social structures.

The sociological imagination enables us to see past discourses that mask significant inequalities and present power relations as reflecting the "natural order," when in fact they reflect the social order, an order that was created through human actions and that can be changed through human actions, however difficult that may be. This awareness does not offer us any simple solutions or magic formulas to follow. However, it does offer us a new level of understanding that should enable us, through critically reflective practice, to explore ways of making a positive difference in, where appropriate, taking account of the structural issues involved. As we noted, PCS analysis can be particularly helpful as an analytical tool in this regard.

Conclusion

This first chapter in Part Two has explored the first element of the SPIDER model of the web of society. We have seen that we live and work in societies characterized by multiple sets of structures, multiple systems of stratification, even though there are social processes at work that tend to place those structures out of focus, fuzzy in the background, while individual factors are highlighted in full focus. We have also seen how these structures interact (intersectionality) in significant ways to produce a complex picture. These structural factors also interact with important cultural factors (that, in turn, interact with personal factors) to complicate the picture further. PCS analysis gives us a framework for making sense of these complex interweavings, a useful tool for our applied sociology endeavors.

In Chapter 4 we will focus on how a number of social processes are also part of the complex social mix. And, of course, we will also see how an understanding of social processes is an asset when it comes to drawing on sociology for practical purposes. It is to these issues that we now turn.

Points to Ponder

1. What would you regard as your class position? How has this affected your life to date in terms of opportunities offered or denied?
2. How would you define or describe your ethnicity? How has this affected your life to date in terms of opportunities offered or denied?
3. And what about your gender? How has this affected your life to date in terms of opportunities offered or denied?

Exercise 3

Our "social location" (where we fit into this complex web of social structures) makes a huge difference to our lives in a number of ways. How might you use a knowledge of social structures to bring about a positive difference in any aspect of working life? List as many possible steps as you can.

Social Processes   4

Introduction

There are countless processes that go on in society, and so it would be hopelessly ambitious to try to capture them all in one chapter. So, this chapter is illustrative, rather than exhaustive, featuring only a selection of social processes. I have chosen to focus on processes that are particularly significant and which, from an applied sociology point of view, present opportunities for using our knowledge of them in practical situations. I am also going to focus on sets of processes, as it is possible, and helpful, to see how some processes cluster together.

But why focus on social processes? What is their overall significance? The short answer is that society is dynamic—that is, it is constantly changing. It is a very easy mistake to make to look upon society as a relatively fixed entity. So, in a sense, the very basis of exploring social processes is a social process in itself, namely social change. This is also an example of what I mean by sets of processes, as social change is not a single, monolithic process. For example, we can identify at least three processes at work:

- *Entropy* This refers to the process of "decay" or unwinding. To put it philosophically, what is is moving towards not being. People get older, physical objects decay, systems start to run down and so on. In this sense, everything is in a state of flux, constantly changing, although many things change so slowly that we assume they are in a steady state. For example, if we look at an apple, it seems as though it is stable and not changing at all. However, each second we look at it is a second closer to it rotting and eventually decomposing. What this means is that change and stability are not opposites. Rather, apparent stability is a reflection of the rate of change, not the absence of change. Everything is changing.

- *Negentropy* As the name implies, this is the opposite of entropy to a certain extent. Negentropy refers to the set of processes that are involved in counteracting entropy. At a very simple level, this relates to the moisturizing cream we put on our skin to try and keep it young and fresh looking or the varnish we put on wood to stop it rotting. At a social level it would include various ceremonies and rituals that we use to keep certain things "alive," war memorials to honor the fallen and to warn of the horrors of war; festivals and celebrations to sustain and revitalize age-old traditions and customs to maintain a sense of shared collective identity. Negentropy therefore refers to the various processes and actions we use to control and counteract entropy as far as we reasonably can. One of its consequences is that it creates an (ideological) illusion that change is not happening, that the existing social order is the natural and inevitable order. It thereby serves to mask the possibility (and ultimate inevitability) of change.
- *Autopoiesis* We encountered this idea in Chapter 2. It is a close cousin of negentropy and operates in a similar way. Autopoiesis refers to how we constantly rebuild things in their own image. An example of this would be an organizational culture. For example, in a workplace where there is a culture of low morale, what sustains that culture is its members each day renewing it through actions, interactions and attitudes that reflect and reinforce low morale. Cultures only exist because their members reproduce them constantly (just as our skin reproduces itself constantly in the original biological meaning of autopoiesis—self-regeneration). This is highly important from an applied sociology point of view. If there is a culture that is problematic, we can look at what people are doing to constantly reproduce that culture and seek to change the processes that are contributing to this autopoiesis. Indeed, this is the basis of leadership, a prime target for applied sociology insights (Thompson, 2016a).

As Sprintzen comments:

Nothing is fixed, nothing is permanent, nothing lasts in spite of our continual need to attach ourselves to that which is infinite, everlasting, and eternal. Energy is ceaselessly at work, only stopping for brief periods when confronted by equal and opposite energy in a state of temporary equilibrium; everything undergoes continual transformations in complex transactions with its ever-changing environs.

(2009, p. 191)

In effect, what we call "social change" is a complex mixture of interacting forces, some processes that push in the direction of change and some that seek to counteract, prevent or slow down change. Stability is something that is *achieved* through social processes, rather than a natural state (it reflects the *social* order, rather than the *natural* order). Here we have a perfect example of the value of sociology at an applied level. Much of the work undertaken in the management and leadership field is around the management of change, but without an appreciation of the complexities involved, it is not surprising that so many change initiatives fail. What we refer to as "change management" is actually a much more complex and nuanced process of balancing elements of continuity and change and the interactions between them.

But this does not apply only in the field of management and leadership. For example, my background in social work has taught me that much of social work involves balancing elements of continuity and change and the interactions between them, and I am sure that there will be other professional disciplines where the same will apply—in fact, I would be highly surprised if that were not the case.

In short, there is much that sociology can teach us about change and continuity and many ways in which we can use those insights in a practical setting. What can perhaps be helpful in guiding us in those endeavors is John Law's notion of a "sociology of verbs" (Law, 1994). Verbs are "doing" words; they refer to actions and processes, and this is what sociology is all about: what seems at first like a "noun," metaphorically speaking, can be better understood, on closer inspection, as a "verb"—that is, as a process or a set of processes. This should become clearer as we make our way through the chapter.

Practice Focus 4.1

Geoff was a community worker in an area undergoing significant redevelopment. There was the original core village that had grown through various stages of development. And now, there was a major redevelopment on the old factory that had closed down over ten years before. There had been conflicts between the "old villagers" and the "new settlers," although nothing major. However, the new development was causing tensions all round, with old and not so old members of the community feeling insecure about what they perceived as their community being over-run, getting too big and crowded for comfort. However, unemployment had been a problem for many people, and the new development was bringing in new jobs. Geoff's background in sociology was helping him to appreciate that what he was facing was an interesting dynamic between changes that were taking place (partly welcome because of the new jobs), and the need to retain a sense of community (that was being threatened by feelings of yet more change). He was now starting to think about how he could use his sociological understanding to help address those tensions.

Social Construction

We have already discussed this, and so it is not my intention to repeat myself here, other than to re-emphasize its central role. We noted earlier that society is often contrasted with nature, but in reality the very notion of nature is itself a social construction. Similarly, the idea of "society" is also socially constructed—developed and defined through social processes of various kinds.

Other examples of social construction are quite easy to find: (i) the distinction between weeds and other plants is a social one, not a biological one; weeds are the plants that have less or no social value as aesthetic objects: (ii) we are used to seeing the rainbow spectrum as being divided into seven colors, but some cultures see only four, while others see eleven—where we draw the "lines" between the different colors is a social matter, not a natural one; and so on.

In a very popular book about humanity and our history, Harari (2011) writes of the "imagined order," by which he means how, as human beings, we have historically created and sustained vast social networks. He argues that these networks offered problems as well as solutions:

> The imagined orders sustaining these networks were neither neutral nor fair. They divided people into make-believe groups, arranged in a hierarchy. The upper levels enjoyed privileges and power, while the lower ones suffered from discrimination and oppression.
>
> *(2011, p. 149)*

His point fits well with a sociological understanding, but I find it misleading for him to use the term, "imagined orders," as this implies that they are not real. As I indicated in our earlier discussion, it is a significant mistake to see socially constructed entities as not real. They are "social facts," and as such, very real in terms of the effects they have on people.

His point none the less remains a valid and important one. He also gives an important example of social construction when he writes about the French automobile company, Peugeot. He points out that the company is not its people (they could be replaced and it would still be the same company). Similarly, it is not its buildings, as it could move to new premises and still be the same company. He adds:

> In short, Peugeot SA seems to have no essential connection to the physical world. Does it really exist?
>
> Peugeot is a figment of our collective imagination. Lawyers call this a "legal fiction". It can't be pointed at; it is not a physical object. But it exists as a legal entity. Just like you or me, it is bound by the laws of the countries in which it operates. It can open a bank account and own property. It pays taxes, and it can be sued and even prosecuted separately from any of the people who own or work for it.
>
> *(2011, p. 32)*

Everything Harari says here is true and important, except that this is not a matter of imagination or fiction; what he is describing is a social construction, a social process at work that produces a social fact.

As we now move on to explore other social processes, we should bear in mind that they too create very real "social facts."

Socialization

It was Durkheim who introduced the concept of social fact. Another of his important contributions was what has become one of the fundamental bases of sociology, namely the idea that each of us is born into a pre-existing society (Durkheim, 2013). Although our human predecessors created society initially and it has evolved through human actions since, each individual is born into a social order that already exists. For example, imagine the birth of a child taking place right now:

- That child will have a biologically determined sex, but what will be just as important, if not more so, he or she will have a socially assigned gender that will have major implications throughout his or her life in terms of opportunities that are opened up or closed off, expectations that are made and "policed," frameworks of meaning that are applied, and so on.
- He or she will be born into a socioeconomic family context. Consider the difference it would make to being born the son or daughter of a billionaire, as compared with being the son or daughter of a billionaire's gardener.

- There will also be racial or ethnic differences (and potential discrimination) that begin from birth.
- The political context will also be significant: contrast being born into a politically stable democracy with being born into a highly unstable war zone.

This is not a complete list, but should be sufficient to illustrate the significance of where and when we are born, at what "social location" we begin life.

Voice of Experience 4.1

I have worked with children from a wide range of social backgrounds, ranging from desperately poor to much more than comfortably off. I've seen what a difference that background makes to the children, to their health, their development, their happiness and, of course their chances for the future. Being poor doesn't stop children being loved, of course, but love isn't the only thing that makes a difference.

Josie, a children's nurse

What this list illustrates is that, while each of us is no doubt a unique individual in our own right, we are unique individuals in a social context (Thompson, 2016a). Sociology helps us to appreciate the significance of that social context. One key aspect of it is the process of socialization. This is the process by which we are, in a sense, "inducted" into our society and culture. It is where we are taught how to be acceptable members of our society. We learn norms and values, expected roles and so on.

Habitus

Through this process we become part of our society and our society becomes part of us, in the sense that we internalize its norms and so on. This is an important part of identity development, as we shall see in Chapter 9. Linked to this is the important sociological concept of "habitus" introduced by the French social theorist, Pierre Bourdieu. As Maton explains:

Habitus is, Bourdieu states, "a socialized subjectivity" and "the social embodied" (Bourdieu and Wacquant, 1992a, pp. 127, 128)—it is, in other words, internalized structure, the objective made subjective. It is also how the personal comes to play a role in the social—the dispositions of the habitus underlie our actions that in turn contribute to social

structures. Habitus thereby brings together both objective social structure and subjective personal experiences, expressing, as Bourdieu put it,
"the *dialectic of the internalization of externality and the externalization of
internality*" (1977, p. 72, original emphasis).

(2012, pp. 52–53)

Habitus is a very useful concept for applied sociology. Giddens and Sutton
helpfully explain it as follows:

> People have embedded, internalized mental structures—their "habitus"—
> enabling them to handle and understand the social world. Habitus is the
> product of a long period spent inhabiting the social world from a specific
> position (such as class location), and individual habitus therefore varies
> considerably.
>
> *(2014, p. 25)*

What makes it helpful is that it can be used as a form of what Maton (2012)
calls a "socio-analysis," a way of revealing the hidden workings of society. In
other words, if we want to understand an individual, we need to understand
their habitus, the way in which they have internalized their social influences
and what they have made of those.

Culture and Meaning Making

A further important aspect of socialization to be aware of is the role of culture
in establishing frameworks of meaning. In Chapter 1 I emphasized the role
of meanings, as meanings are part of what bind us together in collectivities.
Part of socialization is "cultural transmission"—that is, the passing of cultural
norms, values and so on from one generation to the next (see the discussion of
autopoiesis above). Cultures are, of course, built around frameworks of meaning (the C level of PCS analysis), and so we can see that meanings are an important part of socialization. Indeed, we can see socialization as the process of
teaching children what it means to be a member of their society.

Communication

It goes without saying, of course, that communication is an essential part of
society: if there were no methods of communication available to us, there

could be no society. In particular, it is the complexity of language as a communication system and the sophistication it offers that enables us to have such an advanced level of social interaction on a global scale (Mooney and Evans, 2015).

However, although language is a central and hugely important aspect of communication as a social process, it is not the only one. Communication also depends on, for example, transport and supply systems, technology, the publishing industry, the media and so on. Although language will generally be used within these, they are needed to supplement language as a basis of communication. There is also, of course, nonverbal communication, incorporating body language and other behaviorally based forms of communication (violence is a form of communication, for example—Thompson, 2011a).

Practice Focus 4.2

David was a sales rep in a large company. He was doing reasonably well, but not achieving particularly high standards. He met his basic targets but only just, so he was not very happy in his job and was thinking of taking a different career direction. However, this all changed when he attended a training course on nonverbal communication. What he realized from this course was that he was saying all the right things, but his body language was not as effective as it could be. Because he was not happy in his work, he rarely smiled, he rarely made positive eye contact and didn't really make the best use of nonverbal communication. After the course things were different. It created a virtuous circle. His improved body language brought him better results; getting better results made him happier and more confident. That enabled him to do even better, and so it went on, from strength to strength. The training had emphasized that sales work is all about *social connection*, and that was the important message David took away with him.

There is, of course, much that could be said about communication as a social process, but given the limited space available, I will focus on just three aspects in particular:

- *We cannot not communicate* Just our very presence in the social world will tell people something about us. Our clothing, our hair (or lack of it), our tattoos (or lack of them), our body language, our activity (or lack of it), our mode of transport, and so on can all give people "messages" about us, even if those messages are: (i) not what we intended to "transmit;" and (ii) not necessarily accurate. This shows that communication is, by its very nature, a social phenomenon.

- *Communication operates through sociopolitical channels* This is linked to our theme of power. Once again we have to note that it is not a level playing field. The messages of the powerful are much more easily disseminated, whereas the voices of the relatively powerless will generally struggle to be heard. We shall return to this point in Chapter 5 when we discuss the media as a social institution.

- *Sociopolitical processes operate through communication, especially language* This is the other side of the coin from the previous point. Society largely operates through (language-based) communication. For example, it has long been recognized that various forms of discrimination oper- ate through language (he/man language that excludes or marginalizes women, for example, or patronizing and infantilizing language to refer to older people), although it is unfortunate that the oversimplifications of the "political correctness" approach have tended to trivialize the signifi- cance of language by failing to recognize the complexities involved. As I have argued previously, the PC attempts to simply ban the use of certain words (rather than looking more holistically at the issues involved) show a lack of understanding of how language works, how discrimination works and how learning works (Thompson, 2011a).

From an applied sociology point of view, language and communication are a rich seam to mine for insights into how people relate to one another, how they live their lives, how they carry out their work and so on. Whatever prob- lems people are encountering, communication issues will never be far away. Indeed, whatever aspect of society we are trying to understand or trying to act upon, communication is highly likely to be part of the mix. Developing a high-level understanding of communication in general and language use in particular is therefore a worthwhile investment of time, effort and energy.

Social Control

For society to exist there must be some form of control, some processes in place that safeguard society's members and the integrity of the society itself from harm. For example, there need to be mechanisms in place to protect people from crime or abuse—although what constitutes crime or abuse and how they are addressed will vary from society to society as they are, of course, social constructions. This is the positive side of social control, the protective side for society's members across the board. However, there is also a negative side to social control, in the sense that restrictions can be placed on people in certain circumstances that are not for their own protection, but for the protection of the vested interests of powerful groups (consider, for example, repressive regimes that ban dissenting voices against the political elite).

Social control is not, therefore, good or evil, it all depends on what it is being used for and how it is being carried out, the processes that are involved. Let us now look at what some of those processes are and how they work.

Hegemony

One social control process we have already encountered is that of hegemony, which refers to control or dominance, not through force, but through ideas. A contemporary example of this would be the currently dominant political and economic philosophy of neoliberalism, with its twin beliefs that: (i) the market, left to its own devices, will produce the best results; and (ii) public services should be available on a minimal or residual basis only. In reality, of course, this approach produces considerable inequality and fuels a range of social problems (Mendoza, 2015; Thompson, 2017a) and serves mainly to transfer money from the general populace to the most wealthy and powerful groups (Piketty, 2014).

What is significant in terms of hegemony is that this philosophy works because people accept it uncritically, even where it is against their own interests. As we have noted (and will explore in more detail in Chapter 6), ideology works by presenting the social order as if it were the natural order, that it has to be that way (rather than it is this way because it serves the interests of the power elite for things to be presented this way). Piketty captures this point well when he argues that:

> French poet Charles Baudelaire once wrote "La plus belle des ruses du diable est de vous persuader qu'il n'existe pas"—the devil's finest trick is to persuade you that he does not exist. This is the trick pulled by the neoliberal project. Convince billions of people that there is no plan; that we live in a post-ideological world; that there is a free market; that the trickle-down effect means that the best way of increasing the wealth of the poor is to increase the wealth of the rich. This is an absurdity. It flies

in the face of all evidence to the contrary. It is propaganda, a fairy tale told to children.

(2014, p. 181)

One of the reasons critical thinking is so strongly advocated in higher education is that there are so many ways in which hegemony lies in wait, ready to convince us that what serves the interests of the elite is actually good for everyone. Critical thinking in general and the sociological imagination in particular should help us to see through these "fairy tales," or, more accurately, these ideological narratives that tell a biased story, a story biased towards keeping the wheels of power turning and leaving the relations of dominance and subordination intact.

I have used neoliberalism as an example, but it is just one such instance. We could also have explored patriarchy, white supremacism, ageism or any number of other ideologies that work in the same way to exercise a degree of control, and not generally in the interests of the populace at large.

In terms of applied sociology, "consciousness raising" can be a useful tool. That is, by helping people understand ideology and hegemony, you can help them to slip away from their grip to a certain extent (but never completely). For example, helping people oppressed by patriarchal assumptions and expectations to realize that these are socially constructed and are not the "natural order" or inevitable can be, if handled well in the right circumstances, enormously empowering.

Government and Governmentality

Hegemony, by its very nature, operates "behind the scenes," it is largely surreptitious. Government, by contrast, operates on the basis of being open and democratic (although not without hegemony having an influence too). However, governmentality is more than just "government" in the usual political sense. As Lund explains:

> Social constructionism provides a vehicle for examining what Foucault has called "governmentality"—the ways in which governing takes place without seeming to govern. Power is exercised by the creation of "technologies of the self" whereby people absorb socially constructed norms of "responsible" conduct. . . .
>
> *(2011, p. 12)*

There are social expectations that citizens should behave in certain ways (honestly, decently and so on), in line with a set of social values that are endorsed by the society concerned. In this way, it becomes part of socialization as well as social control. Linking Foucault with Bourdieu, we could also develop links between the former's "technologies of the self" (that is, social mechanisms for maintaining a sense of identity) with the latter's "habitus."

In simple terms, government is the process of running a country, but governmentality goes beyond this to include other processes of setting up, and policing, social expectations. In simple applied sociology terms, what is useful about this is that it can help us to understand the problems and challenges that arise when people come into conflict with the social behavior: crime, anti-social behavior, illicit drug use and so on.

Medicalization

The process of medicalization is a form of atomism. It involves taking complex, multi-level phenomena, like mental health problems or addiction difficulties, and presenting them in a straightforward way as symptoms of an illness. This process has been heavily criticized by a wide range of scholars (Davies, 2013), but it continues to be a dominant way of thinking in many quarters. However, from a sociological perspective, we can see that this is a process of control. By focusing on individual factors and neglecting wider concerns, medicalization distracts attention from key issues, such as discrimination, oppression and power relations. Jerry Tew's voice is one of the many now challenging medicalization:

> It is being increasingly recognised that the power issues are closely implicated in the onset of mental distress. Experiences of humiliation, social defeat and entrapment are often seen as precursors of mental distress (Gilbert and Allen, 1998; Selten and Cantor-Graae, 2007). People who have come to see their relationship with the world in terms of an external locus of control—seeing their lives as being largely controlled by the actions of others—are more likely to develop psychosis in adulthood (Bentall et al., 2001; Frenkel et al., 1995). Research into voice-hearing experiences suggests that it is not so much the content of voices that can be problematic, but one's perceptions of the power relations between oneself and one's voices (Birchwood et al., 2000).

> *(2011, p. 47)*

What we can see here is a vicious circle: wider social issues place significant pressures on certain individuals who then develop what come to be seen as "symptoms of mental illness." Further social pressures are then placed on the individuals concerned when a stigmatizing and shame-inducing label is placed on them. The resulting distress is then interpreted as further instances of "symptomatology." The vicious circle of disempowerment continues. Again, this means that sociology can offer insights at a practical level when it comes to rising to the challenges presented by mental health problems. As Tew so aptly puts it: "empowerment and reclaiming personal efficacy are at the core of recovery from mental distress (Chamberlin, 1997)" (2011, p. 47). That gives someone using applied sociology a lot to work with.

Voice of Experience 4.2

My role in the mental health system is to counterbalance the medical perspective, My training emphasized that all health issues have a social perspective, but mental health issues especially so. It can be difficult at times, because our patients have such an ingrained view of their problems as being rooted in "illness." It can be quite a struggle at times to get them to think more holistically about their life circumstances. But, every now and again, we get a huge success when someone is able to break out of that defeatist mentality.

Lal, a social worker in a multidisciplinary mental health team

Institutionalization

The establishing and maintaining of social institutions are what the process of institutionalization is all about. This will be the topic of Chapter 5, and so I will say nothing further here, other than to state that social institutions and social processes intertwine in a number of complex ways.

Discrimination

Discrimination, in its most basic form, is simply the identification of difference—the ability to distinguish between A and B, for example. As such, it is a neutral term; it can be positive or negative. However, in its moral, political or professional sense, it is used to refer to a two-part process: (i) one or more differences are identified among groups of people (ethnicity, for example);

and (ii) the less powerful group(s) are treated less favorably and thereby suffer one or more detriments (that is, lose out in some ways). This is, of course, the basic process underpinning racism, sexism and so on. It is also the source of oppression. It is through processes of discrimination that oppressed minorities are systematically disadvantaged.

Discrimination can be seen to arise through a range of other processes, all of which follow this pattern of identifying differences and then "punishing" minority groups for being different from the mainstream. The following are just some of these.

Marginalization

As the name implies, marginalization is the process of pushing certain individuals or groups to the margins of society, not including them in the mainstream. For example, disabled people can easily find themselves struggling to be included due to ill-informed social attitudes, discriminatory assumptions, stereotypes and so on. This reflects the "social model" of disability mentioned earlier, rooted in the idea that it is social factors that marginalize and exclude disabled people, rather than whatever physical condition they may have (Oliver and Barnes, 2012).

Similarly, ageist assumptions to the effect that older people lack competence and capability, that they are "past their sell-by date," and so on reflect and reinforce power structures that place older people in a subordinate position (Applewhite, 2016). In this way older people are marginalized, separated from mainstream society in a number of ways.

I could give more and more examples of groups or categories of people that are subject to discrimination through processes of marginalization. However, I feel it is safe to assume that it should be clear now that marginalization, although quite common, is actually quite a destructive process. Once again, a sociologically informed awareness of this process puts us in a much stronger position to guard against it and challenge it where possible.

Stigmatization

Literally a stigma is a "mark," and so to be stigmatized amounts to being "marked" in some way. In this regard, a stigma is a mark of shame. It is attached to people who are deemed to have done something shameful, to be inferior or inadequate in some way. Such labels are not necessarily applied fairly, and this is how the process comes to be seen as part of discrimination. Stigmatization converts being "different from" (that is, being a member of a minority group) into being "inferior to" or "of lesser value than." Consequently, we need to be aware of this and use that awareness to spur us to challenge the process. In this way, we can seek to make a positive difference to the lives of people—individually and/or collectively—who bear the brunt of unfair stigmatization.

Pathologizing

Closely linked to the idea of stigmatization is that of pathologizing. This refers to the process whereby individuals or groups are held responsible for problems that are not of their making. For example, people with mental health problems are "pathologized" as "mad axe murderers," even though they are more likely to be victims of crime than perpetrators of it, and, if you were to be murdered, the chances are that the assailant would be known to you and perfectly sane. Another example of pathologizing would be to stereotype black people as likely criminals. In addition, gay men can be pathologized through the assumption that to be gay means being a pedophile. Clearly, this is another area where sociological awareness of the process can offer useful practical insights.

Practice Focus 4.3

Cal was a police officer in a specialist child protection unit. He was in a same-sex relationship, but kept this fact to himself, as he did not want to risk getting any ribbing from his colleagues, some of whom were quite "macho" and insensitive in their attitudes. In his child protection work he was well aware of the unhelpful and misleading stereotype that gay men, by their very nature, were a sexual threat to young boys. He had, on occasions, had to challenge people who seemed to be falling into this trap. However, what he found really distressing was when he was involved in a case where a well-known gay activist was accused of sexually abusing a number of boys. At first, he thought: "Here we go again, more stereotyping going on," but he knew they would have to take the allegations seriously, as that was the policy. However, when the alleged perpetrator was interviewed as part of the investigation, he broke down in tears and admitted having abused dozens of boys over the years. Hearing about what had happened to the boys was difficult enough for Cal to take. Knowing that this gay man really had been a sexual predator made it even harder. But, what was hardest of all was that this man was a gay activist, a strong proponent of gay rights and a strong challenger of anti-gay stereotypes. So, for him to have carried out so much abuse was almost too much for Cal to take. He was intelligent enough to know that the fact that an unfair stereotype about gay men being a threat to children existed did not mean no gay men were a threat. Coming face to face with this situation was heartbreaking. If we are to break down this stereotype, how damaging is it for a gay activist to be an abuser?, Cal thought. Some would have seen this as ironic, but Cal just saw it as tragic. It made him realize how complex these situations are.

Implications for Practice

This chapter has alerted us to the fact that there are numerous social processes that go on; some can be positive and helpful, others destructive. It is important to note too that they do not operate in isolation—for example, marginalization can bring stigmatization, and so on. As applied sociologists we should be able to see complex dynamics operating, with different process interacting with each other, all within a framework of sets of structures characterized by relations of power (dominance and subordination). Our awareness of such matters should put us in a well-informed position to seek to influence these processes, reinforcing the positives and addressing the negatives in whatever reasonable ways we can.

Due to the role of ideology (to be discussed in more detail in Chapter 6), it is generally the case that these processes remain largely invisible—and this is in large part where they get their power from: they operate beneath the surface without challenge, camouflaged by the ideological sleight of hand of presenting the social order as if it were the natural order. The sociological imagination, focused as in this chapter on social processes, should make them visible. They are only invisible until you know where and how to look.

Conclusion

As we noted earlier, sociology revolves around the idea that we are social animals. One of the things that makes us different from other animals, even those who have some form of society, is that we are able to do things on a large-scale collective basis. To reiterate Harari's point:

If you tried to bunch together thousands of chimpanzees into Tiananmen Square, Wall Street, the Vatican or the headquarters of the United Nations, the result would be pandemonium. By contrast, Sapiens regularly gather by the thousands in such places. Together, they create orderly patterns—such as trade networks, mass celebrations and political institutions—that they could never have created in isolation. The real difference between us and chimpanzees is the mythical glue that binds together large numbers of individuals, families and groups. This glue has made us the masters of creation.

(2011, p. 42)

Sadly, it has also made us masters of destruction, but that is a story for another time.

This "mythical glue" is an example of discourse—a narrative that allows millions of people to work together by sharing ideas and meanings. As we shall see in Chapter 5, a key part of that is social institutions. But another important part is, of course, the complex web of social processes we have been exploring together here. Large-scale social networks contribute to, and are shaped by, social processes. Being tuned in to these processes will not give us easy answers to whatever challenges we face, but it will give us invaluable insights and another part of the platform of understanding on which to build.

Points to Ponder

1. What three social processes are likely to be making a significant difference to your area of work, your planned area of work or an area of work that interests you?
2. Choose two of those three processes. How might the two of them interact and influence each other?
3. How might you make use of having a better understanding of social processes?

Exercise 4

The point has been made that communication is a highly significant social process. For this exercise what I want you to do is to: (i) list the forms of communication you use in your current working life / studies; (ii) consider how these can go wrong; and (iii) note down what you could potentially do to prevent things going wrong in relation to communication.

Social Institutions   5

Introduction

In everyday speech, the term "institution" is often used to refer to an organization or part of an organization. For example, a hospital or university may be referred to as an institution. However, in its specific sociological sense, it refers to what some people would call "building blocks" of society. They are entities (social facts) that have developed over time and are now recognized as significant component parts of society. Examples would be the family, the law, the education system and the economy. These are all social constructions, of course, but, while some social constructions can be short lived, the idea of an institution is that it has stood the test of time, in the sense that: (i) it has been around for a long time; and (ii) its longevity gives it a considerable degree of power and influence.

Just as Chapter 4 could not realistically explore *all* social processes, we shall not, in this chapter, be able to cover all social institutions. However, in the space available, we should be able to examine some of the main ones and, in so doing, show their importance and consider how a knowledge of them can be useful from an applied sociology perspective.

Society

My first choice of social institution to consider may seem surprising, but, strange though it may seem, society itself is a social institution. The fact that we think of society as an entity in its own right shows that it is a social institution. For example, it is not difficult to imagine a society that does not think of itself as a society. They may have ideas about social issues, but not have a conception of a unifying whole called "society." Margaret Thatcher, the former UK prime minister once famously (notoriously?) said that there is no such thing as society, only individuals and families. Of course, she was wrong, as she was making the classic mistake of assuming that, because something is socially constructed, it is not real. Social facts are just as real as any other fact, of course. However, what we do have to recognize, is that, just as "nature" is a social construction, so too is society (unless you live among a group of people that does not have a conception of "society"—Thatcherville?).

Within the social institution of society we have the important notion of "social capital" (Lin, 2002). Just as there can be huge differences between individuals and groups in terms of financial or economic capital, there can also be significant variations in terms of what has come to be known as social capital. This term refers to the social and interpersonal resources we have access to. Consider the following two scenarios:

- Lottie is employed in a large organization where she has contacts with a wide range of people, and where there is a very active staff club. She is also a member of a number of social clubs and charitable organizations. She is part of a large, close-knit family and is also very active in her local church. She is still in touch with various people she went to school and university with. She knows a lot of people in positions of power.

- Minnie works nights in a taxi office on her own. The only human contact she has at work is by radio with the taxi drivers. She does not have the chance to make friends with anyone at work. Working nights means that it is difficult for her to be a member of any clubs or societies. She has long since lost contact with the few friends she had at school and she did not go to university. She is not a member of a church. Her parents are no longer alive, and her brother and two sisters live a long way away, and they are no longer close emotionally either. She does not know anyone in a position of power.

It does not take much thought to come to the conclusion that these two people represent the two extremes of the social capital spectrum. If you were called upon to help them in some way, their social capital status could prove to be very significant—for example, in terms of potential sources of support and/or opportunities for empowerment.

The distribution of social capital owes much to individual and familial choices and circumstances, but it would be naive not to recognize that social factors also play a key part. For example, social structures and processes associated with disability, old age, language group, membership of a minority ethnic group and so on can also be important factors.

Linked to the idea of social capital is that of "cultural capital" (Bourdieu, 1986). This refers to the status and power that come from qualifications, accreditations, knowledge, aesthetics, accent and other such elements that can be of credibility value in certain circumstances. There is also "symbolic capital," based on respect and social standing. These forms of capital can, as Bourdieu put it, be "exchanged"—that is, one form of capital can be used to generate another. For example, cultural capital could be used at an interview to secure a well-paid job and thereby increase economic capital (and possibly symbolic and social capital too). As Patricia Thomson explains:

> Bourdieu nominated four forms of capital: economic (money and assets); cultural (e.g. forms of knowledge; taste, aesthetic and cultural preferences; language, narrative and voice); social (e.g. affiliations and networks; family, religious and cultural heritage) and symbolic (things which stand for all of the other forms of capital and can be "exchanged" in other fields, e.g. credentials).
>
> *(2012, p. 67)*

In developing our understanding of society as a social institution in its own right, we can see that the interplay of these different forms of capital creates patterns of differential access to various kinds of resources. Once again we see that an atomistic approach that focuses narrowly on the individual would pay no heed to these powerful and complex interactions. An awareness of these issues gives us further insights that can help us understand people's circumstances, the challenges they face and potential ways of addressing them.

Practice Focus 5.1

Siobhan was a careers officer in a community college. A key part of her job was to help students think carefully about potential future options for careers and then help them move positively in the right direction in terms of what needs to be done to stand a good chance of getting a foothold in that career setting. What she had realized very early in her work in this area was that some of the students were already writing themselves off, even at such a young age. It was as if they knew that their social backgrounds gave them very limited capital in terms of what they would need in order to be impressive in the field of work they would really like to be. A tell-tale example of this was when Joanne, a second-year student, told Siobhan: "Ideally, I would like to be a doctor, but I know that people from where I come from don't get to be doctors. I'll probably end up working in a store." Siobhan recognized that what she had learned about different types of capital was a very real aspect of the world she was now working in.

The Family

The family is a social institution that is generally positively viewed; it tends to get good press for the most part. It is associated with love, support and security, and there is clearly much to be said for what the family offers as an institution. However, we also need to recognize that there is a downside to the family in a number of ways:

- *Conflict and rejection* Some degree of conflict is, of course, inevitable in family life, but in some families, the level of conflict can be alarmingly high. In some cases, this can lead to a family member being rejected, leaving the family home and potentially becoming homeless. Indeed, family conflict is a major source of homelessness.
- *Abuse* Whether we are talking about child abuse, the abuse of vulnerable adults or domestic abuse, the family is a primary site of such problems (Corby et al., 2012). In some families, all three types of abuse can be taking place.
- *Discrimination* A child or adolescent who comes out as gay, a family member who converts to another religion, a family member in a relationship with someone from a different ethnic group—all of these can be scenarios characterized by discrimination, and often bitterly and extensively so.
- *Denial of opportunities* Often families have aspirations for children that the children do not share. This can lead to conflict, of course, but another outcome of such situations is children abandoning their own dreams and fitting in with family aspirations on the basis of "anything for a quiet life," often with profoundly dispiriting consequences.

Shaw captures the picture well: "Families can be warm and supportive; they can also be oppressive, destructive, and harmful to their members" (2013, p. 175).

Of course, it is important to balance out the picture that the family can so often be a safe haven, a source of security, a sound basis for development and a place of joy and contentment. But we should not let the generally positive view of the family blind us to the problems and the challenges that can be part of family life.

We also need to be aware that conceptions of family life change over time, are different in different cultures and take different forms (parents and biological children; step families; foster families; adoptive families; families with grown-up children still living at home; families where children have left home; families, with extended family members resident; and so on). The archetypal nuclear family represents a minority of actual family forms.

From an applied point of view, what this tells us is that we need to look carefully at family issues. We should not assume that family life is necessarily problematic, but nor should we adopt a rose-tinted view of the family as necessarily a safe haven.

Voice of Experience 5.1

I have always been fascinated by family life. I was very lucky to have a very positive upbringing and my family now is a happy one. But right from my school days, through university and even now, I have been aware that not everyone is that lucky. Family life can be hell for some people. It's not all like the way it is presented in the Sunday supplements. It's not all Sunday roasts and happy days. But, what's perhaps most important of all is to know that our families, for good or ill, are a major influence on our lives. That's why I chose a career that involves working with families.

Bernadette, a family therapist

Community

This is another social institution that tends to be seen positively, even though in reality, it too is a mixed blessing. The notion of community conjures up images of camaraderie, and support, a sense of belonging and, in large part a sense of identity. However, communities can also be sources of violence, abuse, exploitation and all manner of negative phenomena. So, as with the family, we are encountering a social institution that needs to be considered carefully. We should not write off communities, but nor should we view them through naive, unrealistically positive lenses.

It is also important to recognize that the term "community" is quite ambiguous, in the sense that it can be used in various ways. Community can mean:

- *The local community* This tends to refer to the local neighborhood, although different people will have different ideas about the boundaries of their local community. Where a particular community begins or ends is likely to be debatable and may be different in different circumstances. For example, children who attend a particular school may regard other children from within that school's catchment area as members of their local community when it comes to school matters. But, for matters outside of school life, those children from further afield may be considered to be from a different community.
- *The regional community* Often the focus of community is broader than the immediate neighborhood. That sense of community can at times be extended to the local region (however defined). For example, if an achievement worthy of pride occurs outside the immediate neighborhood, but within the same region, the sense of pride may be shared across that region: "It was one of our people who did so well."
- *The national community* At other times, the sense of community can extend to a whole nation or even to a set of nations (Europe, North America, Australasia). This sense of community will arise when something happens that reinforces people's sense of national (or cross-national) identity, thereby broadening the focus from a local or regional sense of community.
- *A community of interest* This too is a broad concept, as communities of interest can come in various shapes and sizes. The key element is a sense of belonging, a sense of being part of something bigger than yourself. Examples would include:
    - *An industry community* This could be plastics, telecommunications, health care or whatever.
    - *A professional community* Engineers, law enforcement professionals, social workers, and teachers would all be examples of this.
    - *An academic or intellectual community* This would include sociologists, psychologists, astrophysicists, literary critics and so on.
    - *A shared leisure community* Supporters of the same sports team are likely to have a sense of community, as are people who share an interest in cinema, horticulture, poetry or whatever.

Which communities people belong to, how they relate to them, and how they are treated by them can be significant factors in shaping our quality of life, our health, our relationships and so on. The sociological imagination can therefore be usefully drawn upon to illuminate how community, as a social institution, plays out in people's lives and how people's lives contribute to the creation and maintenance of communities.

Government

In Chapter 4 we explored government and governmentality as social processes, but here our focus is on government as a social institution. The idea that we should have a government, whether democratically elected or not, is something that has evolved historically (think ancient tribes and chieftains; think medieval monarchy). In the overall history of humankind, governments, as currently understood, are a relatively recent development. As citizens we vest power in a number of people to run the country and represent our interests through historically agreed protocols. These vary from country to country, state to state, but the basic principle is the same.

In principle, this is relatively simple and straightforward. In reality, though, there are many complex processes that come into play, and, of course, ideology and hegemony are also key factors. As is generally the case, ideology serves to present the social order (that can be changed) as the natural order (that cannot). This is a way of securing and sustaining positions of power. In a sense, this is typical of social institutions, in so far as they tend to serve as a locus of power. That power can be used ethically for legitimate means, or it can be abused.

Ideology also plays a part in rendering the workings of power largely invisible. Atomism, as a dimension of ideology, focuses attention on individual matters and thereby distracts attention from the wider operations of power, including both legitimate and illegitimate power dynamics within a governmental context. One of the implications of this atomism is a tendency to encourage a sense of powerlessness and disaffection. That disaffection can then manifest itself as a process of depoliticization, producing a lack of interest in political participation and engagement, thereby leaving the status quo intact, with the power elite continuing to hold the reins.

The sociological imagination can help people to become more aware of the role and significance of government and appreciate what options are available for having a voice.

Practice Focus 5.2

Zafar was a trade union official working mainly with public sector employees. A key part of his work was as an education officer for the union. He ran courses, sought out useful online resources and did whatever he could to help members learn and thereby increase their career development options. What he liked to focus on particularly was political awareness raising. It saddened and worried him that the level of political awareness was so low. There were many members who never voted because they were just so disconnected from government and the world of politics. Then there were others who did vote, but had only a very superficial understanding of what they were voting for (or against). A couple of members had accused him of trying to "indoctrinate" them. No, he said, indoctrination is telling people what to think and who to vote for, and he was certainly not doing that. What he was actually doing in fact—or at least trying to do—was playing a part in empowering them by helping them to be better informed about political processes and issues, and indeed about government as a social institution.

The Law

Closely linked to the idea of government is that of the law, mainly because government is the source of legislation. However, it is important not to equate the two. In democratic societies, the two are kept separate and then the law (in the form of the judiciary) can act as a safeguard in relation to government to seek to ensure that governmental authority is not exceeded.

The law can be divided into three main areas:

* *Criminal law* The fact that certain actions (or omissions) are deemed "criminal" in some societies but not others illustrates that crime is socially constructed, and so too is the criminal law. As Leonard explains:

  > Although we typically take for granted the way we think about crime, assuming that our definitions of it are only common sense, things are not as simple or straightforward as they first appear. Crime is not a purely objective, universal, or unchanging category but is instead socially defined, meaning that how we understand and interpret it changes and depends to a large extent on the social context.
  >
  > *(2015, pp. 20–21)*

  Although the focus is on justice, a critical sociological perspective reveals that there are various inequalities and injustices built into the criminal law system. The sociological imagination is therefore an important tool for anyone working in the criminal justice system, probation officers, for example.
* *Civil law* This relates to the process of litigation where one party can sue one or more others. Again this is a field with an explicit focus on

justice, and yet it is characterized by considerable inequality. Whoever has the financial resources to bring a case to court is in a position at least to secure justice, but, of course, there will be many who cannot afford to pursue legal action. It would also be naive not to recognize that ideology and hegemony can have a part to play within the legal system, bringing with them assumptions and perspectives that are far from bias free.

- *Constitutional law* As mentioned above, this is part of the democratic system. The law will generally play a part in safeguarding democracy by making sure that politicians do not go against the constitution of their country. This acts as a protective limitation on the power of politicians. However, the extent to which this operates in practice will vary from country to country, just as the nature and extent of democracy vary considerably across the globe.

The law is a complex area, both in its technical detail and in its operation within society. Sociology can help us develop a fuller understanding of the latter, a useful set of insights in any work context where legal matters are to the fore.

The Media

I emphasized the importance of communication in Chapter 4. We now return to that topic by focusing on the media. Media is the plural of medium, so, when we are talking about the media, we are referring to the various channels (mediums) of communication. The most obvious examples of the media are newspapers, magazines, radio and television (often referred to as the mass media because of the vast numbers of people they can potentially reach). However, there are also other channels of communication that receive less attention, such as cinema and the education system, both of which can have very far-reaching influences, of course.

These are what are now increasingly being referred to as the traditional media. This is because they are now vying for position with the new generation of "social media," such as blogs, online discussion forums, Facebook, LinkedIn, Instagram, Twitter and many more, not least YouTube which is immensely popular as a source of information and entertainment.

Much has been written and talked about in terms of an era of information overload and the fragmentation of social life that occurs because of it, with different people getting their information from very different sources. However, others have a more positive view of the proliferation of channels of communication, with social media having the potential to bypass conventional media that are owned by large corporations that communicate in ways that safeguard the interests and positions of power of their owners and shareholders. For example, Owen Jones, in an important work, highlights the "Establishment" bias of not only the media, but also other social institutions, again reinforcing the message that the playing field is not a level one in terms of various social structures and their uneven power relations of dominance and subordination, even if ideology gives us a persuasive and pervasive message that it is (Jones, 2015).

Similarly, Chomsky writes of the role of traditional media in sustaining existing relations of power:

> So what the media do, in effect, is to take the set of assumptions which express the basic ideas of the propaganda system, whether about the Cold War or the economic system or the "national interest" and so on, and then present a range of debate within that framework—so the debate only enhances the strength of the assumptions, ingraining them in people's minds as the entire possible spectrum of opinion that there is. So you see, in our system what you might call "state propaganda" isn't expressed as such, as it would be in a totalitarian society—rather it's implicit, it's presupposed, it provides the framework for debate among the people who are admitted into mainstream discussion.
>
> *(in Mitchell and Schoeffel, 2002, p. 13)*

This is an important passage sociologically. For example, I have had discussions with people who argue that totalitarian, repressive regimes tell people what to think and thereby close off alternative views, while the media in democratic societies do not do this and are therefore not biased. However, this view is missing the point that bias creeps in through more subtle means, such as choice of which topics are covered on news bulletins, how they are presented, and, as Chomsky notes, in what frame of reference. The language used can also be significant. For example, I remember a television news bulletin some years ago reporting on industrial action in France and stating that French workers are "notorious" for standing up for their rights. The choice of that word clearly indicated disapproval of worker solidarity, and was therefore not at all neutral.

Another example of bias is offered by Chomsky when he states:

> Well, I once asked another editor I know at the Boston Globe why their coverage of the Israeli/Palestinian conflict is so awful—and it is. He just

laughed and said, "How many Arab advertisers do you think we have?" That was the end of that conversation.

(in Mitchell and Schoeffel, 2002, p. 22)

Perhaps social media can make more of a positive difference? While there are now many cases on record of where social media usage has succeeded in getting important messages into the public domain while bypassing the biases of traditional media, social media are not an exclusively progressive force. Communication channels that can be used in empowering ways can also be used in oppressive ways at times—for example, in propagating terrorist messages and hate crime. "Cyberbullying" has become a significant problem in some quarters and, of course, the proliferation of online pornography has done little to challenge the patriarchal tendency to present women primarily if not exclusively as sexual objects.

The media are therefore a complex subject matter, with a wide range of sociological issues associated with them. An applied sociology perspective can therefore give us a more critical, holistic perspective on these very powerful channels of communication and the impact (for good or ill) that they can have on individuals, groups and even whole societies.

Voice of Experience 5.2

I work for a non-profit organization that helps people with alcohol and drugs problems. Every single client I have met has been able to tell a distressing story of tragedy in their life: abuse rejection, homelessness, bullying, exploitation or any combination of these. We do our best to help them, but what makes our work so much harder is the media. They present people with drug problems as the lowest of the low, as if they are some sort of inferior species—at best inadequate and, at worst, evil. What really galls me is that the people producing this rubbish have probably had privileged lives where they would have no idea what our people have been through. People are happier to support animals that have hard times than people who have been through the mill.

Caro, a drugs counselor

Religion

Another very powerful and influential social institution is religion. For a significant proportion of the human population, religion is a major feature of their lives, the source of their moral code, the basis of their spiritual life and, indeed, their whole worldview. It can also be the basis of their social life, affect what work they do or how they do it. Religion can, of course, also be a tremendous force for good in society, while also contributing to significant problems, not least in terms of conflicts between different religions (Cavanaugh, 2009) or different sects within the same religion (McKittrick and McVea, 2012).

I earlier emphasized that an important part of sociology is developing a holistic understanding of meanings and how these arise in a social context. This is clearly relevant to religion, as religions can be understood as major sources of meaning for their adherents. These meanings are, of course, social, as Hamilton explains:

> In providing meaning, religion is often said not simply to address existential questions relating to the individual but also to play a central social role. It provides justification for actions and legitimation of practices, customs and social arrangements. Sociological approaches to religion have usually stressed its role in upholding the social order. It is certainly clear that religious systems have generally been locked into the wider social order. To explain the world in ways that make it meaningful, inevitably entails explaining also the social order in a meaningful way and thereby legitimating it. Thus religion has a social as well as an individual dimension.
>
> *(2001, p. 273)*

Spirituality is, of course, a key element of religion, although it needs to be acknowledged that religion is not the only source of spirituality (Thompson, 2017c). As I have discussed in an earlier work, while spirituality clearly has a personal, even intimate, dimension to it, it is also profoundly social and thus an area of life that sociology can cast light on:

> Existential questions are often addressed at an individual level, concerned with the personal challenges that each of us faces. However, we need to understand these personal challenges in a wider social context, recognizing that there will also be cultural and structural factors to take into account. . . . How religion affects the way we experience grief is sociologically significant, insofar as that experience is fundamentally rooted in society—it does not occur in social isolation, unaffected by social interactions, processes, institutions and structures. To gain a fuller understanding of grief as an existential challenge that religion has

the potential to address, we therefore need to incorporate a sociological dimension.

(Thompson, 2017c, p. 339)

In this passage my focus was on grief and how this raises spiritual questions that are both personal and social. However, this is just one example. We can look more broadly at religion and spirituality as social phenomena in terms of how they relate to a wide range of issues and concerns. It is no coincidence that there is a major body of literature on the sociology of religion (Davie, 2013; Hamilton, 2001), given that religion plays such an important role in society and social processes, institutions and so on arise within religion—it is a two-way relationship.

From an applied perspective, there is considerable scope for the sociological imagination to be brought to bear in dealing with issues relating to religion and, indeed, to spirituality, whether experienced within or without a religious context. One example would be where there are problems relating to religious differences where there is the potential for sociology's critical and holistic perspective to offer a fuller understanding that can be used to develop plans for moving forward constructively. As with other areas of applied sociology, there are no easy, guaranteed answers, but sociology can help us to see the big picture, and that can put us in a much stronger position when it comes to understanding what is happening and responding helpfully to it.

Practice Focus 5.3

Darren was a specialist youth worker seconded to work with the police on a project relating to gangs. The project was based in a strongly multi-ethnic inner city area where there was a long-standing history of different ethnic groups vying with each other for dominance, especially among the young people there (hence Darren's involvement as a youth worker). He was aware that he would need to weigh up the situation quite carefully as it was quite a complex set of circumstances. He therefore did a lot of background research before getting actively involved with young people in the community. What quickly emerged from his research efforts was that there were significant religious differences within the community—in fact, there was no sense of overall community, just a set of religiously based mini-communities. He wondered how realistic it would be to use religion as a way of bringing people together.

He knew from studying sociology that religion can separate out different groups, but could also bring people together. He had read about the "peace and reconciliation" work that had been carried out in Northern Ireland and wondered whether there were any lessons that could be learned from that. He was wise enough to know there wouldn't be any easy solutions, but at least he now had something to work on in what otherwise seemed a hopeless situation of division and strife.

Implications for Practice

What we have explored in this chapter is a selection of social institutions. There are many more such institutions we could have explored if we had the space, but the territory we have covered should be sufficient to make it clear that social institutions are important aspects of society and social life. There will be times when addressing challenges in our working lives will be enhanced by considering the role of one or more social institutions, opportunities to make use of the sociological imagination in ways that give us helpful insights.

By their very nature, social institutions have been around for a while; they are historic social products that have evolved into their present form. This means that they can tell us a lot about society and the forces and processes that have produced them and indeed changed them over time. It would be a significant mistake not to recognize that, however solid and permanent social institutions may be, they are none the less continuing to change, evolving as society evolves. Consider, for example, the family. Our notions now of family life have changed drastically since Victorian times when children were used as chimney sweeps and are continuing to change—for example, in terms of the increasing (but far from universal) acceptance of same-sex relationships as a basis for family life.

As we noted, the media are also changing, with social media playing an increasing role in how people communicate with one another, how they learn about the world and how they live their lives. Social institutions therefore need to be understood as "dynamic," with a constant dialectical interaction of change processes and forces for continuity. Once again, then, we are dealing with very complex matters, and so a basic awareness will not be enough—we need the sort of sophisticated critical and holistic understanding that sociology can offer us. It is for this reason that an understanding of social institutions needs to be part of our applied sociology repertoire. When it comes to "implications for practice," we have plenty of territory to explore as we go about our business in whatever field of work we are engaged in. Consider the complexities of social institutions and the ways in which they influence people's lives and experiences and then contrast that understanding with an atomistic approach that focuses narrowly on the individual and pays no heed to that social context.

Conclusion

We are now halfway through our examination of the SPIDER in the web of society. We have noted the significance of social structures with their constant pronounced tendency to assign people to positions of either dominance or subordination, challenging the ideological notion that society is a level playing field. We have also seen that there are various powerful social processes constantly operating in society, processes that have profound and far-reaching consequences. And, in this chapter we have also reviewed how there are various social institutions, established entities that shape our social experiences in a number of ways. They can be understood as social filters, in the sense that our life experience and our understanding of it pass through those filters. Our information about what is happening in the world comes through the filter of the media; our approach to love, intimacy and relationships will have come through the filter of the institution of the family; and so on. We can reject the influence of those filters, of course, as in the case of people who reject family life and choose to live communally or in isolation. However, their understanding is likely to have come through that filter before they rejected it. Similarly, we may not believe what we read in the newspapers (especially certain newspapers), but that does not mean that newspapers and other media will not have acted as a filter.

It is no coincidence that there are such filters, of course. They work in ideological ways and operate as part of the process of hegemony, as discussed in Chapter 4. They play a part in keeping the wheels of power turning, and turning in the direction that suits the interests of the power elite. This is a key part of what we shall be discussing in Chapter 6 when we focus on discourse and ideology, but before we reach that point what I want to emphasize is that the three topics we have discussed so far—structures, processes and institutions—interact and influence each other. They are part of a complex, dynamic whole and appreciating those dynamics so that we are better informed when it comes to trying to influence those dynamics in a positive direction is exactly what applied sociology is all about.

Points to Ponder

1. Which social institutions (not limited to the ones discussed in this chapter) have the strongest influence on your life? How do they influence you?
2. In what ways can inequality manifest itself within the legal system and therefore within the law as a social institution?
3. In what ways might the media play a part in maintaining existing power relations?

Exercise 5

What role has religion played in social conflicts, historically and currently? How might religion, as a social institution, play a part in addressing such conflicts? What steps could be taken by faith leaders, for example? How might sociological insights contribute to this process?

Social Discourses and Ideologies

6

Introduction

In this chapter we are going to focus on the key concept of discourse and the related concepts of ideology and hegemony. We have already encountered these terms in earlier chapters, but their significance warrants a full chapter of their own. We shall therefore revisit the issues involved and explore more fully how they form part of the web of social life.

I shall discuss each of these key terms in turn before exploring how they manifest themselves in social life, using the "work ethic" as an example.

Discourse

Linguists and others use the term "discourse" in the straightforward sense of a conversation—an interaction between two or more people through language. Sociologists, largely through the influence of Michel Foucault (1972; 1975; 1977), have come to use it in a broader sense, broader in two ways: (i) it refers to how linguistic interactions develop frameworks of meaning, established sets of assumptions, and those frameworks shape actions, attitudes and emotions; and (ii) the frameworks of meaning will generally play a part in maintaining existing power relations—that is, serving the interests of the power elite.

In other words, discourses are forms of language use that influence our thought; our thoughts influence our actions; our actions then reflect and reinforce existing power relations. In this way, power operates through language. This fits with Foucault's view of power as ever-present. It is not just something that arises from time to time, it is a perpetual feature of human interaction, hence the emphasis on language (through which most interaction takes place).

For example, law and order are primarily maintained not by having police officers watching over our every move, but by having a widely accepted discourse of law and order that we are inducted into at an early age. It is the general acceptance that the law should be obeyed that enables law and order to be maintained for the most part. If people did not "buy into" that discourse, policing society would be virtually impossible.

Foucault has proven to be a major influence in sociology (Foucault, 1972; 1975; 1977). Many thinkers adopted his approach to power and saw it as an alternative to structurally based power relations. However, it makes more sense to see these as different forms of power, rather than competing theories (Thompson, 2007). For example, we can understand discourses to be examples of power at the **C** level of PCS analysis, linked to structural power relations at the **S** level.

Language and Power

The relationship between language and power is one that has been recognized for a very long time. For example, Bourdieu wrote about the links between language and social power (Bourdieu, 1988). However, what Foucault's work did was to develop a clearer picture of some of the mechanisms through which power and language interconnect.

Some examples of discourses would be the following:

- *Medicalization* As mentioned earlier, a medical discourse constructs mental health problems as symptoms of an illness (Cohen and Timini, 2008). The widespread use of medical terminology (diagnosis, treatment, prognosis, symptoms) sustains an ideology that gives considerable power to the psychiatric profession and fellow travelers (Tew, 2011). A similar discourse in relation to disability has been strongly challenged by the "social model" of disability—that is, an alternative discourse that speaks of rights, independence and empowerment.
- *Dependency* Much of the language used in relation to older people feeds a discourse of dependency, presenting older people as objects of pity, seen as "less than" younger citizens. Consider how the term "elderly," which

simply means old, is used to mean decrepit or in poor condition. I mentioned earlier Sue Thompson's work on reciprocity, how older people are often denied the opportunity to give as well as to receive, to contribute and be useful. This can be seen to be a direct consequence of a discourse of dependency that creates a framework of meaning that is profoundly disempowering (S. Thompson, 2015; 2016).

- *Parenting* The term "parenting" is gender neutral, in the sense that it can apply to men or women. However, consider what happens when we make the term gender specific. Think carefully about what is implied by the difference in meaning between "mothering" a child and "fathering" a child. This tells us a lot about social expectations in relation to who is expected to do what within a context of parenting.

Unfortunately, it has been common practice in some quarters for the relationship between language and power to be oversimplified, particularly in relation to matters of equality and diversity. I am thinking in particular of the notion of "political correctness," the attempt to make language use less discriminatory. This has mainly focused on seeking to ban certain words and replace them with more acceptable ones. This approach has mainly been a failure because it is based on an inadequate understanding of the relationship between language and power. That relationship is far more complex than the simplistic focus on certain words (Thompson, 2011a).

While it is certainly the case that certain words can "open the door" to a particular discourse, changing a discourse involves far more than simply changing a word. For example, if a social worker speaks or writes of their "treatment plan" for a client, they are invoking a medical discourse and all that goes with it in terms of power dynamics, perceptions of the client, expectations of the interaction and so on. However if their employer were to ban the use of the term "treatment" without any explanation why or any clarity about why it was deemed inappropriate, it is likely that a medical model would continue to operate, despite the term "treatment" no longer being used. Changing a word does not necessarily change a discourse. Any attempt to change a discourse needs to be much more sophisticated than that.

Using the Concept of Discourse

The notion of "discourse" is a useful one from an applied sociology point of view. This is because we can try to make sense of what is happening in any given situation by analyzing the discourse(s) involved. We can explore how language is used, what ideas or meanings are being invoked through that language and what power relations are involved. There are no simple formulas to be followed, but the more we are able to tune in to how discourses work, the stronger a position we will be in to appreciate what is happening, knowing why people are responding in certain ways and so on.

A useful concept in this regard is that of "text." In sociology this is used in a broader sense than its everyday version. In its technical sense it is used to refer to anything that can "contain" meaning. It can be literally a written text, it may be a symbol or set of symbols, a film or audio recording, an object—in fact anything that can be seen to hold meaning. What can happen in practice, then, is that we can undertake a "textual analysis," a review of what meanings are at play, how they are being conveyed, with what effect and so on.

Discourses begin with language, but also impinge on ideas, thoughts, actions and power relations. Language should therefore be our starting point—not just isolated words, as in the political correctness misadventure, but the various ways in which language plays a role in social life (Mooney and Evans, 2015; Thompson, 2011a).

Practice Focus 6.1

Sandra was a newly promoted manager in a financial services company. It was her first experience of management, but she was confident she could do well. However, life proved to be more difficult than she had anticipated, as she met a lot of resistance. Members of her team would not recognize her authority and tended to treat her quite disrespectfully. Fortunately, she had a supportive manager that she could talk openly to. Her manager, Jean, had had similar experiences when she had become a manager. Jean didn't use the technical term of discourse. Instead, she talked about her all-male team having a "mindset" that did not recognize women as managers. Women, so this mindset/discourse goes, do not belong in positions of authority. They then set about discussing how to develop strategies to change that mindset and to challenge that discourse.

Ideology

"Ideology," as I noted earlier is a term that is used in different ways by different theorists, but it is commonly used to refer to sets of ideas that have the effect of sustaining existing power relations. Renowned sociologist, Stuart Hall expresses it like this:

> the term "ideology" has come to have a wider, more descriptive, less systematic reference, than it did in classical Marxist texts. We now use it to refer to *all* organized forms of social thinking . . . It certainly refers to the domain of practical thinking and reasoning (the form, after all, in which most ideas are likely to grip the minds of the masses and draw them into action), rather than simply to well-elaborated and internally consistent "systems of thought". We mean the practical as well as the theoretical knowledges which enable people to "figure out" society, and within those categories and discourses we "live out" and "experience" our objective positioning in social relations.
>
> *(1996, p. 27)*

Ideologies operate in a similar way to discourses, in so far as they provide frameworks for making sense of the social world. They play a part in constructing sets of meanings that give us a coherent thread or perspective.

Dominant and Countervailing Ideologies

We can identify two main categories: dominant and countervailing. An ideology is described as dominant if it reflects (and reinforces) existing power relations. A countervailing ideology, by contrast, is one that challenges and seeks to displace one or more dominant ideologies. For example, patriarchy (literally "the rule of the father") can be seen as a dominant ideology, while feminism would be seen as a countervailing ideology, one that is in direct opposition to the dominant ideology. In this way, we can envisage an ideological battleground, in the sense that people are not just mindless passive puppets being led in one direction by the dominant ideology. There will be some who are committed fully to that ideology, some who are set against it, and some who accept elements of the dominant ideology plus elements of the countervailing ideology.

Ideologies and Theories

Although ideologies are sets of ideas, we should not confuse them with theories. This is for two reasons:

(i) Ideologies succeed when they achieve the status of not being questioned, when they are accepted uncritically as "common sense"—for example, the idea that it is natural for women to be caregivers because of their nurturing "nature." By contrast, theories succeed when they are open to challenge, but manage to survive any such challenges. So, theory and ideology are both sets of ideas, but they operate in vastly different ways. Theories try to extend our understanding ("Verstehen," as Weber called it), while ideologies try to establish unthinking adherence, unquestioning acceptance (see the discussion of hegemony below).

(ii) It is not uncommon for ideologies to involve contradictory or logically incompatible ideas, without their power being diminished in the slightest. Ideologies do not rely on rational argument—that is not the basis of their effectiveness. Theories, by contrast, need to be logical and avoid contradiction, otherwise their appeal will be severely limited.

Interpellation

Where the appeal of an ideology lies is in what is called "interpellation," a concept deriving from the work of Althusser (1971). It refers to the way ideologies "call out to us," the way they manage to "win hearts and minds"—that is, to win us over in some way. Through our upbringing and other channels we become constantly exposed to the dominant ideologies around us and, through the process of socialization discussed in Chapter 4, we internalize much of them, in the sense that they become part of our way of seeing the world ("Weltanschauung," to use the technical term).

We have already noted that ideological assumptions often manifest themselves as "common sense," "natural" or "obvious"—that is, taken for granted as beyond question. This is part of how interpellation works. Because the ideas within the ideology "ring true" for us, because we have come to feel "at home" with them, they have a profound influence on us. They become the norm, the foundation of our worldview unless and until they are challenged.

The Role of the Media

It should come as no surprise to recognize that the media play an important role in this. The mass media constantly put forward ideological messages that reinforce existing power relations (Mooney and Evans, 2015). This is not necessarily a deliberate strategy or ploy; it is a state of affairs that has evolved historically. What now exists is an ideological system. By system, I mean a set of interrelationships that "keep the wheels turning." Powerful groups are in a position to put forward and reinforce ideas that are in their interests, ideas that protect the status quo with its established power relations of domination. These ideas are transmitted through the media which helps them to come to be established as "normal" and "natural" and, again, as common sense. The fact that they are seen as common sense makes them very difficult to challenge.

The rise of social media presents the opportunity for countervailing ideologies to gain a stronger voice, although it would be naive not to recognize that social media are also complicit in disseminating the ideas that support dominant ideologies. So, what we are seeing once again is a complex mix of continuity and change. Dominant ideologies serve to sustain existing power relations and therefore play a conservative role in terms of ensuring a degree of continuity. However, there are also two elements of change: (i) the dominant ideas change and adapt over time—for example, the ideas that sustain patriarchy may be different from the ones that played this role in the 1950s, but patriarchy continues to be alive and well (albeit maintained in more subtle ways than would have been the case in the 1950s); and (ii) there will be continuing battles of ideas due to the role of countervailing ideologies. In this way ideologies evolve over time, but they continue to play the same role of exercising power through ideas.

From an applied sociology point of view, ideology is a useful concept. It helps to give us a broader picture of how power is operating, how ideas are being put across in ways that protect the status quo. We can make sure that we are not passive consumers of ideology and are prepared to look at it critically and holistically. There may also be times when we can help others to do this where this can help them with the challenges they face. For example, much work has been done to help women disempowered by patriarchal ideology to have much more control over their lives by recognizing the insidious effects of sexist ideas that seek to assign women to a narrow and restrictive set of social roles.

Similarly, many people have been helped to develop more fulfilling lives by being helped to understand that capitalist ideology encourages a strong emphasis on material goods, generally at the expense of more spiritual pursuits (Thompson, 2016c). In this way, some people can adopt a more critical and holistic perspective on their lives, recognizing that there can be more to life than securing more and more material goods or accumulating more and more wealth.

Voice of Experience 6.1

I work mainly with people who have been traumatized in some way, so they are feeling that their life is in disarray. They have lost sight of familiar landmarks and are all at sea. They usually want to get back to normal as soon as possible, but what I have noticed is that there is the opportunity for people to do better than to get back to normal, especially if their previous "normality" was not the happiest of states. I have seen people get annoyed with all the ads that are telling them to "buy, buy, buy." They have started to want more than what they wanted before, not more possessions, but a more satisfying life. A lot of the discussions I have with patients are about helping them to find more in life than materialism can offer them. For some, that's religion, but it doesn't have to be.

Dan, a chaplain in a specialist psychological trauma unit

Discourse and Ideology Compared

It should be apparent that discourse and ideology are similar concepts. Indeed, they overlap to a large extent. Because they have grown up in different theoretical traditions, they use different terminology and have different emphases (for example, the language that leads to certain ideas in discourses, but the ideas themselves in ideology). I am aware from my work with students that this can cause considerable confusion. This is why I am about to discuss how the two concepts interrelate. However, what I want to emphasize is that the similarities are much greater than the differences and that it is the common themes that are important when it comes to applied sociology.

Macro and Micro

One way of trying to understand the relationship between discourses and ideologies is to see the latter in macro terms and the former in more micro terms. This involves seeing ideologies as being on a much broader scale than ideologies. This would involve seeing discourses as some sort of sub-ideology, a component part of a wider ideology. An example of this would be to see capitalism as an ideology and consumerism as a discourse within it. Zygmunt Bauman has explored the role of consumerism. He likens it to a form of addiction:

In consumerist society, we can say that all shops and service outlets are first and foremost pharmacies—whatever, rather than drugs, they display on their shelves and stands and put on sale for present and prospective customers.

(2010, pp. 68–69)

A consumerist discourse around the appeal of buying materialist goods (and thus "buying into" a materialist discourse) propagates ideas around buying and consuming being good. These in turn encourage people not only to spend money, but also to spend money on the latest fashions in clothes, the latest perfumes, the latest IT gadgets and so on. The result is not just an emphasis on buying, but also on keeping buying, as trends change and new gadgets become available. This helps to create a "treadmill" of purchasing.

In this way, a discourse of consumerism becomes self-perpetuating. Consumerist language promotes the acceptance of consumerist ideas, and the transmission of those ideas (through the media, for example) then promotes consumerist behavior (buying). The buying keeps those who benefit from consumerism in profit and therefore serves their interests and protects their position of power.

However, if we look closely, we can see that consumerism, as a discourse, supports capitalism as an ideology. The success of consumerism as a discourse keeps the wheels of capitalism turning. It is in this sense that a discourse can be seen as a micro level manifestation of a macro-level ideology.

A further example would be neoliberalism as an ideology, and managerialism as a discourse within it. The managerialist discourse of focusing on targets and performance indicators reflects and reinforces a wider ideology of neoliberalism, with its emphasis on a reliance on the market and the minimization of public services. Making public services more like businesses (managerialist discourse) makes it easier to privatize public services (neoliberal ideology).

This is a useful model of the relationship as far as it goes. However, it is to a certain extent an oversimplification of a complex relationship between the two. But, the good news is that, from an applied sociology perspective, the relationship need not concern us too greatly. As I mentioned earlier, the important point is that the common ground between the two provides fertile soil for applied sociology interventions.

As I have stated in another work:

To summarize, ideology and discourse are concepts that:

- describe clusters of ideas and assumptions that help shape our understanding of the world;
- form the basis of the frameworks of meaning we develop to make sense of our lives;
- are closely linked to the concept of power . . .

(Thompson, 2018, p. 39)

By focusing on these commonalities we need not get bogged down in the subtle details of the relationship between the two. What we can usefully focus on is how our understanding can inform practical problem-solving activities at an applied level. The basic theoretical lesson here is that: (i) language informs ideas, particularly ideas that serve to maintain the status quo; (ii) those ideas inform actions; (iii) these actions in turn reflect and reinforce the status quo, thereby serving the interests of those in positions of power—the power elite. In practice situations there will be many opportunities to break these power links, to disrupt the process where it is causing harm and create opportunities for greater empowerment. Having an understanding of the common ground between ideology and discourse will therefore give us a good basis for exploring where and how we can intervene where appropriate.

Practice Focus 6.2

Lisa was a university professor teaching media studies. She had always been fascinated by how "social messages" are disseminated through the media. Her particular interest was cinema, and the way that movies subtly, and sometimes not so subtly, portray men as the action heroes, the ones who "do" things, while women are portrayed as the vulnerable ones who need rescuing or protecting or whose main role is to look gorgeous and be the love interest that motivates much of the "action hero" stuff—faint heart never won fair maid and all that, as she saw it. But, overall, she was interested in any way in which social messages were put across and how those messages suited the interests of the wealthy and powerful. She enjoyed doing various exercises with students to help them become alert to the processes involved and the consequences of those processes. She occasionally had a student who "didn't get it," but for the most part the response was a very energized one as the students became more and more aware of the subtle ways in which, as Lisa put it, powerful ideas are powerfully expressed in ways that reinforce existing power relations.

Hegemony

As we discussed earlier, hegemony refers to the idea of maintaining dominance through ideas, rather than through force, extortion or any other means. Having now explored discourse and ideology in more detail, it will be useful to revisit hegemony in order to see more clearly how it fits into this picture.

Many students when they first come across ideas like discourse or ideology find them difficult to grasp. In a sense, this is a sign of how effectively they are working, as a key part of what makes discourses and ideologies so successful in what they are doing is that their operations are rendered "invisible," in the sense of being masked or camouflaged. This masking or "camouflage" is precisely what hegemony is all about.

Central to the process of hegemony is the idea that, if we do not know we are being influenced, we are more likely to be open to that influence. For example, if someone were to approach you and say that they are trying to sell you something, then you are less likely to buy than if they approached the subject more indirectly. The same applies at a sociological level. Ideologies and discourses influence us in more subtle ways. I am not suggesting that this is a deliberate conspiracy or set of tactics, but, rather, something that has evolved historically.

One of the main ways in which hegemony works, and we have noted this on a few occasions already, is to present the social order (which can be changed) as if it were the natural order (which cannot be changed). Sometimes this is explicit, as when people say things like: "White people are naturally superior to black people . . ."; "It is normal for women to be caregivers . . ."; "Homosexuality is unnatural"; and/or "it is normal for old people to be less involved in society as they get older." At other times, this message is put across more indirectly, where it is simply implied that certain things are "not right" or "not supposed to happen."

Similarly, challenging hegemony can result in ridicule, stigma or just outright rejection. This is very clear historically; consider the initial hostility to the people who started the anti-slavery movement and the early suffragists. Today, the negativity towards challenges can be more subtle, but not always so. Consider how dissenting voices, in the political arena, for example, can be marginalized by the media, squeezed out to a large extent. In some regimes, of course, dissent can be punished very severely, by loss of liberty or even death.

A further example of hegemony at work is the way in which people can find themselves voting or acting against their own interests. For example, it is not uncommon for people to support policies or initiatives that mainly serve the interests of the rich and may actually make their own lives more difficult. Such is the effectiveness of hegemony as a social process.

Interestingly, what also happens in terms of hegemony is that some dissenting voices can be "incorporated," they can brought into the mainstream. As Duncombe explains:

> The dominant system is one of such complete ideological and material hegemony than any cultural expression, even if it appears rebellious, is, or will soon be repackaged and transformed into, a component of the status quo.
>
> *(2002, p. 6)*

Consider how bands like the Rolling Stones were originally perceived as "anti-Establishment," "rebellious," and a threat to the moral order. Both rock and blues in their time have been described as the Devil's music, and yet both genres are now part of the mainstream—they have lost their "edge" and their "edginess."

One of the implications of this in applied terms is that any efforts to address power imbalances and promote empowerment have to be very carefully handled. A simplistic approach that has not been thought through is unlikely to make a dent in hegemony and may well provoke reprisals of some kind. This territory needs to be navigated carefully and thoughtfully.

Voice of Experience 6.2

I used to challenge things head on. I could see through all the BS and wasn't taken in by it. I spoke my mind and told it as it is. Of course, I paid a heck of a price for doing that and got no end of grief and hassle from the powers that be. Eventually I learned that I had to be a bit more subtle, a bit more strategic in raising my objections. I wasn't selling out; I was still letting people know when things weren't right; I was just being more tactful. Why? Well, basically because it works much better. I realized that I was able to cut through all the you know what, just the same as before, but now without giving people the opportunity to dismiss me or put me down. Power works in subtle ways, so you have to be subtle in working against it too.

Chris, an events coordinator and campaign manager

The Work Ethic

The notion of "work ethic" is a well-established one. It is closely associated with Max Weber's classic text, *The Protestant Ethic and the Spirit of Capitalism* (Weber, 1930). If that book were to have been written today, it would probably be called something like *The Protestant Discourse around Work and the Ideology of Capitalism*. But, historical terminology issues aside, the work ethic can be a useful example of a discourse in action.

In Chapter 10 we shall explore in some detail how sociology can be helpful in addressing organizational factors, so in some ways the discussion here foreshadows that chapter.

What is particularly interesting about the work ethic is that it is so firmly established and so widely accepted. The capitalist system works on the basis of employees selling their labor in return for a wage. The owners of capital generally receive far more benefit from that labor than the employees do. While a minority of employees may work on a piece rate basis, and thereby operate along the lines of the harder they work, the more they get paid, most people are on a fixed rate. The harder someone works, the greater their opportunities for advancement, in principle at least. However, in general terms, the link between working hard and achieving just deserts for doing so is not a particularly strong or direct one. The work ethic remains a dominant discourse, none the less.

The reason I am highlighting this is not some effort to bring down the capitalist system, however problematic it may be in terms of health and well-being (James, 2007; 2008), nor am I trying to discourage anyone from working hard. Rather, it is a case of wanting to highlight how potent a discourse can be and how it can fit into a wider ideological framework. In "buying into" this discourse and supporting its "parent" ideology, employees are obtaining benefits for themselves, but creating even greater benefits for their employers and thereby sustaining the system that offers differential rewards and perpetuates the inequalities involved.

If we take this as an example of a much wider process, we should be able to recognize that discourse, ideology and hegemony are important features of social life. We can learn much about how society operates by being aware of frameworks of meaning (whether discourses or ideologies) and how they both reflect and reinforce power relations. We would do well to remember that the process is a hegemonic one—that is, the dominance is achieved through language, ideas and meanings, not through force or any other means, and so any changes we may need to bring about at any time, will also need to be achieved through language, ideas and meanings—and that is where a solid foundation of sociological knowledge can be of value.

Practice Focus 6.3

Wes was a loss adjuster in an insurance company. His job was to make sure that any insurance claims made were appropriate in line with the terms of the particular policy and to guard against any attempts to make fraudulent claims or fraudulently increase the value of claims. What he liked about the job was that he was able to get out and about quite a lot. He would have hated being behind a desk all day, even though this job did involve a lot of paperwork. However, what he didn't like was that he felt like "piggy in the middle." This was because he was under pressure from his employers to keep payment levels down in order to keep profit levels up—the name of the game was after all maximizing profits for the shareholders—while also being under pressure to do right by the claimants. Some claimants were clearly trying it on, trying to take him and his company for a fool, but generally he was dealing with people who had been through terrible difficulties and experienced a major loss of some description. He felt for them and wanted to do right by them, but he knew that he would get flak from his manager if he was perceived as being too generous, too much of an easy touch. He was caught in a complex system that was trying to make money by meeting people's needs after some sort of terrible incident. It was a really difficult balancing act, but he knew that it was not an even balance. He was not naive enough to think that there was any way the company was going to lose out, but sometimes claimants clearly did.

Implications for Practice

A key concept underpinning this chapter has been that of meaning. Discourses are based around meanings; ideologies are based on meanings; hegemony works through meanings. These are biased meanings, biased in favor of the status quo and the power structures involved. These meanings are put forward through social processes (for example, socialization), social institutions (for example, the media) and, as we shall see in the next two chapters, social expectations and social relations. Their power is both a cause and effect of their prevalence through these channels.

A key part of this is access to channels of communication. The more powerful a person or group is, the easier it is for them to gain such access. Bernstein captures this well when he argues that:

> Once we are aware of the connection between political power and access to communication technology, it becomes obvious throughout all of human history. These technologies are not in and of themselves oppressive or liberating. Rather, it is relative access to them that determines political reality.
>
> *(2013, p. 11)*

Consequently, one of the practice implications to arise from this chapter is that the ability to communicate countervailing "messages" is essential. If we are not able to do this, people will be left to fend for themselves in a system of meanings that reinforces inequality and injustice, that privileges the rich and powerful at the expense of ordinary people. Being able to overthrow the system of hegemony is unlikely to be a realistic aim. However, sociological understanding of the processes involved and the meanings that are being framed by those processes creates opportunities to make a positive difference in certain ways at least.

Another practice implication, as noted earlier, is that these issues are complex and need to be weighed up carefully and approached strategically. Just diving in to make a positive difference in a sense of outrage at the inequalities involved may be understandable, but it is unlikely to be productive—in fact, it is much more likely to prove counterproductive, for you and for whoever you are trying to help. An intelligent, sociologically informed approach is called for.

Conclusion

A question students have often asked me is: Why is atomism so pervasive? Why is there such a strong tendency for people to focus narrowly on individual matters and disregard all these other sociological issues that we have been discussing in class? The answer, of course, is because atomism is a powerful discourse, a well-established framework of meaning that people are inducted into from an early age. By focusing narrowly on individuals, the wheels of power can keep turning uninterrupted, untroubled by any challenges.

In a sense, atomism is a meta-discourse. What I mean by this is that it is a discourse that does the groundwork for other discourses. Atomism basically says: wider issues need not concern you; they are not important—just focus on individual matters. Sociology, as a listening art and a seeing art, helps us to look beyond atomism and start to see what is going on in the background—to see who is gaining and who is losing.

One of the things discourses and ideologies do is to establish social expectations, to create meanings about what we should and should not do. It is therefore to the topic of social expectations that we now turn in Chapter 7 as we continue exploring our SPIDER in the web of society.

Points to Ponder

1. In what ways might older or disabled people be characterized in a discourse of dependency? What forms of language might be used?
2. How might the frameworks of meaning created by discourses and ideologies create problem and/or restrictions for people?
3. Why might it be dangerous and counterproductive to challenge hegemony "head on," rather than in a strategic way?

Exercise 6

Hegemony operates primarily by "camouflaging" power relations and the inequality they create by presenting the social order (that can be changed) as the natural order (that cannot). How do you think this is brought about? Think carefully about this and list below as many ways as you can think of. Bear in mind that this is not a test, so feel free to consult with others to help you think these issues through.

Social Expectations   **7**

Introduction

The issue of social expectations is one that we have already encountered a number of times. Social structures create social expectations (consider the notions of "knowing your place" and "not getting above your station"). Your social location not only opens or closes certain doors in terms of opportunities (or "life chances," to use the technical term), it also sets up expectations about how you should act, think and feel. These expectations are powerful influences on us, and the sanctions for not abiding by them can be severe (not least stigmatization). Social processes also set up expectations. Consider how socialization inculcates the child into their society and, in so doing, leads to the child internalizing the norms, values and expectations of their particular culture and of wider society. Social institutions likewise create expectations. An obvious example is the role of the media. Think about how the fashion pages of a newspaper give strong messages about what is currently expected if you are not to be considered out of step or behind the times. And, of course, discourses and ideologies are characterized by sets of expectations, the frameworks of meaning they construct bring with them strong messages about what is expected of us.

Social expectations can therefore be seen as a key part of the web of society, which is precisely why we now have a full chapter to explore their significance and consider what role they can play in terms of applied sociology.

Perhaps the first point to emphasize is that social expectations are hugely powerful. Consider the distress that can be experienced when people feel the shame of not living up to social expectations. For example, returning to the theme of the work ethic discussed in Chapter 6, there is a strong expectation that honest, decent citizens should be gainfully employed. Consequently, unemployment can bring great stigma and distress. This is also an example of hegemony, as the distress is arising from ideas that have been inculcated into us through the work ethic discourse. Some people manage to escape this hegemony and do not feel significant distress as a result of unemployment, but they are in the minority, of course, such is the power of the discourse.

What is also significant is that failing to abide by social expectations can invoke significant "penalties," as we shall see below. We therefore need to recognize that social expectations are matters we need to take seriously. We should not underestimate the effect they can have in (i) shaping human action directly through the expectations that have become internalized through socialization and other influences: (ii) motivating people to avoid the negative effects of not abiding by social expectations; and (iii) sanctions when social expectations are breached. The significance of these three sets of issues should become clearer as we make our way through the chapter.

We begin by exploring an important "branch" of sociology, namely symbolic interactionism, a theoretical approach that focuses specifically on how people interact with one another (interactionism) in a context of shared and emerging meanings (symbolic). We shall also discuss the related approach of role theory before moving on to consider some example of how social expectations operate in relation to gender and age. Once again, I will relate the key issues to their usefulness in an applied context from time to time.

Symbolic Interactionism

Much of sociological thought has focused broadly on macro-level phenomena. However, there is also an important contribution to our understanding of the web of society to be made by sociological approaches that focus on the micro-level of social interaction, as evidenced in the work of such sociological stalwarts as Erving Goffman (1922–1982), George Herbert Mead (1863–1931) and others in what came to be known as symbolic interactionism.

Goffman's work has proven very influential and it would be beyond our scope in this chapter to attempt a comprehensive overview. I shall therefore limit myself to a small number of examples of his key contribution. I have already mentioned a number of times the significance of stigma. Our understanding of this owes much to Goffman's work (Goffman, 1990b). Avoiding the shame associated with stigma is a powerful source of motivation. This is because status or social standing is highly prized (another set of social expectations arising from a discourse), and so to lose status is very costly in emotional terms. People will go to considerable lengths to avoid losing such status. This immediately introduces an applied dimension, as an awareness of this will tell us a lot about the behavior of individuals, families, groups and even whole communities.

Face Management

Mead (1967) introduced the notion of "face management," using face not in the literal sense of part of our anatomy, but as a metaphor for respect, as in the notions of "losing face" or "saving face." As we interact we present a front, we put forward an image of ourselves that we want others to see (what Goffman, 1990a, called "impression management"). A key factor in those interactions is the careful maintenance of face. We have some very complex rituals and interaction patterns that have evolved to help us manage our own face and that of others (for example, manners or etiquette). We engage in a sort of dance where we try to protect our own "face," while also being careful not to make other participants in the interaction lose face (unless, in certain circumstances, we are deliberately trying to offend someone or to make their life difficult). We do not have to look far to see evidence of this "dance" going on.

What can complicate matters is that ideas about appropriate behavior to manage face can differ from culture to culture. What is considered appropriate and acceptable in one culture can be unacceptable in another (Jandt, 2015). For example, I once met a man who studiously avoided eye contact with me, which, from my own cultural perspective, made me feel uncomfortable. However, shortly after meeting him, I was formally introduced to him and we shook hands. After that he had no difficulty making eye contact, we got on well and enjoyed each other's company. I later discovered that, in his culture, it was considered rude to make eye contact with someone you do not know. So, once we had been introduced, it was no longer a problem for him to make eye contact. I learned an important lesson from that interaction. In Chapter 8 we shall discuss the significance of conflict, but for now we should note that cultural differences in face management can be a significant source of conflict if they are not handled sensitively.

> *Practice Focus 7.1*
>
> Clare was a mediator in a large legal firm. The culture in the legal system was basically adversarial. The name of the game was doing battle to try and win your case. Saving face was something you might want to do for yourself, it did not apply to your opponent. It wasn't quite "no holds barred," but it could get very rough at times. Mediation, however, was very different. It was about finding common ground. It was about establishing a basis of mutual respect where possible. This involved trying to make sure that both parties in the dispute were able to maintain face and not do anything that would lead to the other party losing face. This meant being ready to interrupt if either party started going down a road that would bring about a loss of face. It was about keeping both parties within the boundaries of respect and dignity. Face management had been a part of Clare's mediation training, and she found that very useful. It gave her a clear and helpful framework to guide her work.

Symbolic Meaning

Sociology, as we have seen, is often concerned with meaning, the various ways in which social meanings emerge and operate. Symbolism is an important part of frameworks of meaning, and so to develop an adequate understanding of meaning, we need to consider how symbols work, how they play a part in social interactions. This is what the school of symbolic interaction in sociology has set out to do and made a lot of progress with. Hopkins explains it in the following terms:

> Symbolic Interactionism posits that our daily routine of interactions are not spontaneous creations of our own making. Rather, they are "symbolic enactments" that reflect our knowledge of cultural rituals. With this knowledge, people can coordinate their behavior and create meaning amongst one another (Cupach and Metts, 2008, p. 204).

(2015, p. 1)

This is to say that we operate within frameworks of symbolic meaning that establish set patterns of ritualized interaction. For example, consider what happens when a telephone call is made. Person A calls Person B. Person B picks up the phone and initiates interaction by saying "hello" or equivalent, stating their name and/or organization. Saying their name or whatever—that is, they acknowledge that the contact has been made and may also identify

themselves in the process. Person A then speaks, usually identifying themselves, possibly giving a greeting and then stating the purpose of the call:
Person A rings the number.

Person B (answers the phone): "Hello, Kim West, Sales Department; how can I help you?"
Person A: "Hi Kim, it's Sam here from Reception. I just wanted to let you know that your 10 o'clock appointment has arrived."

Superficially, this all seems very straightforward, but if we look at it more closely and more critically, we should be able to see a number of rules of interaction being followed here:

1. *Order of speaking* Imagine how unnerving and strange it would be if Person A rang Person B and started speaking before Person B has had a chance to say anything. Imagine Person B's surprise because a rule of interaction has been broken.
2. *Phatic communication* This is the technical term used to refer to the "small talk" we use to have smooth interactions. It includes greetings and comments like "How are you today?," even though we may not particularly want to know how well that person is doing. It is a form of social lubrication. Anyone who dispensed with it would soon be labeled "rude"—a sanction for breaking a social rule.
3. *Turn taking* We are so used to this that we generally do not notice it happening. Sometimes people talk over each other a little bit in conversation, but there is clearly a social rule that people in conversation (whether by telephone or more broadly) take it in turns to speak and to listen. Again, somebody who infringed this rule would be considered rude and perhaps self-centered also.
4. *Purposive interaction* There is generally a purpose underpinning social interaction, even if that purpose is only to enjoy human contact. Again a social rule would be infringed if someone were to initiate an interaction for no apparent reason. For example, if I were to approach someone in the street and simply tell them my favorite color, it is likely I would make them feel uncomfortable as I would be breaking the rule of purposive interaction (see the discussion of mental health below).
5. *Closing rituals* Another significant rule is that we go through a closing "dance" of phatic communication. For example, in the case highlighted above, if Kim were to simply put the phone down after hearing what Sam had to say, it is likely that this would create ill feeling. Similarly, if Kim were to say: "Thanks, Sam, I'll be down in a minute. Bye," and Sam were

to simply put the phone down (without saying something like "Thanks, Kim, bye"), that too is likely to be considered rude.

These "rules of interactions" are, of course, sets of social expectations. They will vary from culture to culture, but, whatever the cultural context, where rules are broken, there will be consequences, generally adverse ones.

Symbolic interactionism is therefore a potentially useful tool for applied sociology. It can give us a lot of insights into human interactions, especially where they go wrong and may require some sort of intervention. It can give us some helpful clues as to what went astray and why, and therefore potentially give us some ideas about what needs to be done to rectify the situation.

The understanding offered by symbolic interaction has wide application. For example, Cox illustrates how society uses symbolic interaction to address matters relating to death:

> How a person dies has also become a major symbolic phenomenon. The meanings attached to how a person dies are major social issues. A person who suicides is mourned quite differently from a person who dies in his or her sleep at an elderly age. A person who dies a traumatic death in an accident, terrorist event, natural disaster or violent gun incident is interpreted quite differently from a person who dies from natural causes.
>
> *(2017, p. 65)*

Symbols and rituals associated with them contribute frameworks of meaning that subsequently inform our view of the world and our interactions with it. This again highlights the inadequacy of an individualistic approach that focuses narrowly on the individual and largely neglects the significance of the complex, multi-level social context in which we operate as individuals. It also highlights how rich symbolic interactionism can be as part of a commitment to an applied sociology that seeks to make a positive difference. These insights are in addition to those discussed in earlier chapters, as there is no contradiction between this micro-level approach and the other, macro-level aspects of the web of society.

Role Theory

Part of symbolic interactionism is role theory. What makes role theory relevant to this chapter is that a role is basically a set of expectations. There can be various sets of roles, not least the following:

- *Familial* Mother, father, brother, sister and so on—all of these carry sets of social expectations.
- *Occupational* There can be job roles (engineer, nurse, banker), function roles (manager, leader, supervisor) and activity roles (chair of meeting, minute taker).
- *Cultural* Different cultures can assign different roles to individuals or groups—for example, arbiter of disputes, source of advice or wisdom, and so on.
- *Sporting* Back, forward, referee or umpire, coach, and so on are sport-related roles.
- *Gender* Men and women are, of course, assigned different roles in different circumstances. We shall discuss this issue in more detail below.
- *Situation specific* There will also be roles that arise in specific situations as and when required—for example, bridesmaids at a wedding, mourners at a funeral, customers when out shopping.

This is not an exhaustive list, but it does show that roles, as sets of social expectations, are common features of social life.

What is also significant are the interactions of such roles. For example, when we consider the topic of workplace stress, we can see that it can arise from role issues: conflicting roles, too many roles, unclear role expectations, and so on (Thompson, 2015b). An understanding of roles is therefore a distinct advantage when it comes to applied sociology.

Consistent with symbolic interactionism, we should note that roles do not operate in isolation; they interact. Sometimes roles will be linked by their very nature, complementing one another: teacher—student; doctor—patient, and so on. However there will also be times when roles interact purely as a feature of social interaction. For example, imagine this scenario:

Marie is upset when she finds that her brother has been assaulted. She feels the need to talk about her distress (she adopts the role of a person needing help). Bob recognizes her distress and wants to help and support her (he adopts the role of helper). As a result of this he offers Marie advice about how to help her brother make sure he is safe from attack in future (he adopts the role of advice giver). Marie becomes angry and tells Bob she does not want advice, she wants somebody to listen to her. In clarifying what she wants, she is adopting the role of negotiator—seeking to secure a more appropriate response from Bob. Bob responds by no longer offering advice and, instead being supportive by just listening (adopting the role of listener).

This is a typical example of how roles can interact and how a change in one role can elicit a change in role from someone else.

Like other sets of social expectations, not sticking to what is supposed to happen within a particular role comes at a price—there will be adverse social consequences. Parents who do not fulfill their parenting role may be accused of neglect and may, ultimately, have their children removed from their care for their own good. Similarly, someone who does not fulfill their role as a law-abiding citizen is likely to face sanctions and may lose their liberty—or even their life.

Being able to analyze what roles are being occupied, how differing roles are interlocking or conflicting, how people are managing their roles and so on can be a very useful applied sociology tool that can be implemented in a wide variety of situations. This can be done informally as you go about your everyday business or it could form the basis of a formal study—for example, as part of a consultancy project.

Gender Roles

When considering roles in particular and social expectations in general, there is much to be gained from considering gender and its role in shaping differential social expectations across the sexes. We noted in Chapter 3 the significance of gender as a social structure, how it divides people into categories and then assigns them differential levels of power accordingly.

You do not need to be a sociologist to recognize that gender roles have changed over time. However, what has not changed is that there are still clear gender roles in place. Consider, for example, the bullying, ridicule and stigma that a boy is likely to receive at school if he behaves in ways that are perceived as reserved for girls. While what is considered appropriately masculine or appropriately feminine has been changing, and will no doubt continue to change over time, the fact that there are differential expectations of masculinity and femininity remains the case, as does the fact that there will be costs for "transgressing" those expectations.

What complicates matters is that it is not a simple binary relationship, as captured in the classic notion of blue for a boy and pink for a girl. Simone de Beauvoir, in her highly influential work, *The Second Sex* (de Beauvoir, 1972) discusses the concept of "alterity" or otherness. What she meant by that was that men are seen as the main reference point, as the norm, while women are then defined in relation to them. This is why feminist scholars and activists have challenged he/man language ("every man for himself," "may the best man win," and so on). Women are expected to fit in with male terms. Women are the "spare rib," the deviation from the norm. It is not uncommon, for example, for women to be referred to as the "chairman," but it is highly unlikely that anyone would refer to a man as the "chairwoman." Clothing would be another example. A woman wearing trousers is unremarkable, but a man wearing a dress is likely to be seen as inconsistent with expectations of men's roles and activities in most social spheres. It is as if men occupy the positive pole *and* the neutral, while women are the negative pole, defined in relation to (not being) men. Woman is the "other."

For much of history gender roles were fixed and rigid. One of the changes that has emerged since the development of the women's movement and feminist thought is that roles are now much more flexible, the boundaries much less distinct in some ways. There are now far more opportunities for women and men to explore gender territory that was previously "out of bounds." However, we should not let this fool us into thinking that gender roles have limited significance in this day and age. The situation is far more complex than that.

Wrestling with that complexity can be part of the challenge of applied sociology. Exploring how gender expectations are shaping behavior and interactions, looking at what problems or limitations these may be leading to and exploring positive ways forward can all be part of an applied sociology approach.

Voice of Experience 7.1

I found the theoretical work at university quite interesting and undaunting, but when I went out on placement I really found life difficult at first. I was constantly finding myself in very tense situations. I kept wanting to make light of the situation, to start joking and easing the tension, like men usually do—or at least men in my social circles—but I knew that wasn't appropriate. Then there were also the stories I was hearing of terrible situations people had been through, and there was nothing I could do about them. I felt so frustrated. All that talk in my childhood about "This will make a man of you," and "Big boys don't cry" had left me very ill-equipped for the challenges I was facing in social work. I could see now why, back at the university, there was so much of a focus on social structures in general, and gender in particular.

Martin, a social work student on placement in a
child protection team

Culture, Ethnicity, and Race

It is not just gender that has a hand in creating differential role expectations. If we know where to look we can see that this applies to all the "social divisions," all the ways in which social structures divide us up into groups or categories and assign higher or lower levels of power accordingly. Culture, ethnicity and race are prime examples of this.

Cultures will, of course contain sets of social expectations within them— established customs, rituals and so on. Our ethnicity is closely linked to culture and reflects our sense of heritage and belonging, and that too involves sets of social expectations, of course. From a biological perspective, there is only one race, of course, the human race. However from a sociological perspective, it would be naive not to recognize the social construction of racial groups, even though they have no basis in biology—they are "assumed" groupings, which is why many authors always place the term race in inverted commas. Unfortunately, alongside the social construction of "race" is the social construction of racism, a social fact. One of the ways racism operates is through the process of assigning discriminatory and oppressive expectations to minority ethnic groups. This is usually in the form of stereotypes—rigid, distorted expectations of a particular group that generally have no basis in reality (for example, that black men are oversexed and/or that Asians are not to be trusted).

Applied sociology can play an important anti-racist role by highlighting such stereotypes and the misleading expectations they generate. Racist assumptions operate at the **C** level of PCS analysis, and so this can be a useful analytical tool for revealing and exposing racist social expectations.

Practice Focus 7.2

Irma was a race equality adviser in a multinational corporation. As well as the usual duties of an adviser in helping to promote racial equality and educate people about the value of diversity, Irma was regularly called upon to deal with issues arising from the international nature of the organization. There were people from different countries, different cultures, different religions and different backgrounds. The plus side of this was that the benefits of diversity were very much in evidence, but the downside was that issues kept cropping up due to people from one group making assumptions about members of other groups—a sort of culture clash. Irma realized that all staff had basic training in diversity and cultural competence, but that was part of the problem, it was only basic training, and some people needed much more than the basics. For some staff and managers, their views (and expectations) of some groups of staff were deeply ingrained after being brought up in a family and community where racist beliefs and assumptions were quite common. She knew that basic training wasn't enough for this sector of the employee groups, but she also knew that her requests for funding for fuller training were falling on deaf ears and would continue to do so unless and until there was a major incident and/or a litigation case. So, she resigned herself to having to deal with each issue on an ad hoc basis as and when it arose.

Act Your Age!

There are many other sets of social expectations that are worthy of exploration, but, for reasons of space, we must limit ourselves to just one more, and that will be the social expectations associated with ageism. Older people are subject to a wide number of social expectations, most of which reflect ageist assumptions and stereotypes—for example:

- *Disengagement* At one time in the not-too-distant past it was proposed that it was right for older people to "disengage" from mainstream society (Cumming and Henry, 1961). This was presented as serious scholarship, despite the major discriminatory underpinnings of this view of the role of older people in society. Although such an approach would now be rejected in academic and professional circles as unacceptably ageist, it would be naive not to recognize that the expectation that older people will feature less in society is alive and well in the popular consciousness.
- *Reduced competence* One prominent ageist stereotype is that older people are less competent than their younger counterparts, less intelligent and generally less capable. While it is true that aging can bring some degree of decline in intellectual and physical performance over time, this tends to be exaggerated for the most part. Examples of memory difficulties or other elements of decline in old age tend to be overextended, so the struggles some older people have easily come to be seen as struggles older people in general have. For example, while the incidence of hearing loss is higher in older people than in the general population, this is a far cry from assuming that older people *in general* are deaf and therefore need to be shouted at.
- *Dependency* This is an extension of the reduced competence assumption. As we discussed in Chapter 6, it is a mistake to assume that independence is not a realistic goal for most older people.

- *Lack of sexuality* The idea of sexuality in old age is often the butt of humor. An older man who has a healthy sexual appetite is likely to be referred to as a "dirty old man." What these facts indicate is that old age is perceived as a sex-free zone, yet another misleading and potentially damaging stereotype.

I have focused here on old age, as that is a time of life that tends to provide the most salient examples of ageist stereotypes. However, we need to bear in mind that ageism is discrimination on the grounds of *age*, not just old age. The idea of "Act your age!" is significant across the life course. Children can be held back by misleading assumptions about what is or is not appropriate at a certain age, but then so can other age groups. Ageist stereotypes promote limiting social expectations that can easily be internalized (Thompson, 2018). That is, people can feel under considerable pressure to fit in with these expectations, for fear of being told to "act their age," or may even reach the point where they feel that these age-related restrictions are right and proper.

An applied sociology perspective can make use of these by highlighting where such expectations are operating, exploring what problems they may be causing and considering ways of helping people to address any such concerns. For example, you may encounter organizations that have ageist assumptions built into their policies.

Voice of Experience 7.2

When I first came here the place was unbelievably stereotyped in pretty much every aspect. I had to make a lot of changes and manage a lot of resistance, but it was worth it in the end. The place is much better now. We've ditched all the limiting stuff and we focus on helping people explore what they are capable of. There were people sitting with their backs to the wall waiting for the tea and coffee trolley to come round. Now we have people sitting in groups and they take it in turns to sort out the teas and coffees. And, instead of waiting and hoping that someone will offer them a piece of cake, we support them in baking cakes and sharing them around. It wasn't rocket science, it was just a case of looking critically at what assumptions and expectations were creating unnecessary barriers and then dismantling those barriers by challenging the assumptions they were based on.

Lee, manager of a day center for older people

Implications for Practice

Like so many other aspects of the web of society, social expectations are unavoidable. They can be positive and helpful at times—for example, by giving people ambitions to strive for, something to live up to. However, as we have seen, they can also be negative, limiting and disempowering. The main implications in terms of applied sociology practice are twofold. First, being aware of these social expectations and how they influence people's thoughts, feelings and actions can give us important insights into "what makes people tick." It can help to give a more holistic picture, whether we are working with individuals, families, groups, communities or organizations. It can explain things that might otherwise remain obscured—for example, how fear of being stigmatized may prevent people from getting involved in certain activities, whatever those may be, if involvement would risk going beyond the limits of social expectations.

Second, there may be situations we encounter where someone has broken social rules and is now paying the price for that (for example, by being ostracized). This may be an individual or a whole group—for example, working with gay schoolchildren who have come out and are being bullied. Or it may be, as in Practice Focus 7.3, working with people with mental health problems. Indeed, mental health issues and social expectations are closely interlinked. This is because:

- Some mental health problems manifest themselves in behavior that is deemed "abnormal" or even "crazy." That behavior may not be doing anybody any harm (walking through a shopping mall with no shoes and socks on, for example), but is sufficient to unnerve people to the point where they feel "something must be done." The behavior goes against social expectations of "normal" behavior. In this respect, such behavior invites, unfortunately, a degree of social disapproval, stigma, rejection and even, at times, violence (Thornicroft, 2006).
- Social disapproval, stigma and rejection can then prevent people with mental health problems being involved in things that can be of benefit to them: employment, leisure activities, housing and so on. They are therefore denied helpful ways forward, while experiencing additional pressures arising from the social expectations issues.

In effect, a vicious circle has been established. Sociology does not give us any ready-made solutions to this problem, but it gives us a basis of understanding to explore strategies for potentially breaking that vicious circle. It is not easy work, but it is important work.

One consequence of this vicious circle is that it can assign people with mental health problems to a life of poverty, and that can then trigger another vicious circle, whereby poverty-related pressures may make recovery from mental health problems less likely. Interestingly, those poverty-related pressures are also linked to social expectations. As Tew explains:

> International comparisons would suggest that there is relatively little adverse impact on mental wellbeing if one is poor within a context where everyone is poor, or within a culture where one is valued for who one is rather than what he owns. Instead, it is suggested that it is experiences of injustice, in terms of *relative* disadvantage (and the negative social connotations that may go with this), rather than *absolute* levels of deprivation, that may be more pernicious in their effects on mental health (Dohrenwend, 2000).
>
> *(2011, p. 37)*

What this means, then, is that, while poverty brings problems of its own in general terms, its impact on mental health is particularly related to being in poverty relative to wider society—raising issues of exclusion, stigma and social expectations once again. And, once again, we can use our awareness of these issues to adopt a critical, holistic approach to the issues involved with a view to making a positive difference in whatever ways we reasonably can.

Practice Focus 7.3

Vaughan was a mental health recovery worker. He was part of a specialist project set up to try and improve the recovery rate for people experiencing mental health problems. The project arose from concerns about a research study that showed that the recovery rate for people with mental health problems was much lower than recovery rates for physical health problems. This reflected an increased emphasis on recovery in mental health. Vaughan was "dual qualified"—that is, he held qualifications in both psychiatric nursing and social work. He could see that the social issues were most prominent when it comes to recovery. He had seen how medication could stabilize people's conditions, but recognized that what really made a difference was changes to their social circumstances: housing, employment, social connections and so on. When he was appointed to the project he made himself aware of the research on these matters, so he was well informed. He was able to make clear plans for how best to help people work towards recovery. However, the problem he came across time and time again, was social attitudes, people's expectations of anyone with a diagnosis of "mental illness." But tackling this stigma and these restrictive and disempowering expectations was only half the battle. Just as important was trying to work directly with the patients to try and help them move away from the negative and limiting assumptions that they had internalized. It wasn't just about convincing employers that people with mental health problems could hold down jobs if they had the right support; it was also about convincing the patients themselves that they could hold down a job in the right circumstances. It was an uphill struggle, but Vaughan knew it was much more fruitful than just using medication to keep people in check.

Conclusion

As with the other chapters in Part Two, drawing on sociological understanding of the issues involved does not give us simple or straightforward steps to follow. Rather, it gives us a basis of understanding, a set of insights to guide our critically reflective practice, as discussed earlier. It equips us to think carefully and clearly about the complexities involved, rather than risk making situations worse by getting involved without really appreciating what we are dealing with or what is happening.

Social expectations are powerful; they are also unavoidable. Managing them is a highly skilled undertaking, illustrating how much skill is involved in everyday social life, the skills that can be taken for granted by an atomistic approach. Applied sociologists can play a part in helping to develop those skills where needed, can help to address problems where social expectations are breached, where social rules of interaction are infringed, for example, and offer an understanding of what is happening that an atomistic approach would in all likelihood miss.

We have now covered five of the six elements that make up our SPIDER of the web of society. In the final chapter in Part Two we explore the sixth element, that of social relations. How people relate to one another is partly about the structures, processes, institutions, discourses and expectations that we have already explored together. However, there are other aspects of social relations that we have yet to examine, and so those matters will be precisely what we focus on in Chapter 8.

Points to Ponder

1. What sanctions can be brought to bear for anyone who "transgresses" what society expects of them? That is, what might the adverse consequences be of "breaking the social rules"?
2. How are social expectations transmitted? That is, where and how do people learn what is expected of them?
3. Consider what age group you are part of? What are the social expectations of that age group? Do those expectations place any unnecessary limitations or restrictions on you?

Exercise 7

Think of three roles you have played in the past seven days. What expectations are associated with those roles? Map them out in detail. Where do you think those expectations have come from—that is, what purpose might they serve? What would the likely consequences be if you did not fulfill those roles or you fulfilled them in a way contrary to social expectations? Having explored these issues, are there any conclusions you can draw about how roles and social expectations play their part in the web of social life?

Social Relations $\quad$ **8**

Introduction

Every time people come together it is a unique encounter. However commonplace the circumstances may be, that specific combination of factors will be unique to that particular situation. However, despite that uniqueness, there will be recurring themes that can be detected whenever people come together. The study of those recurring themes is what social relations (and this chapter) are all about.

Of course, we have to handle the uniqueness of each situation as it arises, but an understanding of the themes of social relations will give us an important platform to work from. This is an important platform because social relations are all around us; we are constantly interacting with other people, whether face to face or virtually. Such relations are not incidental; they will play a key part in shaping various aspects of our lives. It is for this reason that we shall be exploring such important issues as friendship, love, groups and conflict.

A key concept in this regard is "connectedness." This is a term that originates in the spirituality literature (Hyde, 2008). It refers to the fact that each of us is part of a broader whole—groups, communities and even humanity as a whole. It is a mainstay of sociology that, whatever we do, we do in a social context. We have explored various aspects of this social context through our SPIDER model in the web of society in earlier chapters of Part Two. Connectedness, in the form of social relations, is now a further aspect of that web for us to explore,

It is important to emphasize right from the start that social relations are not separate from the other features of society that we have been examining, They reflect (and embody) social structures; they interact with social processes; they influence and are influenced by social institutions; they operate within a context of discourses and ideologies; and they engage with social expectations in various ways. In other words, social relations are part of the complex web of society, and so we need to look closely at them to see what we can learn about them and from them.

What contributes to this complexity is the basic principle that what unites us divides us. This can apply to groups (which we shall discuss below) where being a member of one group (supporters of a particular sports team for example) unites us with fellow members of that group, while also setting us apart from members of groups that support other teams within that sport. It can also apply more broadly to cultures and nations. Feeling proud of being a citizen of your country unites you with other citizens of that country, but sets you apart from citizens of other countries. As we shall see, that setting apart need not be a basis for conflict, but it easily can be. This is why the widely used idea of "unity in diversity" is important. What unites us separates us is therefore an important point to bear in mind when considering social relations.

It is also important to be aware that social relations can be positive, negative or neutral; they can be empowering or disempowering. This is where the applied sociology element comes into its own, as a knowledge of social relations can put us in a stronger position when it comes to promoting positive, empowering social relations and addressing negative, disempowering ones.

Similarly, we need to acknowledge the central role of conflict (and its management) in social relations. It would be naive to think that there will always be consensus and harmony. Understanding how conflict arises within social relations and how it can be handled is a distinct benefit of adopting an applied sociology approach. Conflict can be constructive at times, but it can also escalate into aggression and violence. Which direction it goes in will generally depend on how the social relations involved are handled, and that is where sociological insights can be invaluable.

We shall focus on the significance of conflict and its management later in the chapter, but first we must set the scene by examining more harmonious aspects of social relations.

Friendship

Making friends is a basic feature of human experience. Friendships are generally seen as a "natural" phenomenon. However, our focus here is on their *social* nature. There will, of course, be random elements of pure chance in terms of who meets whom, who engages with whom and so on. However, there are also social patterns that can be discerned. That is, people are more likely to befriend people from a similar class group, similar cultural background and so on. This is partly because of "opportunity pathways"—that is, a greater chance of meeting someone that you have a great deal in common with in the first place. But it is also partly because you are more likely to be on the same wavelength as someone who shares a similar background in terms of social location, more likely to have compatible frameworks of meaning and outlooks.

How friendships operate will also be a sociological matter, of course. Consider, for example, class differences between friends who share time at the opera and at cocktail parties and those who frequent the same bar or take their children to the same crèche. There will also be gender differences in terms of how people meet, how they become friends and how such friendships are sustained or fade over time. Gender will also be a significant consideration in terms of male–female friendships. Some people steer clear of these in case they are confused with (or evolve into) romantic or sexual relationships, while others welcome them.

The list could go on in terms of how aspects of social structure can shape how friendships develop. They are clearly, then, social matters.

Friendships can also be (and often are) couples based—that is, not just individual to individual, but a four-way friendship involving two couples. This reflects that friendship relationships often revolve around groups—sets of couples, for example, and/or groups of individuals. Such groupings can arise in a variety of ways, including the following:

- *Shared work* Friendships often arise from the workplace and can continue after the individuals have left the work setting where they originally established their relationship. Again, these friendships can be individual to individual or group based.
- *Shared education* Many friendships begin at school, at college or at university. Some of these will be long lasting and continue long after the educational connection has been lost, while others will fade away once their shared educational experience is over.
- *Shared interests* These can be intellectual, professional, leisure or sporting interests, or a combination of them. The interests may also arise from shared experiences—for example, being the parents of a disabled child or having been victims of the same crime.
- *Shared space* People may become friends because they live in the same neighborhood, attend the same church or share some other physical or social space.

- *Shared adversity* People who have experienced the same problems can also become friends in recognition of their shared journey through their challenges.

Friendships, however they arise, can be important contributors to well-being, although tensions that arise from time to time can also undermine well-being.

Friendships are part of the social capital we discussed in Chapter 5 and are therefore potentially significant from an applied sociology point of view. Understanding the network of social relations people have puts us in a better-informed position to appreciate "where they are coming from" and may at times give us ideas about how best to intervene—for example, where someone may benefit from developing a higher level of social capital.

Practice Focus 8.1

Brenda was a youth worker. Part of her job was to develop projects to help young people in various ways. A key element was to reduce youth offending where possible. One thing that was receiving more and more attention was bullying among young people—ranging from cruel teasing to criminal assault. She consequently decided to see what she could do to reduce bullying. It did not take long before it became apparent that it was mainly the young people who had limited contact with others who were the main "targets." She had come across the concept of social capital on a training course, and thought it could be very relevant for this project. She therefore decided to speak to her colleagues to explore ways in which they could help some young people to boost their social capital by developing new friendships in the hope that they would be less open to the bullying attentions of others.

Love

Love can take many forms, such as parental, romantic or sexual, and friendship based. While the feelings involved may be felt biologically in physical sensation and have significant psychological effects, we should not lose sight of the fact that love is socially constructed. Consider, for example, the different understandings of love in different contexts. Is parental love the same as romantic love or are they different entities that, in certain cultures, share the same name? What does it mean for friends to "love" each other? These are all matters of social meaning.

Illouz offers an interesting analysis of love when she argues that:

> The most arresting claim made by feminists is that a struggle for power lies at the core of love and sexuality, and that men have had and continue to have the upper hand in that struggle because there is a convergence between economic and sexual power.
>
> *(2012, p. 5)*

This echoes Sartre's claim that love is the struggle for possession (Sartre, 1958). However, Illouz goes on to suggest that this view is too simplistic, as it does not recognize love as a potentially positive force to challenge patriarchy (rather than simply be a reflection of it).

Love, of whatever kind, is, of course, a powerful motivator and a significant factor in a variety of social relations. It can be a very positive force. However, as with friendship, it can also have negative elements. For example, love can generate jealousy that, in turn, can create a wide range of problems (such as relationship tensions). It can also distort perception, leading to unhelpful biases at times.

There is a certain irony that we talk and write so much about *romantic* love, and yet the subject can often be treated "romantically," in the sense of being romanticized—that is, in a way that is not grounded in reality. It is something of a cliché to say that romantic love is a form of madness, but it is none the less fair to say that some forms of love can affect perceptions, and sometimes in a way that causes problems—for example, when a "romanticized" view of someone prevents a foolish course of action they are pursuing from becoming apparent.

Voice of Experience 8.1

> In our society we put so much store in this thing called love, and yet it is incredibly complicated. Anyone trying to understand people without having a good idea of the role love—or the lack of it—is playing in their lives is missing an important part of the picture. Love can do so much good and quite a lot of harm too. In my job part of what I need to do is to help couples work out whether their love is going through a difficult time and needs revitalizing or whether it has died and it is time to move on.
>
> *Karena, a marriage guidance counselor*

Groups

How many groups we are part of will depend on our level of social capital, but most, if not all, people will be in at least a small number of groups.

Groups will generally serve as a social microcosm, as they will normally reflect wider features of society—for example, social structures, discourses and social expectations. However, it would be an oversimplification to see them as simply shrunken versions of wider society. This is because groups have dynamics of their own. And, of course, they are infused with social relations, hence our interest in them in this chapter.

Groups can be formal or informal. The former refers to groups that have an agreed, explicit purpose, whether for business or leisure (a society or association, for example), whereas the latter is likely to be a case of people gathering together around shared interests, but without a specific purpose or constitution (people who regularly play cards together, for example).

As with the other social relations we have mentioned, groups can be a great force for good, but they can also do harm. Groups can bring people together in empowering ways to achieve much that could not have been achieved by the individuals alone. However, groups can harm their own members (through intimidating behavior, for example, or through ridicule and rejection) or harm other groups or individuals (by using their collective power in unethical or even illegal ways).

There is also a significant distinction between open and closed groups. An open group is one that can accept new members at any time—for example, a club that receives any new members who meet their membership criteria. A closed group, by contrast is one where membership is limited. For example, a workplace team may have a particular complement of staff, and so a new member could join only if an existing member leaves. Membership of closed groups, because of the scarcity element, tends to be valued more than membership of an open group, but this can vary.

There is a significant literature on groups and ways in which: (i) the performance of groups can be improved; and (ii) groups can be set up specifically to tackle a problem or bring about a positive difference (see, for example, Doel and Kelly, 2014). In this regard sociological insights can have much to offer, whether this is in a human resources context (team development or troubleshooting in teams, for example—Thompson, 2011b), a sporting context (improving team spirit and performance) or a helping professions context (a therapeutic group, a parent support group, a dementia caregivers support group and so on). These are all areas where applied sociology can have a part to play.

Practice Focus 8.2

Rick was a probation officer based in a prison. The traditional method of practice in the prison was to work with prisoners on a one-to-one basis. Rick could see the value of that, but he could also see how group work could be of value too. He could see that many of the prisoners were facing the same issues and could potentially support one another in exploring them and looking for solutions to their challenges. When he first suggested this to his manager he encountered a degree of resistance, as this was something that had been used in other prisons, but not in this particular one. However, after a while, Rick's manager relented, as he could see how keen Rick was, and he was also impressed with the research evidence that Rick had collated to make his case for a group work approach. Rick was delighted with this change of heart, but was nervous in case his plans did not live up to expectations when finally implemented. However, he need not have worried, as things went very well. As is often the case with group work, it took a while before the group settled down and trust was established, but once that lift off point had been reached, things took off nicely. Rick got great job satisfaction by seeing how positively the group was working and what a big positive difference it was making. He knew it would be no substitute for the one-to-one work he was used to carrying out, but he recognized that it was a very fruitful use of his time and prison resources.

Conflict, Aggression, and Violence

I made the point earlier that it would be naive to expect social relations to be entirely harmonious. Indeed, if we look closely, we can see that conflict is part of everyday life. Many people see conflict as a breakdown of normality, whereas in reality it is very much a part of that normality. The misperception tends to come from the fact that so many people associate conflict with hostility or aggression, and so in the absence of such difficulties, they assume that there is no conflict. However, if we look at this sociologically, we should be able to see that there are multiple conflicts in social relations long before any hostility arises. Conflicts can range from civilized disagreements, through awkward tensions to outright hostility and on to extreme physical violence. Whether or not a conflict escalates from minor disagreement to major confrontation will depend on how the situation is managed—and that will depend, to a large extent, on how the social relations are handled.

So, whether it someone acting informally as a peacemaker, a mediator in a formal mediation session, a negotiator in an arbitration or a judge in court, what is involved is some degree of trying to manage the social relations involved—for example, helping the warring factions to appreciate the other person's point of view and/or foresee the consequences of continuing the conflict. There are various techniques for doing this (Coleman and Ferguson, 2014), but what it is important to recognize is that a sociological understanding of social relations can be a distinct benefit whenever we encounter conflict situations.

This applies not only in addressing third-party conflicts (that is, where you are the third party to a conflict between two or more people or groups), but also direct conflicts that you may find yourself in. Either way, the understanding of social relations offered by sociology should stand you in good stead.

Sociology can also help us to "tune in" to conflict situations that may not be seen initially as matters of conflict. For example, it is not uncommon for people to say something like: "Rhian is such a difficult person to deal with, always being awkward." In such circumstances, however, it is not uncommon to find that Rhian feels she is being perfectly reasonable and that it is the person who described her as "awkward" who is being difficult. What we are likely to have, therefore, is not a case of one or perhaps two people being "awkward" towards each other, but, rather, a conflict situation. It could well be that the problem lies *between* them, in their social relations, rather than in either party's personality or behavior, but each party sees the other as the problem, and neither is adopting a critical, holistic perspective that looks at the bigger picture. And this is precisely one of the ways in which applied sociology can be helpful in addressing conflict situations, by helping the individuals concerned to look at the situation with fresh eyes that may be able to help them move away from their entrenched positions (that are likely to lead to more conflict if they are not changed).

Conflict can at times be a positive thing: it can help people broaden their horizons and move away from entrenched positions by appreciating another person's point of view; it can lead to learning that may not otherwise have taken place; it can lead people to have greater respect for one another because of the way they skillfully handle the conflict with each other; and/or it can highlight differences that could have proven very problematic if they had not arisen until much later. And, of course, trying to bring out, and capitalize upon, the positives of conflict can be a role for applied sociology.

However, conflict can also be extremely destructive: it can ruin what were previously positive relationships; it can destroy morale in a team; it can distract people from what they should be focusing on; and, of course, it can also escalate to the point of aggression and violence.

Aggression

We use the term aggression when someone is trying to get their own way at someone else's expense. They may try to mask their aggression to a certain extent (what is often referred to as being passive-aggressive) or express their aggression openly and forcefully, but the process remains the same; it is one of somebody trying to get what they want and is prepared to abandon normal social mores, customs, manners and conventions to get it.

There is a major psychological literature about aggression (Bushman, 2016), but what has featured much less is a focus on the *sociological* dimensions. Understanding what is happening in the aggressor's head or heart can be important and helpful, but so too can knowledge about the social relations issues involved. When someone becomes aggressive, they are abandoning conventional social ways of negotiating; they are dispensing with the usual "face management" we engage in when interacting with others (with both parties losing face in an aggressive encounter); they are exercising social power in ways that are socially disapproved of and thereby flaunting social expectations. Aggressive behavior is therefore very clearly a sociological phenomenon as well as a psychological one. Preventing and defusing aggression can therefore also be seen as legitimate territory for the use of sociological insights. It can complement well what psychology can teach us about such matters.

Violence

Aggression and violence are concepts that are often used interchangeably, but there is an important distinction that can be drawn to avoid confusion. Aggression, as we have noted, is a process whereby Person A seeks to achieve their aims at the expense of others and is prepared to abandon normal social behaviors and break social rules in order to do so. Violence is a similar process, but one where the use of physical force is included—it therefore goes a step beyond aggression.

Some people temper this distinction by using violence in a metaphorical sense to refer to when, for example, emotional harm is done through aggression (the "violence" of emotional abuse, for example). Without getting bogged down in detail, what I can emphasize is that aggression does not do any harm necessarily (for example, police officers or security guards may encounter it regularly, but will usually take it in their stride without being harmed by it), but violence, by its very nature, will do harm.

One of the most common "triggers" of violence is humiliation (Walker and Knauer, 2011). This is, of course, a psychological matter, but there is also a sociological dimension to it, in so far as the sense of humiliation relates to social expectations (as discussed in Chapter 7) and the process of stigmatization discussed in Chapter 4. Efforts to prevent violence and defuse it if or when it does arise can therefore also be part of the applied sociology repertoire.

Sociology can also help us to understand conflict in general and aggression and violence in particular in terms of the operation of power within social structures: racist violence, sexual violence against women, "gay bashing," and so on. In more positive terms, we can also see how the sociological phenomena of discourses, social expectations and "rules of interaction" play a part in reducing conflict-related problems. For example, it is likely that we would have far more hostility if we did not have: (i) discourses around acceptable social behaviors; and (ii) the "sanctions" (stigma and so on) against not abiding by social expectations.

Clearly, then, there is much that sociological thought can contribute to the field of conflict, aggression and violence, to those situations where social relations have become problematic, if not catastrophic.

Abuse and Exploitation

Social relations can also be problematic in terms of abuse and exploitation, and so it is worth considering how sociology can cast light on aspects of this equally troubling and troublesome subject matter.

We can think of abuse in terms of three main categories (Thompson, 2017a):

- *Child abuse* This includes physical abuse, sexual abuse, emotional abuse and neglect.
- *Abuse of vulnerable adults* Mistreatment of older people, people with disabilities or others who for whatever reason, may struggle to protect themselves.
- *Domestic abuse* Physical violence or emotional abuse towards a spouse or partner.

Of course, although I have listed these types of abuse separately, for ease of exposition, we need to realize that they do not necessarily operate in isolation. Sadly, it is not uncommon for two or even all three of these forms of abuse to be taking place in the same household. What we should also note is that what all three of these have in common is that underpinning them all is the abuse of power.

Abuse arises when one or more people transgress a boundary in terms of what are considered socially acceptable social relations. Indeed, abuse can be seen to be a form of social relations in which there is an unequal distribution of power resulting in one or more people being treated in a harmful and degrading way. Problematic social relations are therefore at the heart of abuse,

Sociology can cast considerable light on these issues. For a long time, abuse, particularly child abuse, was conceptualized in medical terms. There was (and still is, to a certain extent) a medical discourse that spoke of symptoms, diagnosis and treatment. What is now developing is a more holistic view of child abuse, and sociology is playing an important part in that development. Indeed, the whole field of childhood studies is now being strongly influenced by sociology (McNamee, 2016).

Sociology has yet to make such an impact in relation to the abuse of vulnerable adults, but there is a significant sociological contribution to our understanding of domestic abuse already in place (Lombard and McMillan, 2013). Consequently, in whatever workplace setting abuse issues are being addressed, applied sociology has the potential to make an important contribution.

Exploitation

In a sense, much of the abuse mentioned above is a form of exploitation (consider the sexual abuse of children, for example). However, there are many other forms of exploitation besides these: human trafficking; fraud and embezzlement; some forms of bullying; child labor; and so on. It should come as no surprise to learn that exploitation is a sociological matter, in the sense that it reflects power dynamics, discourses and other aspects of the web of society.

We can also see that exploitation is a further example of social relations, a further instance of how social relations—so positive and enriching in so many ways—can also do immense harm. As I mentioned in the Introduction to this chapter, social relations can be positive and empowering or negative and disempowering. Both abuse and exploitation are examples of the latter.

Whether in a law enforcement setting, the caring professions or wherever else, we should not forget to include a sociological perspective when seeking to address issues of abuse and exploitation.

Voice of Experience 8.2

In addition to my basic training, I received specialist training around domestic abuse issues, and much of that was rooted in sociology. I really found this useful; it really captured my imagination. As a woman of color I could see how domestic abuse was not just some nasty things going on behind closed doors. I could see how various aspects of society were reflected in abuse situations. Some of the men on the course yawned every time the word "patriarchy" was used, but the point was not lost on me that so much of abuse in the family home was an extension of the power relations that exist in most homes. Don't get me wrong, I'm not saying that makes it acceptable—far from it. What I am saying is: if we had more equality in our family relationships, perhaps we would have less abuse too. Anyway, what I do know is that our everyday understandings of domestic violence are way too simplistic. Sociology helped me to appreciate the complexities involved. It certainly opened my eyes.

Parmita, a specialist police officer in a domestic violence unit

Work Relationships

The whole of Chapter 10 is devoted to exploring the significance of the workplace and the organizational context more broadly, and so I am not going to go into great details here. However, what I do want to do, briefly, is to highlight that relations at work are also significant from a social relations point of view.

There are three aspects I want to discuss: paid work; domestic labor; and civil labor. Paid work involves complex social relations in terms of: (i) employer–employee relations; (ii) peer relationships; and (iii) organization-customer relationships.

In terms of (i), there are significant issues here in terms of the operation of power; trade union relations; leadership; and team development. These are complex issues that I will explore further in Chapter 10.

In terms of (ii), the focus of work studies has tended to be on paid work, with work in the home largely being ignored. However, social relations apply to housework; household management (organizing meals and so on as well as preparing them); financial management (sorting out the regular bank payments; renewing the insurance policies; child care; care of dependent relatives; maintenance of household equipment; gardening; and so on). How decisions are made about household work issues is a social relations matter. There is a significant sociological literature on these issues demonstrating the subtle and complex workings of various social factors that contribute to these social relations. We are not likely to have an adequate understanding of household social relations without drawing on sociology and putting the sociological imagination into practice.

In terms of (iii), civil labor refers to unpaid work undertaken within a community—as a volunteer, committee member and so on. Highly respected sociologist, Ulrich Beck argues that we should not confuse this type of work with workfare-type schemes:

> Civil labour should by no means be confused with the pressure being put everywhere on benefit claimants to undertake work in the community. Civil labour is voluntary, self-organized labour, where what should be done, and how it should be done, are in the hands of those who actually do it. The democratic spirit that animates civil labour, and with it the society of self-active individuals, will perish if one commits the centuries-old mistake of confusing it with compulsory labour.
>
> *(1999, p. 127)*

Civil labor raises a number of issues about social relations. Who does and does not get involved; who exercises what power and in what ways; how wider social structures, discourses and so on manifest themselves within it; and so on.

What is also of sociological interest is how these three domains of work-related social relations interact and influence each other. There is therefore no shortage of issues for an applied sociologist to consider. As we shall see in Chapter 9, work is a fundamental basis of identity, as well as a major contributor (positively or negatively) to our well-being and even to our health.

Practice Focus 8.3

Rob was a researcher for a government department. He had been involved in various studies, ranging from what he found to be quite boring, tedious ones to some that he found fascinating. The study on different work patterns came into the latter category. The main focus was on paid work with a view to reducing unemployment levels, but domestic and civil labor were to be considered also. This was because the team that put together the funding bid for the research were well informed enough about work issues to know that studying paid work in isolation would give a partial picture of the scene and not do justice to the complexities involved. One of the interesting themes to emerge from the research was that the de-industrialization that had been occurring in the region had removed a lot of full-time jobs, some of them quite well paid (that had been mainly occupied by men), and what had replaced them were mainly part-time, low-paid jobs (traditionally mainly occupied by women). What also emerged was that, despite higher levels of male unemployment, there had been no significant increase in men's involvement in domestic labor and only a small increase in involvement in civil labor. Rob was keen to explore what the impact of all this was in terms of social relations, in the home, in the community and in the workplace.

Implications for Practice

Social relations infuse every aspect of our lives. Wherever there are people, there will be social relations. Applied sociology involves bringing the sociological imagination to bear in relation to whatever activities we are engaged in. This means being tuned in to the complex array of social relations that affect social life in so many ways (including, but not limited to, the ones we have covered in this chapter).

In Chapter 9 we shall discuss the myth of the isolated individual, and we need to challenge that myth because it fails to take account of the vitally important role of social relations. In our world so strongly influenced by atomistic thinking, when we look round we tend to see individuals. Until we start to think sociologically, what we will not see is the multiplicity of sets of social relations that are so significant in shaping various aspects of our lives. So, when it comes to implications for practice, the main one is to start seeing what has been there all along (remembering that sociology is a seeing art as well as a listening art) and to see what differences that makes to the problems we are facing and the potential solutions.

Conclusion

This now brings us to the end of Chapter 8 and therefore to the end of Part Two. By exploring some of the complexities associated with social relations in their various forms and settings, we have completed our SPIDER model of the web of society. We have now seen how six particular features of the social world affect, in their own ways, our experience of social life. We have seen how complex these issues are and how their interaction with one another makes them even more complex.

At times we have paused to look briefly at how these issues might inform an applied sociology approach and how applied sociology, in turn, can be useful in addressing the problems and challenges involved. I have emphasized that there are no easy solutions, there is no direct link between sociological understanding and practical strategies. But, what sociological knowledge in general and the sociological imagination in particular can offer is a critical, holistic perspective that offers more insights than a narrow, atomistic approach could.

All this sets the scene for Part Three where we will be exploring in more detail two particularly important sets of consideration for applied sociology, identity (sociology is about people, not just an abstract "society") and the organizational context (most applied sociology will take place within organizations). Those considerations will, in turn, set the scene for the final chapter where I will be summing up the challenges of using sociology in applied ways.

Points to Ponder

1. Friendships are an important part of social relations. How can they affect quality of life and possibly even health?
2. How might a sociological approach to conflict management influence any steps you might take in dealing with a conflict?
3. What might the significance be of the interrelationships across the three domains of paid work, domestic labor, and civil labor?

Exercise 8

Imagine that you became aware of a situation involving abuse of some kind and that the matter was reported to the appropriate authorities. They now need to develop an assessment of the situation in order to have an informed basis for deciding how to proceed (abuse issues are complex and sensitive, and so they need to be handled very carefully). How might sociological insights into social relations help inform their assessment?

PART THREE

Sociologically Informed Practice

Introduction to Part Three

Part One set the scene by laying the foundations of our exploration of applied sociology. Part Two then built on those foundations by exploring, in turn, each of the six elements of our SPIDER model of the web of society. Now, in Part Three, it is time to put our metaphorical roof on what we have constructed so far by considering areas of social life that applied sociology can help us with.

In this third and final part of the book there are three chapters. In the first (Chapter 9) we focus on the individual in social context. I have emphasized at various points that focusing narrowly on the individual (atomism, as it is known) is not enough; we also need to look at the social context that has such a vitally important part to play in shaping actions, reactions and interactions. However, this is not to say that we should neglect the individual or assume that sociology has nothing to say about individuals. On the contrary, there is much that sociology can tell us about the individual.

In Chapter 10 the subject matter that interests us is the organizational context. Applied sociology, as we have seen (and as we shall explore in further detail here in Part Three) can be used in a wide variety of occupational settings and professional roles. For the most part these settings and roles will be within the context of an employing organization. That very context is socially significant in itself. We would be making a major mistake to omit consideration of how sociology can help us understand the workplace, regardless of what type of workplace it is or what activities go on within it. This is because organizations and organizational life have various characteristics that are shaped by their location within the web of society, and so sociology can help us make sense of them and leave us better equipped to handle the challenges of working life.

Chapter 11 is concerned with "holistic practice" and its aim, basically, is to pull together some of the main strands of the discussion so far and give as clear a picture as it can of how sociology can be beneficial, not just as an academic discipline, but also as a profoundly useful set of tools in real-life practice situations. The chapter title refers to holistic practice because one of the main strengths of sociology is that it enables us to see the big picture and not focus down too narrowly on one aspect of human experience.

The Individual in Social Context

9

Introduction

Every one of us on the planet is a unique individual—a combination of biological, psychological, social and spiritual factors makes sure of that. There are some ways in which we are all the same—for example, in terms of our biology: we all need oxygen to survive and we all bleed when cut. There are also social factors that apply across the board. For example, we all live within cultural contexts that will have shaped our perspective on the world (our *Weltanschauung*). And those cultural contexts will also ensure that we share certain things with certain groups, but not with others. If we want to understand people, whether individually or collectively, we need to understand how we are all the same, how we are the same as some people, but not others and how we are all unique. If we miss out one or more of these dimensions, we leave much of the human story untold.

What Does It Mean to Be an Individual?

One of the first development tasks of the new-born child is to start the process of creating a boundary around self, to know where they finish and the rest of the world starts (Edward et al., 2015). At first, everything is a buzz of stimuli, a confusing range of inputs that the infant needs to make sense of. Thankfully, the way the human brain has evolved allows us to do this for the most part without too much difficulty.

One very important point to recognize here is that the very process of establishing a sense of self, a sense of what is me and what is the rest of my environment, is a social process right from the start. This is because: (i) this process of delineation of me-not me takes place in a social environment, in the sense that so many of the stimuli the child has to make sense of are social in origin; (ii) that environment is not neutral: there will be people within it who will be shaping the child's perceptions (smiling, cuddling, talking and so on); and (iii) we need to return to Durkheim's important point that society precedes us—that is, at birth we are "inserted" into a particular place in society (social location again) in terms of economic position, gender, ethnicity, language group, religious context, political stability or otherwise, and so on.

It would be naïve not to recognize that all three of these elements are profoundly social, and therefore the very roots of identity formation are social (and thus of sociological interest). Durkheim's point is particularly important. Consider, for example, the huge differences in terms of social influences at a crucial time of maturation between, say: (a) a boy born in peacetime into a wealthy family that speaks the dominant language in a patriarchal society and are members of the main faith in that society; and (b) a girl born during a lengthy war into a poverty-stricken family who speak a minority language that is stigmatized and who are from a minority sect in a highly sectarian and equally patriarchal society. This begins to paint a picture of how complex these issues are, how many social variables there are and how dangerous and misleading it is to see just an individual in isolation without taking account of the immensely powerful influences and constraints (for good or ill) that are brought to bear in the development of our identity and our perspective on life, as well as our life chances—the opportunities and challenges we face that are not evenly distributed across society.

I have focused so far on identity formation in childhood. However, sociology can help us to challenge the dubious Freudian notion that identity development is largely over by the age of five. A sociological approach to lifecourse development can help us to see that identity development is a lifelong process; we continue throughout our lives to have opportunities to grow, develop and change (Hunt, 2016).

So, it is very much the case that every one of is unique, we each have our own definitive sense of who we are. However, we should not make the mistake of assuming that we are, therefore, somehow separate from society in splendid isolation. What it is much wiser to recognize is that what makes us unique is: (i) the complex mix of social variables as we have seen; and (ii) our own distinctive reaction to them. This reflects the idea of structure and agency, as discussed earlier. We are not immune to the influences and constraints of the social world around us (even though atomism ideologically serves to camouflage the fact by promoting a conception of an autonomous individual divorced from his or her social context), but nor are we puppets pushed around by social forces with no say in the matter—we have agency.

In an earlier work on the subject of leadership (Thompson, 2016a), I made the point that there will always be constraints, things that we cannot prevent or remove ("facticity," to use the technical term), but there will always be *agency*, always things we can do in response to those constraints ("transcendence," in technical language). In simple terms, whatever circumstances we find ourselves in, there will always be things we can do about them in terms of how we respond to the situation—there will always be choices.

The social nature of identity is captured well by Sprintzen when he argues that: "The autonomous individual is a fiction. Individuality is always partial, embedded, historical, and transactional" (2009, p. 113). The "interactional" element is particularly important, in my view, as it moves us away from an essentialist notion of selfhood—that is, the notion that we are who we are and there is nothing we can do about it because personality is largely fixed. This oversimplification of some highly complex dynamics neglects the fact that our sense of self is flexible and fluid, depending on the circumstances we are in and the way people relate and react to us. I think the existentialist social theorist, Jean-Paul Sartre, got it right when he said: "we are what we make of what is made of us" (Sartre, 1973). By this he meant we cannot escape social forces and their effects on us (what is made of us), but how we react to them (what we make of them) will shape our sense of who are and how people relate to us. That is, who I am is basically shaped (and reshaped over time) by the choices I make and the attitudes I adopt to the set of social circumstances I find myself in. I am not total master of those social circumstances, but nor am I simply a passive victim of them (Thompson, 2017b).

So, it is fair to say that individual factors are very important, but they need to be understood within a social context. As Bauman and May so aptly put it: "Sociology thus stands in praise of the individual, but not individualism" (2001, p. 11), and by individualism they mean what I have been referring to here as atomism.

Practice Focus 9.1

Bill was a workforce development manager in a large company. He had been trained to focus on individual learning needs and learning styles, so his approach focused very much on individuals. However, he began a relationship with Sophie, an anthropologist. He found her work fascinating and was keen to know more and more. Her focus was on how culture affects parenting practices. Before long, Bill could see that her research had implications for his work. As a result of this, he started to read up on learning cultures and the influence of wider factors on learning (and obstacles to learning). Sophie's more holistic, socially focused approach to her work had helped him realize he was being too narrow in how he approached workplace learning.

The Role of the Social Context

So far, then, I have indicated that an atomistic approach to identity is not helpful; a much broader, socially informed approach offers a more realistic picture. In this section what we are going to do is explore these issues further by looking in more detail at how the social context shapes individual experience.

The Sociology of Brushing Our Teeth

Many years ago I taught a distance learning introductory social science course for the Open University in the United Kingdom. One element of the course was built around the social significance of brushing our teeth. The point the course was making was that, while brushing our teeth is something we see as very personal, private and intimate, it is also very much a social phenomenon. Consider the following:

- The water used is not likely to come directly from a natural source; in most cases it will be through a plumbed system linked to a water company. There will be payment involved for the water, and therefore economic aspects to bear in mind. The supply in the vast majority of cases will be part of a complex water supply network that is clearly social in its origins and operations. That water supply will probably also be regulated, in the sense that it will have to pass governmental or industry-specific water quality tests and be subject to health and safety legislation.
- The toothpaste will have come through a socially organized manufacturing process that is also part of the economy. It too will be subject to regulation and legislation. It will not have been given away free, and so there will be socially significant processes involved, such as sales and marketing activities. The toothpaste will also, more than likely, have been through

complex transportation systems: raw materials to the factory; finished product to the warehouse or depot; and distribution first to the whole-saler and then to the retailer. These systems could well be international in scope. There will then be the interactive processes involved in buying the product, and this will take place within a context of consumer protection legislation. Similar issues will apply to the toothbrush, of course.

- There will also be "social rules" (see Chapter 7), social expectations about, for example, not using someone else's toothbrush, allowing a person privacy when they are brushing their teeth and, of course, social disapproval of people who do not clean their teeth or not often or well enough. That sense of disapproval is likely to have emerged from the process of socialization.

So, this personal, private, intimate activity is, in reality, also a highly social one in a variety of ways. However, our atomism-infused society is likely to mean that we will normally see the personal, individual aspects, but filter out the social elements, despite their clear significance—they have been ideologically camouflaged by a discourse of atomism. We therefore need to stop thinking about "individual vs. society" and think more clearly about "individual *in* society." This simple, but highly significant, step then gives us a platform for an applied sociology that can address individual issues and concerns, rather than just macro-level ones.

A Complex Fusion

Earlier I referred to the "coffee and cream" perspective on the individual and, in so doing, emphasized that it is not, as traditionally, believed a case of soup (the individual) in the bowl (the backdrop of society), with each remaining relatively untouched by the other. Rather, the two blend together like coffee and cream to create a "psychosocial" entity. There can be no society without individuals, but we also cannot separate individuals from society, such are the profound and far-reaching influences and constraints of wider society—hence the idea that we are dealing with a complex fusion (coffee and cream, individual and society), rather than a simple juxtaposition (soup and bowl, individual and environment).

When I trained as a social worker many years ago, I was taught that social work operates where the individual and society meet and so, to be an effective social worker, you need to understand individual, psychological issues (psycho) and wider sociological issues (social) and how the two sets of factors interact (psychosocial). To this day I still see social work as precisely that psychosocial enterprise. However, I have long since extended my understanding to see that it is not just social work that operates at that intersection, it is human experience in general that does so. Social work deals with some of the problems and challenges that arise at that intersection, but not all. In a sense, then, applied sociology can be seen going beyond conventional social work and being prepared to adopt a psychosocial perspective on all human problems and challenges, not just those that traditionally come within the ambit of social work—hence the idea that applied sociology can be used in any setting where there is a concern with people, problems and potential (a point to which we shall return below).

Habitus and Field

Earlier we drew on some of Bourdieu's ideas. It is worth returning to them here as the "fusion" I have just mentioned is where he was coming from. In particular, two of his concepts can help us understand the significance of the individual *in* society, rather than the individual vs. society, namely habitus and field.

Maton describes them in the following terms:

> *habitus,* the subjective element of practice. This concept signifies the "generative schemes" . . . acquired in the course of individual life trajectories. *Field:* the objective network or configuration of relations . . . to be found in any social space or particular context . . . Both concepts should be seen as being inseparable, mutually constituted and always interpenetrating.
>
> *(2012, p. 47)*

By "generative schemes" what he means is ways by which we generate our reactions to the situations in which we find ourselves, our established patterns of response and attitude. A habitus, then, is a set of characteristics (and characteristic responses) that have developed around us and, in a sense, become part of our identity, a subjective filter through which we approach the objective world around us.

A "field" is an area of social life where we operate, and we basically adapt our habitus to suit the field we are in. For example, how we react in a work situation (work field) may be very different to how we would react at home (family field) or if we were out with a group of friends (leisure field). As Maton goes on to say:

We cannot understand the practices of actors in terms of their habituses alone—habitus represents but one part of the equation; the nature of the fields they are active within is equally crucial.

(2012, p. 51)

To understand an individual, therefore, we need to take account of not only the wider social context in all its different (SPIDER) forms, but also the specific social *field* (or set of fields) that are also part of the equation.

Voice of Experience 9.1

I did a sociology module as part of my degree, but I always thought it was about things beyond the individual, the background, I suppose. But I started to see it in a new light when I started working here, because this place is very much about helping individuals, but the approach is based on a sociological understanding, with a fair bit of politics thrown in.

Leigh, a fundraiser at a refugee support center

PCS Analysis Revisited

In Chapter 3 we looked at how I had taken Giddens's structuration theory which emphasized the dialectic between structure and agency and extended it to a "double dialectic" between, first, the personal and cultural levels and, second, the cultural and structural levels. If we consider the significance of that analytical framework for a moment, it should become clear that it can cast a great deal of light in the individual in society:

- Each individual is a person in their own right; they have their own *personal* perspective, outlook, focus, values, priorities, and so on. And, as we have already noted, each individual is unique. However, the different elements of the personal level do not just appear out of the blue; they arise from interactions between the individual and the wider social issues (SPIDER).
- The interactions between the individual and the web of society operate through frameworks of meaning (first dialectic). These sets of meaning are captured by the notion of the *cultural* level, the level of shared meanings, taken-for-granted assumptions and unwritten rules. However, these do not arise in a vacuum either. These reflect (and end up reinforcing) the wider structural power relations (second dialectic).

- We therefore need to include the *structural* level in our analysis, to make sure that we are aware that the issues at this level also play a part in shaping human experience at the **P** level.

We can therefore use this framework to understand (and analyze) the position of the individual not as one of isolation, but one of social location in terms of being embedded in a wider cultural framework of meanings(s) that, in turn, are embedded in wider structural relations of power—very much a case of the individual *in* society, rather than the individual vs. society.

PCS analysis is not a panacea for making sense of the complex interrelationships between individuals and various elements of society, but it does offer a strong beginning and a sound foundation on which to build.

Practice Focus 9.2

Anwen was a social worker in a multidisciplinary child protection team. As part of her social work degree she had learned about PCS analysis. She had initially seen it as a useful concept to discuss in her essays as appropriate. However, now as a fully qualified worker facing some really difficult and complex situations, she was fully aware that she would need some help making sense of these complexities. So, her familiarity with PCS analysis was a big bonus, as she could start to use that straight away. For example, she could see that each individual in the family had their own personal issues and perspectives. But, she could also see how cultural issues were relevant too—not just broad cultural issues around societal attitudes towards abuse, but also cultural differences about what was perceived as abusive or not, plus how families acted according to their own sets of cultural meanings, a bit like the family "scripts" she had read about when she studied family therapy. And, of course, it wasn't long before she could see how structural power relations (around class and poverty, for example), were very relevant, as were structural issues around gender role expectations in relation to sexual abuse. Anwen knew PCS analysis would not give her the detailed plan of action she would need to develop in each case, but it did give her a very powerful tool for thinking holistically and clearly about cases.

People, Problems, Potential

The people/problems/potential theme was introduced in the Introduction. As you may recall, it was built on the recognition that the complexity of human life is such that, where there are people, there will also be problems—but there will always be potential. Part of the core argument of this book is that applied sociology can help us to: (i) understand and address those problems; and (ii) nurture and realize that potential. Sociology is therefore a very powerful tool in a variety of work settings. It can be helpful at a macro level (for example, in policy development and/or bringing about culture change—see Chapter 10), but also at a micro level in addressing the problems and challenges of individuals. It is worth exploring some examples of how this applies, as this is very relevant to our theme of the individual in society.

There is a common, but misleading assumption that personal problems are the domain of psychology, while social problems are what sociology is supposed to be concerned with. However, in reality, sociological insights can cast light on personal problems to a large extent, as we are about to see, and psychology can be seen to offer insights into certain aspects of social problems (the psychological effects of being a victim of crime, for example).

Problematic Drug Use

There are many misleading stereotypes of people whose use of drugs is problematic in some way, one being the deranged addict in a world of their own and beyond help. In reality, problematic drug use can be traced back to a number of social issues, including poverty, abuse, discrimination, social expectations (peer pressure), homelessness and stigma.

These can all contribute to a sense of social rejection and therefore alienation. As I have explained in an earlier work:

> The causes and consequences of the problems associated with drugs and alcohol are many and varied. However, one important factor is the significance of alienation, a feeling of not belonging, of not fitting in and of not being valued. This is especially the case with illegal drugs where there will tend to be subcultures associated with the use of those drugs. The 1960s notion of "dropping out" and belonging to an "alternative" society is strongly associated with the development of drug cultures and associated problems.
>
> (Thompson, 2017a, p. 151)

Similarly, Harris locates addiction in a social context when he argues that: "Addiction is not simply the biological action of the drug, but the cultural context in which the drug is taken" (p. 43, 2005). Of course, there are clear biological aspects to problematic drug use, but we should not allow that to seduce us into thinking that social factors are non-existent or marginal. Problematic drug use is profoundly social for a number of reasons (socially different access to drugs, for example).

Unfortunately, though, a common response to drug-related problems has been to individualize (and pathologize) drug use, through individual drug treatment programs and the criminalization of drug use and supply (what is often referred to as a "war on drugs").

Sociology, by contrast, can offer a focus on addressing the social factors involved (drug cultures, for example); access to drugs (in prisons, for example) and even by developing social programs that seek to address the underlying factors—seeking to stem alienation through greater social inclusion, for example. Much of the best anti-drugs work has been informed by more holistic sociological approaches that question a medicalized "treatment" approach, and conceptualize drugs-related problems as public health concerns, rather than medical and/or criminal ones.

In a parallel manner, Hari (2015) points out that the illegal drugs industry is a major economy in its own right, one ruled by violence and murder. If we really want to put an end to the immense misery and suffering that illegal drug use brings to so many people, perhaps more attention needs to be given to the macro-level issues of the drugs economy.

Furthermore, although there is much emphasis on illegal drug use, this can tend to cast shadows over another significant problem, namely the abuse of prescription medication—an example of "iatrogenesis," a problem caused by tackling a complex, multi-level issue as if it were simply a matter of a medical ailment that needs treatment. For example, depression is a complex condition, with complex causes and contributory factors (Rogers and Pilgrim, 2014). However, an approach rooted in a medical discourse oversimplifies the issues involved, leaving a major emphasis on anti-depressant medication as a "treatment" option. It is ironic that much of the medication that is being used through apparent addiction is intended to "treat" depression and anxiety.

There have been voices of dissatisfaction in relation to how drugs issues are dealt with for quite some time, but the dominant approach remains individualistic, partly medical and partly criminalizing (and therefore strongly pathologizing).

Workplace Problems

When it comes to individual identity, we should not neglect the significance of work (which is partly why Chapter 10 focuses on workplace issues). For very many people, of course, work is a core part of their identity. Problems in the workplace can therefore be highly destructive because they can undermine self-image, self-esteem and self-efficacy, and thereby contribute to alienation and its harmful consequences.

Workplace problems can include, stress, bullying, conflict, aggression and violence, unresolved grief and/or trauma and various other threats to our well-being and even health. This should be unsurprising for large workplaces which can have a population equivalent to a small town, and which could be expected to have the full range of problems you would anticipate finding in a small town.

Sociology can be of help in addressing how these problems affect individuals in a number of ways. The concept of workplace well-being has emerged much more prominently in the last decade or so (Thompson and Bates, 2009). Many people interpret this initiative very narrowly, and it is not uncommon for employing organizations to offer confidential counseling, spa therapies and other such approaches that are: (i) predominantly individualistic in their focus; and (ii) largely focused on the "symptoms" of the problem, rather than the underlying social processes and power dynamics that are operating. We shall return to this topic in Chapter 10, but for now we should note that sociology can help individuals experiencing workplace problems by looking at the issues more holistically and more critically.

Emotional Challenges

Emotion is another area where the focus is primarily, if not exclusively, on psychological aspects. This is unfortunate, as there is a sociological dimension to emotion that is largely ignored (Turner, 2011), a dimension that can help us to develop a fuller understanding.

This applies to emotional issues in general, but can also relate to emotional difficulties or challenges. There are two of these that I have already mentioned earlier, but it is worth revisiting them here to highlight their significance in terms of applied sociology.

The first of these is stress. The dominant approach to stress had traditionally been an individualistic one, based on the idea that stress arises when someone fails to cope with the pressures they face. It is therefore an approach that pathologizes people who experience stress. However, we can look more holistically at stress by asking such questions as:

- Is the individual's workload reasonable in the circumstances?
- Is it clear what is expected of the employee?
- Is there sufficient autonomy or is the work unduly constrained?

- Is appropriate support available?
- Is the leadership offered of a sufficient quality?

These are questions that go beyond the individual in order to see the bigger picture, and thereby avoid pathologizing that can make the problem worse. We can see stress as being parallel to pain in the body. Pain is a warning that something is wrong in the body and needs attention. Stress is also a warning that something is wrong and needs attention. An atomistic approach would have us interpret this as something wrong with the *individual*, hence the pathologizing. However, the more critical approach of applied sociology would have us interpret the question more holistically, looking at the individual *in context*.

The second emotional challenge to consider is that of grief. We have already explored just how *social* grief is, despite the very strong tendency for it to be seen in atomistic terms. Grief will vary according to gender, culture, class and so on. How people react to other people's grief will also vary, depending on a number of social variables. Furthermore, if we think about it, grief arises when we lose someone we love, so a social relationship can be at the heart of it, heart being the appropriate word, of course.

The two areas of emotional challenge, stress and grief, can therefore be understood as sociological as well as psychological phenomena, and so there is the potential for applied sociology to make a positive difference.

When we combine the three main areas—problematic drug use; workplace problems; and emotional challenges, we can see that there is considerable scope for a sociological approach to have a significant impact if well used. Illouz regards it as an urgent matter for us to address:

> Precisely because we live in a time when the idea of individual responsibility reigns supreme, the vocation of sociology remains vital. In the same way that at the end of the nineteenth century it was radical to claim that poverty was the result not of dubious morality or weak character, but of systematic economic exploitation, it is now urgent to claim not that failures of our private lives are the result of weak psyches, but rather that the vagaries and miseries of our emotional life are shaped by institutional arrangements.
>
> *(2012, p. 4)*

She is here making an important point, in so far as a great deal of harm can be done by atomistic approaches that ignore the wider social context and thereby run the risk of pathologizing, disempowering and thus oppressing people, robbing them of their dignity and self-respect. Sociological insights are therefore of major significance when it comes to helping individuals. Consequently, we cannot allow the continuance of the stereotypical view that sociology is just about abstract things in the background that may be of some academic interest, but of no practical value.

Voice of Experience 9.2

My manager left and was not replaced for months. I ended up doing a lot of her work as well as my own. I also took a lot of the flak for some of her work that didn't get done, even though it wasn't my responsibility anyway. Things started to get really difficult, and what turned out to be the last straw was that two temporary workers we had with us decided that this was not the place they wanted to work, with such unreasonable workloads, and so they contacted the agency they worked for and arranged to be placed elsewhere. The situation then went from incredibly difficult to just plain impossible. I ended up going off sick for six weeks because I was totally frazzled. But, do you know what the worst thing was? After I went off sick, head office pulled out all the stops and reduced the pressure in various ways. Why couldn't they have done that before I went off sick and prevent the indignity of it all for me? Why did they totally ignore me when I told them about the unrealistic pressures and then find they could do something about it after all? They then had the cheek to offer me confidential counseling. I didn't want counseling, I wanted justice for the dreadful way they had treated me and my colleagues.

Sam, a section leader in a logistics company

Beyond Psychotherapy

Therapy of or for the mind is what psychotherapy literally means. During my career I have come across enough people who have benefited from psychotherapy to know that it can be immensely powerful in making a positive difference. However, it is not without its problems.

Where I have seen it work well has been where circumstances that were being addressed were amenable to this approach and where the approach was quite appropriate and legitimate. However, Furedi is one author among others who has expressed concern about how it can be overextended, and how it can therefore contribute to inappropriate responses:

Through the language of psychology, therapeutic culture frames the way that problems are perceived. "The result is that social problems are increasingly perceived in terms of psychological dispositions: as personal inadequacies, guilt feelings, anxieties, conflicts and neuroses", concludes Beck (2002) . . . Of course, understanding the self and the internal life of the individual is important for comprehending individual behaviour and the wider life of the community. However, a one-dimensional preoccupation with the self often leads to overlooking the social and cultural foundations of individual identity. This approach leads to a novel and specific representation of the self—one that the American sociologist John Rice has characterised as an "asocial self" [Rice, 1996]. From the standpoint of the asocial self what matters is its internal life. The significance of social and cultural influence is discounted in favour of a narrow psychological deliberation of personal emotions.

(2004, p. 25)

At times, there is a need for a "sociotherapy"—that is, for problems to be viewed more holistically when their roots are in the wider society, rather than, as Furedi quite rightly bemoans, presenting a distorted atomistic picture of the situation.

I am not arguing by any means against psychotherapy, but it is important to hear what Furedi is saying about the dangers of trying to fit social problems into an atomistic framework, thereby contributing to further pathologizing and distracting attention away from the important social roots of social problems.

Practice Focus 9.3

Ken was a freelance workplace well-being consultant. He had a strong background in trade unionism and had specialized in helping organizations get the best out of their staff by treating them properly. He was well respected as a consultant and had a steady flow of work coming in, although he could always take on more if available. One day he was approached by a large consultancy company inviting him to be an associate senior consultant with them. He was flattered by the approach and excited about increasing his throughput of work. However, his positive feelings were shortlived. He was invited to the company's headquarters for an informal discussion. He did not like what he heard. As a former trade unionist, he was well aware of the significance of organizational issues, the importance of support and leadership and so on, However, this company's approach was very different. They were being commissioned by large companies to provide "well-being services," but what they were offering was entirely individualistic (massage, alternative medicine approaches and so on). The very clear message coming across to him was: We focus on helping individuals to recover from their pressures and difficulties; we do nothing to look at those difficulties holistically and look for strategic solutions. So, he decided to continue on his own and to carry on making a positive difference to employing organizations by looking well beyond just individual presenting problems.

Conclusion

The value of making use of sociological insights is fundamentally what this book is all about. In this chapter we have looked at how sociology can be helpful in addressing a range of problems and strategies individuals can encounter. In doing so, we have been challenging the notion that such areas are the exclusive terrain of psychologists. As we shall see in Chapter 11, psychology and sociology work best when they are complementing each other, when they are based on the idea of the individual *in* society, rather than going down the path of the long-standing well-trodden pitfall of thinking in terms of the individual vs. society.

As part of our discussions, we have touched on the significance of the workplace setting. This sets us up nicely now for Chapter 10 where we will explore in more detail what applied sociology can tell us about the workplace and working life.

Points to Ponder

1. Consider your own identity. Can you identify ways in which your social circumstances have helped to shape who you are?
2. What difference does it make to think of the relationship of the individual to society as coffee and cream, rather than soup and bowl?
3. What harm is likely to occur if stress is seen narrowly as the sign of someone who does not cope very well, rather than holistically to encompass wider social and organizational issues?

Exercise 9

What might a "sociotherapy" look like? How might it differ from psychotherapy? What actions could it involve to bring about progress? What situations might it apply to?

The Organizational Context   **10**

Introduction

Applied sociology, as we have seen, offers a helpful foundation of understanding that can be used across a wide variety of occupational settings and activities. Those work activities will, of course, take place within an organizational context for the most part. The main focus of this chapter, therefore, is on that organizational context. We cast our sociological spotlight not just on work activities, but on the very context in which those activities take place.

We should note that, in terms of applied sociology, the organizational context is doubly significant—first, because, as I have just noted, it is likely that the practical application of sociology will take place within an organizational setting; and, second, much of the attention of applied sociology will be on helping organizations to tackle the problems, issues and challenges they face. In this regard, we can say that the organizational context is relevant to applied sociology because: (i) applied sociology takes place *in* an organizational context; and (ii) will often involve working *on* an organizational context—that is, trying to make changes to bring about improvements and address concerns.

A key factor in this regard is organizational culture. Indeed, the culture of an organization (and its various subcultures within various sections and teams) will be a major influence on working life at a number of levels. It is for this reason that a review of the key aspects of organizational culture will act as the foundation for this chapter.

Following on from this we shall also consider how the world of work has been changing and how it is likely to continue changing. This will lead into a discussion of workplace well-being, its importance, and the role applied sociology can make in promoting it. Next will come a consideration of leadership, an issue (or set of issues) that I see as fundamental to organizational success (or otherwise).

Organizational Culture

Cultures are shared frameworks of meaning. To be a member of a culture involves subscribing to the meanings involved, the unwritten rules and taken-for-granted assumptions. It is "the way we do things round here." Organizations have cultures, or sets of (sub-)cultures. For example, a large company may have its overall culture shared across the whole organization, but different offices, sections and/or teams may have variations on the same theme—or may even have elements of culture that run counter to the overall organizational culture.

Some elements of organizational culture will be deliberate. For example, a company may have particular values that are explicitly part of its strategic plan, and there may be consistent concerted efforts to instill those values and firmly embed them within everything that is done in the company's name. However, much of culture is emergent—that is, it evolves over time. It is rooted in habits and unquestioned assumptions, but that does not mean it does not change over time.

Cultures in organizations are exceptionally important because they influence people without their awareness for the most part. For example, a new entrant to a team will quickly become acclimatized and start following patterns of action, reaction and interaction that have been laid down previously as the existing culture developed. While some of this may well be intentional as part of an effort to "fit in" and feel at home, much of it will happen fairly spontaneously—a process of "socialization" (or "enculturation") will occur. We become "inducted" into the culture by becoming part of the various discourses involved.

Cultures can both help and hinder, depending on the circumstances and the nature of the culture—and this is where applied sociology can be of value, Foucault argued that:

A critique is not a matter of saying that things are not right as they are. It is a matter of pointing out on what kinds of assumptions, what kinds of familiar, unchallenged, unconsidered modes of thought the practices that we accept rest.

(1988, p. 155)

Cultural critique is therefore value-neutral, in the sense that it is not necessarily critical in the everyday sense of criticizing. It is not a matter of liking or disliking a culture. It is about being able to pinpoint how the culture is operating and what impact it is having on its members and possibly on others outside the cultural circle. This is where applied sociology can be helpful in highlighting different aspects of a culture—things that members of that culture may not be able to see clearly because they are part of that culture, they are members of the "club." In this respect, an applied sociology intervention could help to identify strong points of the culture, positives to build *on*, while also highlighting problematic areas to build *up*.

In an earlier work (Thompson, 2017b) I introduced the notion of a "culture audit." This is a tool that can be used to get a sense of what is important in a culture and to highlight potential problem areas. It involves reviewing the culture in terms of seven dimensions as follows:

- *Negative vs. positive* This is a reflection of morale. Motivation is a psychological matter, in large part down to the individual, but morale is a sociological phenomenon—it is about shared feelings of positivity or negativity. As we shall see below, negative, low morale cultures can be very destructive.
- *Dependency vs. independence* How much autonomy do members have? Is it mainly a matter of following orders (an algorithmic approach) or is there scope for autonomy (a heuristic approach—Pink, 2011). The less autonomy people have, the less engaged and productive they are likely to be.
- *Tramlines vs. creativity* Are members encouraged to be creative and to explore innovative solutions or are they discouraged from doing so and restricted to established patterns of work?
- *Problem avoidance vs. problem solving* As the 3P model (people/problems/potential) highlighted for us earlier, where there are people, there will be problems. Is the culture realistic about this? Does it encourage a problem-solving approach or does it encourage sweeping problems under the carpet (problem avoidance)? This will include how the culture sets people up to manage mistakes. As Friedman comments:

> Having a team that's afraid of admitting failure is a dangerous problem, particularly because the symptoms are not immediately visible. What appears on the surface to be a well-functioning unit may, in fact, be a group that's too paralyzed to admit its own flaws.
>
> *(2014, p. 19)*

- *Resisting change vs. capitalizing on the opportunities presented by change* It is often assumed that people fear and resist change. Is that true, or is it the way that change is managed that can generate fear? Cultures can range from a strong fear element, at one extreme, to positively engaging with change and trying to make the best of it at the other.

- *Unsupportive vs. supportive* Do staff feel valued, appreciated and supported? Do they feel safe? Cultures play a key role in shaping people's perceptions of the workplace, their morale, their level of commitment and so on. Friedman again makes apt comment: "Helping the people who work for you feel appreciated seems easy enough. So it's surprising that plenty of workplaces get it wrong" (2014, p. 161). This fits with my own experience, as I have come across so many organizations that have not managed to get this basic requirement right (and have paid the price for it in terms of low morale and its deleterious effects).

- *Closed vs. open* Is there a culture of gossip and issues being discussed behind closed doors? Or does the culture encourage openness and transparency? For example, if an instance of dangerous practice were to emerge, would employees feel it is safe to raise it as a matter of concern or would they be more likely to "bury" it and thus allow the danger, and its associated harm, to persist?

To these seven dimensions we can also add a further set of issues to consider, namely: What does the culture encourage in relation to learning and development? From my consultancy work I have been able to identify three distinct types of culture in relation to learning and development:

1. *A learning culture* This is where learning and development are valued, supported and encouraged. There is a genuine commitment to employees achieving their potential through learning and thus producing the best results.

2. *A non-learning culture* There may possibly be a rhetorical commitment to learning and development, but this is not borne out in practice. The ethos of the organization, section or team is rooted in a culture of "just get on with the job." Time expected to be committed to learning and development activities is seen as a cost, rather than an investment. Any learning is partial, sporadic and inconsistent.

3. *An anti-learning culture* This is the type of culture that goes a step further and actively discourages learning and development. It is as if there is a fear of learning, as if development is somehow threatening. It is characterized by comments like: "If you've got time to think, you haven't got

enough work to do" and/or "What do you want to go on a course for, they won't increase your salary for it?" People who are keen to learn are likely to leave or remain and become disillusioned and possibly burnt out. People who are not learning feel safe in that type of culture, even though not learning is actually a very risky undertaking.

This type of audit is a good example of an applied sociology tool that can be used in various contexts to help bring about positive change and to address existing problems. Influencing organizational culture in a positive direction is a key part of effective leadership, and so we will return to this topic below when we consider how applied sociology can inform leadership practices.

Practice Focus 10.1

Ken was an independent workplace well-being consultant. He had experience of working with a wide variety of organizations. Who engaged his services reflected a degree of "polarization," in the sense that it was organizations at the two extremes that tended to come to him for help: (i) those that valued workplace well-being and appreciated its benefits, so they were prepared to invest heavily in it, recognizing that it was an investment, that they would get their money repaid and with interest, through improved productivity and fewer workplace problems: and (ii) those organizations that were "in trouble" when it came to their people management practices, with problems such as a high turnover of staff, high levels of sickness absence, low morale, high levels of conflict, tension, discrimination, bullying and, of course, stress. What had become crystal clear to Ken was that what distinguished these two types of organization was their culture. Type (i) organizations had a positive and supportive culture, whereas Type (ii) organizations tended to have negative and destructive cultures.

The Changing World of Work

As we noted in Chapter 9, work is often an important part of people's identity; it can take up a significant proportion of our waking time. As such, it can be a very positive aspect of our lives (consider the detrimental effects of unemployment, by contrast) or it can be highly problematic and a considerable source of suffering and harm. There is therefore scope for sociological insights to be of value.

The Changing Landscape of Work

What is also important to recognize is that the world of work is not static; it is constantly changing. Some of those changes are positive, some are negative, and many bring a mixture of positives and negatives. Applied sociology can play an important role by being aware of workplace changes and helping people to: (i) make the best of any positive elements, while (ii) safeguarding people, as far as possible, from the negative effects of change.

In 1999, Ulrich Beck argued that what he called the "work society" was coming to an end. He felt that this was because more and more people were being ousted by "smart technologies." Although he was certainly right that technological development has had (and continues to have) a huge impact on working life in so many different ways, whether or not this is changing the fundamental basis of work in society remains more of an open question.

Changes in the world of work over the past 20 or so years include (but are not limited to):

- *Job (in)security* The idea of a "job for life" no longer seems to apply for most people. Contract-based work, temporary contracts and other schemes that offer flexibility to employers, but insecurity to employees are becoming increasingly common. Beck relates this development to changes in how risk is managed in the economy:

    > The upshot is that the more work relations are "deregulated" and "flexibilized", the faster work society changes into a risk society incalculable both in terms of individual lives and at the level of the state and politics, and the more important it becomes to grasp the political economy of risk in its contradictory consequences for economics, politics and society.
    >
    > *(1999, p. 3)*

- *A move from employment to self-employment* More and more people are involved in what Beck terms "Me & Co.", offering their knowledge and skills on a freelance, contractual basis, rather than on an employment contract basis. This also offers employers greater flexibility, while shifting the risk to the contractor, in the sense that any loss of revenue through "slack time" is borne by the contractor, not the contracting organization. What also shifts to the contractor is the cost of the "tools of the trade." For example, a company employing someone who needs a computer to carry out their duties is likely to provide it for the employee, whereas it is likely that a self-employed contractor would be expected to provide their own. For some specialist work this can prove prohibitively expensive.

- *Increased use of computer technology* As more and more tasks can be automated, the silicon chip and its cousins become more and more central to manufacturing, service industries and public service. This has introduced a new skill set relating to information technology and created an even bigger gap between those with marketable skills and those who have only their labor time to offer. It has also created a bigger gap between older generations, many members of which will have limited computer skills (and, importantly, confidence) and younger generations being brought up with a mouse in one hand and a smart phone in the other. Further inequalities are thus arising.

These changes and the insecurities and uncertainties they bring create opportunities for applied sociology to make a contribution to: (i) making sense of the changes holistically; and (ii) capitalizing on benefits afforded and addressing problems and challenges generated.

A New Work Vista?

I mentioned earlier Beck's view that "the work society" is dying out. He explains it this way:

> The counter-model to the work society is . . . a multi-activity society in which housework, family work, club work and voluntary work are prized alongside paid work and returned to the centre of public and academic attention.
>
> *(1999, p. 125)*

Gorz (1999) is another theorist whose work has been associated with a new approach to the role of work in society—a new vista. However, to achieve such a society, major changes would be needed in social organization and in the ideologies that underpin the current social order. Whether this is what will emerge at some point remains to be seen, but we can certainly see that work is a complex social domain, a multi-layered aspect of social life that brings both benefits and problems, positives and negatives.

Voice of Experience 10.1

I have been self-employed for over five years now. I enjoy the freedom it brings, but that freedom comes with a certain amount of insecurity. When I was employed, I knew that my salary would be there at the end of the month, but now I not only have to find the work and do the work, I also have to make sure I get paid, and that isn't always easy—some people need a lot of chasing up before they eventually honor the invoice, and that takes up a lot of time I am not getting paid for. I am lucky in that I generally have plenty of work coming in, but I have come across lots of self-employed people who really struggle, but regular jobs are really hard to come by in some industries now.

Pat, a freelance training provider

Workplace Well-Being

One of the important messages I have been at pains to put across in my published work and my other professional activities is that there is a world of difference between trying to get the *most* out of employees, and trying to get the *best* out of them (Thompson, 2013). The former refers to putting pressure on people with a view to getting as much work out of them as possible. This is highly likely to be counterproductive for a number of reasons:

- It can lead to employees not feeling valued, feeling that they are just a dispensable cog in the wheel; morale can therefore suffer.
- It can contribute to stress, as there is no clarity about boundaries between a reasonable, manageable level of work and one that is unreasonable and unrealistic; the result can be work overload and stress, and, consequently possible litigation.
- It can encourage sabotage and resistance by people who resent being treated in this way; these "disloyal" activities can prove very costly at times.
- It can contribute to staff turnover; people will be motivated to seek employment elsewhere in places where the levels of pressure and support are more conducive.

By contrast, trying to get the *best* out of people means supporting them, valuing them and making sure they feel safe and secure in what they are doing (Thompson, 2016b). This more enlightened approach brings with it a number of benefits, including the following:

- More highly motivated staff who appreciate the support they receive.
- A higher level of morale that contributes to both increased productivity and improved quality.
- Greater levels of creativity and a greater chance of innovative approaches developing.

- A more positive atmosphere in which learning and development can take place.
- Fewer conflicts, tensions and related problems.
- Fewer work-related health problems.
- Lower levels of staff turnover.
- Lower levels of sickness absence.

The "getting the *best* out of people" approach is clearly a much wiser option, and this is the basis of what has now come to be known as the "workplace well-being" approach. It is based on the old adage that if you treat your staff well, they will treat your customers well.

Practice Focus 10.2

Debbie was the manager of a team of administrators in a large company. She had recently joined the team from a rival company. She was quite concerned when she realized how much pressure team members were under. To her, their workloads seemed unreasonable, and the whole atmosphere in the team was very tense and unpleasant. She spoke to Vince, her manager, about wanting to change this, but he was not very supportive of the idea initially. "We have to make sure the work gets done," he insisted; "if we reduce the pressure we will reduce the throughput, and then where would we be?" However, he didn't want to fall out with Debbie within days of her arrival, so he agreed reluctantly to let her try a different approach for a month "on a trial basis." But a month was all she needed, because, during that time she was able to convince the team that what she wanted was to get the best out of them by supporting and valuing them, not squeeze the most out of them and wear them out in the process. Very quickly the tense atmosphere disappeared, people felt more relaxed and more confident. Sickness absence levels dropped almost immediately and Debbie was quite convinced that staff turnover would now be severely reduced also. As she fully expected, the net result was an increase in throughput, not a decrease, partly because there were fewer mistakes that were time consuming to put right and partly because staff were more motivated and engaged.

As I mentioned in Chapter 9, some organizations have interpreted workplace well-being very superficially, reducing it to offering staff perks like spa treatments, equating well-being at work simplistically with a vague notion of "happiness," based on a principle to the effect that the happier people are the better. Ironically, Friedman sees too much happiness as a problem to be avoided:

> research suggests another downside to excessive happiness: an increased tendency for making mistakes. When we're happy, we grow confident, which at times can lead us to overestimate our abilities and ignore potential dangers. We can become more trusting, less critical, and occasionally unrealistic.
>
> *(2014, p. 96)*

Happiness is indeed part of the well-being equation, but there are some complex issues and subtle dynamics involved that need careful handling. Just equating well-being with happiness is a problematic oversimplification. Others have regarded well-being quite cynically as simply a matter of ensuring compliance with employment legislation. In both cases, the point—and value—of workplace well-being has been missed (Haworth and Hart, 2012).

Much of workplace well-being (or the lack of it) will stem from organizational culture. Some cultures are well-being friendly, while others are not and may actively contribute to exacerbating workplace problems (for example, negative, low morale cultures that breed cynicism and stress, thereby fueling burnout). This is a matter for leadership, and so we will return to this point shortly.

While the benefits of workplace well-being may be self-evident, evidence of its absence is generally not hard to find (Schnall et al., 2009; Thompson and Bates, 2009). As Friedman explains: "A 2010 study spanning 120 countries found that, internationally, 84 percent of employees are disengaged at work" (2014, p. 267). This presents immense opportunities for applied sociology to offer critical analyses of workplace practices that run counter to workplace well-being and to offer more constructive approaches.

Leadership

Leadership is one of those terms that is used in different ways by different people. Here I am using it to mean the role of significant organizational players (not just managers) to influence the culture in a positive direction so that everyone benefits: employees; managers; clients, customers and patients; and other stakeholders (Thompson, 2016b).

Management and Leadership

One way of looking at it is to say that management involves keeping the wheels turning, while leadership makes sure they are turning in the right direction (and that the people who need to be "on board" are indeed on board). Leadership is therefore not a substitute for management. However, it is not only managers who can or should be involved in leadership. For example, all members of a team can play a part in shaping the culture positively, rather than sit back and just wait for the manager to do that.

This fits with the idea expressed by Mary Parker Follett as long ago as 1924 that part of the role of a leader is to empower others to become leaders. An effective manager skilled in leadership will therefore discourage any "us-them" attitudes and try to create an atmosphere where people want to be part of a positive culture and, indeed, to contribute to it.

Sociologists as Leaders

Bearing in mind: (i) my description of leadership above in terms of shaping cultural development in a positive direction; and (ii) culture being a key part of sociological intellectual territory, there is a basis for arguing that sociologists can be leaders. What I mean by this is that it is not just members of an organization that can shape a culture. This can also be done up to a point by consultants, advisers, researchers and, in some cases, inspectors. Even a student on a field placement or practicum can have the potential to influence a culture in a positive direction.

It is also possible for members of an organization who have some degree of background in sociology to play an important role in shaping in-house culture by drawing on their sociological knowledge to develop a critical and holistic understanding of the culture and its impact, and thus the potential for it to be changed in a positive direction. The example given earlier in this chapter of a culture audit (Thompson, 2017b) can serve well as an illustration of this potential. At times, an independent person who is not part of the culture can offer insights into its workings that members of that culture do not see because they have become part of their taken-for-granted mindset. This can be an example of sociology as a "seeing art," as well as a listening art. However, while some degree of independence can be of value, it is possible— although difficult at times—for a "cultural insider" to use the sociological imagination to make sense of the culture and identify any possible positive changes that could be made.

Distributed Leadership

The traditional model of leadership is a straightforward hierarchical one, with the "leader" at the pinnacle of an organizational chart and the "followers" of various grades on various rungs below. However, what has emerged more recently is a model of "distributed" leadership (Harris, 2014). Part of this approach is an emphasis on leadership skills and activities being more evenly spread across the organization, which makes this a model much more in keeping with what I described above.

This more diffuse model of leadership opens up possibilities for people in various parts of the organization to use sociological insights to help them exercise their duties within their particular leadership "domain."

The Organizational Operator

In my *Promoting Equality* book (Thompson, 2018), I use this term, "organizational operator" to refer to how members of an organization do not have to sit back and hope that the powers that be address discrimination and promote equality. There are ways and means of influencing organizations subtly, skillfully and sensitively without inviting reprisals and other unwanted responses—and anyone who does this is what I would call an organizational operator.

We can extend that notion of organizational operator to apply to any process of influencing an organization in a positive direction. Of course, this could be seen as a form of leadership, especially where it involves seeking to influence the culture, rather than just directly influencing policy, for example.

Again, there is great scope here for applied sociology to feature, to serve as a basis for acting as an "organizational operator" in a spirit of distributed leadership.

Voice of Experience 10.2

I have long been a campaigner against discrimination in the workplace, having experienced more than my fair share of it myself. I was lucky to have an excellent mentor in my early days who taught me the value of learning how to work towards change without making enemies or creating an unnecessary fuss that will annoy people. I have seen some people adopt the "bull in a china shop" approach and all they have achieved is to alienate people. Your tactics need to be much more sophisticated than that if you are going to get anywhere.

Malik, a community development worker

Building Teams

Not everyone works in a team, but they do represent the most common configuration of staff. We often use the term "team building," although it is not the most accurate term, given that teams are more like organic entities than buildings. Perhaps "team nurturing" would be a more apt term.

Teams can do a lot of harm or a lot of good. The difference normally comes down to the quality of leadership. Effective communication is essential, of course. As Friedman helpfully points out:

> Research conducted by the Gallup organization suggest that the strongest predictor of employee retention isn't salary or perks or confidence in a company's future—it's the quality of the employee–manager relationship. And a major component of that relationship is the way in which a manager communicates.
>
> *(2014, p. 184)*

And, of course, we can extend this beyond staff retention to include any aspect of effective leadership: if you cannot communicate effectively, you cannot successfully lead.

But, there are other leadership issues that are significant too. Friedman's views are again very apt:

> We rarely need employees to simply do routine, repetitive tasks—we also need them to collaborate, plan, and innovate. Building a thriving organisation in the current economy demands a great deal more than efficiency. It requires an environment that harnesses intelligence, creativity, and interpersonal skill.
>
> *(2014, p. xv)*

That "environment" is not just the physical location, of course, it is also the human environment, the culture. So, we are back again to the notion of leaders as culture shapers.

Teams function best when they have: (i) a sense of shared endeavor (Thompson, 2011b); and (ii) a sense of security generated by having faith in their leader. Leadership therefore involves shaping the culture in such a way that people feel "on board" and feel safe because they are in safe hands. Shaping a culture involves having the skills to analyze the dynamics going on within the culture (the interpersonal interactions, the social processes, the power relations and so on) and develop strategies for influencing them. These are, of course, sociological matters and our ability to manage them effectively can be enhanced by sociological knowledge in general and the use of the sociological imagination in particular.

Tackling Cultural Problems

We have already focused on how workplace well-being can be a positive development with a view to getting the *best* out of employees, rather than making the common mistake of focusing on getting the *most* out of them. It reduces the likelihood of problems arising, but, of course, cannot prevent them altogether. So, if there are still going to be workplace problems associated with the organization's culture, what can be done about them? The full answer to that question could easily take up a full book in its own right. However, the following comments should give at least the beginnings of a picture as to how that question could be more fully answered:

- *Group work* This could involve setting up a sort of focus group to explore what the problems are and what the potential solutions could be. This could be useful in situations, for example, where there have been communication difficulties. Proposing more effective communication systems could be potentially very useful. The "culture audit" discussed above could also perhaps be used in certain circumstances.
- *Mediation* If the problem has arisen through an unresolved conflict, then a formal mediation process may prove very helpful. This involves a neutral mediator giving each party the opportunity to "tell their story" and air their grievance uninterrupted. Once each party has an understanding and appreciation of the point of view of the other person(s) involved, there is a much stronger basis for moving forward constructively. The aim of mediation is to produce a written agreement that is expected to be binding on the signatories, but its main benefit is getting individuals to understand each other's perspectives and concerns.
- *Narrative therapy* This involves identifying a person's understanding (their self-story or "narrative") and how it may be causing problems for them or for others, and then helping them to develop the narrative to make it more empowering. For example, if one or more people lack confidence and this is leading to significant problems, this approach may be helpful. Giving reassurance and positive feedback is likely to be helpful, but it is unlikely to be enough on its own.
- *Team development activities* These can range from outward bound-type exercises, through team-building games and exercises to focused discussion around issues and challenges.

This is just a selection. My book, *The People Solutions Sourcebook*, contains an extended essay about problem solving and 88 tools or techniques that can be used in a problem-solving context. Many of these can be used in an organizational problem-solving context.

The Problem of Low Morale

One particular cultural problem that merits special attention is that of low morale. This is because a culture of low morale: (i) distorts perceptions in the negative direction (positives get filtered out, negatives get amplified); (ii) saps motivation and confidence and fuels a sense of defeatism and an attitude of cynicism; (iii) blocks communication; (iv) discourages creativity and innovation; (v) serves as an obstacle to learning; and (vi) encourages defensiveness and risk-averse approaches;

All of these are important issues to address, but (vi) has a particular resonance, as Friedman notes:

> When avoiding failure is a primary focus, the work isn't just more stressful; it's a lot harder to do. And over the long run, that mental strain takes a toll, resulting in less innovation and the experience of burnout.
>
> *(2014, p. 18)*

Tackling issues of low morale and the cultures that feed them should therefore be recognized as a priority for leaders where such issues arise. It should also be crystal clear that these are (applied) sociological matters, as they can be seen to relate to various aspects of social functioning.

Practice Focus 10.3

Vince was both surprised and delighted by the positive changes Debbie had made so quickly. He had never been a particular fan of Debbie's predecessor, but he had not had any particular concerns about him either—he seemed quite a competent manager. However, what Debbie had done was to show that she was not only a good manager, but also a good leader, an excellent one in fact. She had recognized very quickly that the culture in the team was not helpful. She saw her chance to change the culture and seized it, producing very positive results very quickly. She knew very well that cultures are not always that easy to change, but realized that, in this case, the high level of tension and unhappiness in the team meant that her approach was likely to be well received—and Vince was so pleased that it had been. In a way, Debbie's changes had amounted to a case study of positive leadership in action, whereas her predecessor had settled for management and not really made any effort to go beyond that to establish good leadership practice as well.

Conclusion

Organizations are complex social spaces. In many ways they are a microcosm of wider society, with all its social structures, processes and so on, but there are also, as we have seen, aspects of organizational life that have their own "rules" and need careful attention.

This chapter has sought to show how organizational life can be understood sociologically and how, therefore, there is considerable scope for applied sociology to make a valuable contribution to addressing workplace problems and capitalizing on the potential that is to be found in any organization.

The costs of getting workplace issues wrong are quite considerable, as Hames points out:

> In organisations, morale, trust and loyalty are almost impossible to recover once they have been eroded by a dysfunctional work environment, where individuals feel devalued or discounted altogether in comparison with profits.
>
> *(2007, p. 93)*

The benefits of being able to highlight problems and address them—or better still, nip them in the bud and prevent them doing any harm in the first place—are vast, and so the importance of investing in workplace problem solving is huge. This is why the notion of "workplace well-being" has become such an important one, despite the superficial and cynical use of it in some quarters.

Organizational psychology has made important contributions to our understanding of the workplace, its problems and its potential solutions. There is no good reason why organizational sociology cannot also offer an invaluable contribution to improving organizational life.

Points to Ponder

1. In what ways can work influence (for good or ill) a person's quality of life?
2. What might explain why a "getting the *most* out of people" approach seems more common than a "getting the *best* out of people" approach?
3. From your experience, what do you see as the factors that distinguish a good leader from an ineffective one?

Exercise 10

Think of an organization you are familiar with. What would you see as the main hallmarks of its culture—that is, shared assumptions, unwritten rules and so on? How do these affect the behavior of the employees? Try to think of some examples of where this influence would be positive and some where it might be negative.

Holistic Practice   11

Introduction

In this final chapter our focus is on holistic practice, and, by "holistic," I mean practice that is based on seeing the "big picture." This is what is sometimes known as "helicopter vision," the ability to rise above a situation and get the overview, and then be able to descend back into that situation and deal with it (Thompson, 2012b). Academic sociology helps to provide the helicopter perspective, the overview, and so *applied* sociology is about the second part, namely descending into the situation and using the insights gained to address the issues involved. It is not necessarily easy, but it is certainly important and can be immensely valuable and constructive.

Following on from Les Back's (2007) view of sociology as a "listening art" (giving voice to the people whose views are silenced by dominant ideologies and restrictive discourses), I described sociology as also a "seeing art," in the sense of being able to see past those ideologies and discourses that paint a picture of inequality and social exclusion as normal and natural. In particular, this "seeing art" can help us to identify power dynamics at work and see how they stack the odds in favour of dominant groups and disadvantage ordinary people who are not part of that "power elite."

Part of this holistic perspective is the recognition that profoundly personal and intimate experiences are social too, whether we are referring to everyday activities like brushing our teeth or less frequent occurrences like grief. Sociology warns us against being seduced by the notion that something that is personal is therefore not social; we should not allow ourselves to be led down a path that is built on an individual vs. social model, and, instead, embrace the significance of the more accurate person *in* society model. This latter model opens up new vistas and enables us to have a much fuller picture.

This does not mean that we should see sociology as an alternative to psychology. To try to explain everything in sociological terms, thereby squeezing out other perspectives is known as "sociologism," parallel with the idea of psychologism which refers to the tendency to explain everything in individualistic, psychological terms and thereby ignore the significance of the social context.

Dennis Wrong, in what has come to be recognized as a classic article, wrote of the "oversocialized conception of [wo]man," by which he meant the tendency to recognize the social issues, but to neglect or dismiss the personal aspects, those that are unique to each individual (Wrong, 1961). In a sense, sociologism is the mirror image of atomism, in so far as it sees the social context that atomism ignores, but fails to see the person in that context (all coffee and no cream, to return to my earlier analogy).

Sociologism fails to see human existence as profoundly *psychosocial*. A much wiser, and more useful, approach is to recognize psychology and sociology as complementary to one another, each contributing to the insights of the other, and not as competitors for intellectual territory or professional status.

When it comes to being holistic, we should also note sociology's strength of offering a critical, questioning approach, one that does not take things at face value, as that would leave us prey to ideologies and discourses that are biased in favour of dominant groups, messages that "tell the story" from the point of view of the people who benefit from the story being told in that way. Sociology is not about finding the "true" story, but rather, hearing the multitude of stories in order to get a fuller picture, rather than be taken in by the dominant story.

This critical questioning is one of sociology's great strengths when it comes to being an applied discipline. This is because it enables us to avoid falling in line with dominant assumptions and adopting a partial, distorted view fed by ideologies and discourses that favour the status quo and thereby resist movements towards social amelioration that benefit those who are not members of the power elite.

This chapter covers some of the key ways in which sociology can inform holistic practice—that is, actual practices in real-life situations that can benefit from the wider perspective offered by helicopter vision. In order to do this I shall adopt the H-5W framework. That is, I shall explore the how, who, where, when, what and why of applied sociology. We shall address each of these areas in turn.

HOW Is Sociology Useful?

In a sense, the whole of the book has been geared towards answering this question. I will therefore restrict myself here to commenting on a small number of highly significant issues about how sociology can be useful as an applied discipline.

Beyond Atomism

As we have noted several times, a narrow focus on the individual is likely to present us with a partial and misleading picture—one that distorts and over-simplifies the issues involved. One of the unfortunate consequences of this is "pathologizing." Atomism presents a false picture of causality, in the sense that its narrow focus blurs out wider factors that will often play a highly significant role in terms of causality of any problems being experienced.

One example of this that we noted earlier would be the experience of stress. It is commonly assumed (from an atomistic perspective) that stress is a sign of a weak or inadequate person, someone not capable of coping with their life demands. However, if we look at the situation holistically and critically, it may well turn out that the stress has more to do with: an excessive workload; unclear, unrealistic or contradictory expectations; poor or non-existent management support; ineffective leadership; workplace conflicts and tensions; bullying or harassment; discrimination; or any combination of the above. Reducing this complex set of factors to an individual "weakness" is not only surprisingly unintelligent, but also dangerous, in so far as it is likely to make a bad situation worse and create a vicious circle that can harm the individual and their employing organization (Thompson, 2015a).

In this respect, going beyond atomism can also be of value in preventing us from being judgmental towards others. It can help us understand that each of us has a unique story, a set of circumstances that most people are unaware of. We should therefore be wary of forming moral judgments about people without knowing the "back story." For example, the person we perceive as "rude" because they do not return our friendly smile or greeting may be wrestling with after-effects of a traumatic experience. Of course, it may well be that they are indeed simply being rude, but the point I want to emphasize is that we do not know—if we are being judgmental, we are making assumptions that could turn out to be not only false, but also unfair and discriminatory. It is no coincidence, for example, that being non-judgmental is a long-standing feature of the social work value base (Thompson, 2015c).

Contextualizing

By going beyond atomism we are entering the territory of "contextualizing." What I mean by this term is the process of clarifying the important factors in the context concerned that are influencing the situation. This will include all six elements of the SPIDER model of the web of society. How are these factors, and the interplay, helping to shape the current circumstances? What problems are they contributing to? How can they be used to bring about positive change?

It can at times be helpful to break it down into three important aspects of human experience:

- *Thoughts* How are the social context factors influencing people's thoughts? How can an understanding of social issues, influences and constraints help us make sense of what people involved in the situation are thinking? For example, what discourses may be influencing their thinking?
- *Feelings* How are social issues playing a part in the emotions operating in this situation? How are they contributing to the mood, the level of tension and so on? Are there, for example, any gender or ethnicity dimensions of emotion at work here?; and
- *Actions* What is happening here? What needs to happen here? In what ways is the social context playing a part in shaping the actions involved? For example, what are the power dynamics influencing people's actions (or inactions)?

Across all three of these dimensions we can question and note the role of ideology and "interpellation"—that is, the way ideologies "speak" to people and make the social order appear as the natural order and thereby serve to block routes to changing the status quo. This "interpellation" or appeal to hearts and minds that makes social relations that are biased in favour of dominant groups appear natural, normal and fair, is generally a major factor in maintaining the existing power relations. These are important contextual factors that can easily be missed if we do not draw on the sociological imagination— they become "camouflaged."

Contextualizing can also help us to appreciate the significance of diversity. For example, Smart challenges the notion of childhood as a single, monolithic entity when she argues that:

> the new sociological approach quintessentially recognized that there are many different childhoods if the experiences and standpoints of the

children are taken as a starting point. Hence, there may be, in a Western society such as the UK or the USA, disabled childhoods, Chinese childhoods, girls' childhoods, the childhoods of adopted children, poor childhoods and so on.

(2011, p. 101)

Adopting a stereotypical (ideological) model of the family as a "one size fits all" not only fails to do justice to the complexities involved, but also sets up people who are in minority family forms to be perceived as "deviant" or "abnormal," rather than just another example of the rich diversity of family forms across society. Again there is a danger of pathologizing in which "different" gets ideologically translated into "deviant" or "deficient" (and therefore dangerous).

Empowerment

Helping people gain greater control over their lives is what empowerment is all about. It is a positive process of supporting people in emancipating themselves from restrictive and self-defeating circumstances, structures and discourses, opening up new possibilities and vistas, shrugging off discriminatory and oppressive shackles and offering a strong platform for growth and development.

What sociology is very good indeed at is making power visible through its holistic and critical approach. It is the invisibility of power through ideological processes that makes it such a significant issue in social life and makes it so effective. The more visible power is, the less force it has. The more aware people are of the "loaded dice" of power relations, the less likely they are to be taken in by the discourses that present inequality, unfairness and social injustices as natural and normal.

Practice Focus 11.1

Carla was a rights adviser in a socially deprived and disadvantaged suburb of a large city. To begin with, it was not really the job she wanted, but because of the high levels of unemployment in her area, it was the best she could do at the time. In the early days what didn't appeal to her was that she saw it as a very technical job, and therefore not very interesting or challenging. However, her initial impressions gradually evolved into a much more positive perception of the role. She began to realize that it wasn't just a matter of telling people what their rights were, based on the guidance books they had available for reference or the websites on the list pinned to the noticeboard near her desk. She soon realized that, as the saying goes, "knowledge is power." She saw so many cases of people really benefiting from the knowledge, advice and guidance she was able to give. She came across example after example of people who were being exploited, ill-treated and discriminated against, and she became quite passionate about her job, seeing her role as an important one in contributing to the empowerment of people who were being treated unfairly in one or more ways. Even though her being there was down to serendipity, she decided that this was not just a job to pay her bills; this was to be her career, her vocation.

WHO Can Use Sociology?

I partly answered this question in Chapter 1, but it is such an important question that it is well worth revisiting it here and paying it further attention. I am going to answer it by identifying three main groups of people who can benefit from what sociology has to offer.

The People Professions

There are various professional groups who are called upon to work with people and their problems. This will include social workers and other social services professionals; health care professionals; counselors and psychotherapists; youth and community workers; probation officers; clergy and chaplains; police officers, probation officers, prison officers, and various others. The linking theme here is human relationships. Sociology can cast light on person-to-person interactions in a variety of ways.

Leaders across All Workplaces

In Chapter 10 we noted that leaders are an important part of organizational success (or failure). We also noted that it is not just managers who can play a part in shaping the culture in a positive direction. So, whether a manager or not, if you are in a position to influence the culture of an organization (one you are employed by or providing services to), you are in a position to make use of applied sociology and what it has to offer.

Everyone: Self-Awareness

But it is not just in a direct occupational context that applied sociology can be of value. Everyone can achieve improved self-awareness and self-understanding that can benefit us in our private lives and, indirectly at least, benefit how well-equipped we are to handle the demands of our career and our workplace setting. For example, sociology can help us understand our own "social filters," the various things that shape how we see the world and how we act upon it.

Clarity about our identity can be helpful, in the sense that "identity awareness" can help us understand our strong points, our areas for development and our values—the things that matter most to us. Being tuned in to who we are and how we fit into the world is, of course, an aspect of spirituality, but it is also part of sociology, in so far as these are very much socially rooted areas.

Voice of Experience 11.1

I had always thought of myself as having a fixed personality, which meant that I had to take the rough with the smooth. I knew I had my flaws, but just assumed that I was stuck with them: "That's just the way I am." So, when I started the new semester and got stuck into the sociology module, my eyes were really opened. The idea that identity is *social*, and that it was fluid over time was something I had never thought of before. But, the more I thought about it, the more I realized how true it was, the more examples I could think of where my sense of who I am had changed and of where the social circumstances of where I was at any given time affected my sense of self. Fascinating stuff, and all totally new, as I had never given it any thought at all.

Marv, a marketing consultant

WHERE Can Sociology Be Used?

The breadth of applicability of sociology is really quite vast. The following are just some of the types of work or work settings where a sociological perspective could be of value:

- *Casework* Many jobs will involve what can be loosely termed "casework"—that is, one-to-one work with an individual who has a problem or challenge of some description and needs the help of a professional to address it. There can be both micro-social issues to consider (as per symbolic interaction and role theory, for example) and macro-level ones in terms of broader social structures, processes, expectations and so on.

- *Policy development* The holistic and critical basis of sociology can be a really positive and useful foundation for policy work, whether in an organization you are employed by or one that you are providing services for. This can include policy formulation, implementation, review and evaluation.

- *Research and analysis* Sociology has a strong tradition of social research to draw upon, using social surveys, for example. Many organizations use sociological research for a variety of reasons, and such research and analysis can be put to good use in shaping strategy, problem solving and/or any other aspect of organizational life where the intelligence offered by social research can be highly informative.

- *Consultancy* Buying in expertise where needed is a well-established practice in some industries and public services. Much of that expertise can and will be informed by sociology.

- *Education and training* Whether school-based education for children and young people or adult education, sociological insights and a critical perspective can be of value in a number of ways. For example, meeting special educational needs is an area where sociology has much to say (around inclusion policies, for example).

- *People awareness* This is the equivalent of the "any other business" item on a meeting agenda, that can include a wide range of possibilities. Any occupational setting that relies on having a good understanding of people can be enhanced by a sociological perspective. People are indeed social animals, although the social element can often be forgotten. If people (rather than machines, interest rates or budgets) are of key interest, then sociology can offer us invaluable insights. Such areas would include: health care; the military; politics; and/or the media. An example of this would be the significance of communication. The need to communicate effectively at all levels is not simply a matter of communications skills, but also communications systems and, of course cultures, and is therefore a matter that comes within the purview of sociology.

Practice Focus 11.2

Paulo was a senior manager in a large not-for-profit organization. It was apparent to him that there were major communication difficulties that were causing problems for very many people. Consequently Paulo got in touch with Val, the training manager and asked her to arrange some communication skills training for staff across the board. This was quite a big investment for an organization that had a very limited budget, but the problems were so bad that Paulo felt it was a good use of limited funds. Roughly half way through the planned series of courses, Paulo and Val were both at the same meeting. During the coffee break, Paulo asked Val how the training was going. "Very well," she replied, but then added that, interestingly, the trainer had commented on the fact that the existing levels of skills were quite high and he was wondering whether the problem was actually not in the communication skills arena, but, rather, in the communication systems arena. "It doesn't matter how skillful your staff may be in communicating if the communication systems don't work or are even non-existent in places." What a really good point, Paulo thought, while also feeling concerned that he may have been investing scarce funds in training when what was really needed was an overhaul of their communications systems.

WHEN Can Sociology Be Used?

There are various times when sociology can be of use, but here I am going to focus on just three of them for present purposes: problem solving; managing change; and social amelioration.

Problem Solving

The 3P model we discussed earlier (people/problems/potential) is an example of when sociology can be put to good use. Problems people encounter will often have a psychological component to them, but we must make sure we do not slip into "psychologism" by seeing the issues as purely psychological and thereby neglecting the social context that could be significant—for example, in relation to stress, grief, conflict and/or issues of spirituality.

Managing conflict is a particularly good example, as conflict involves the "social space" between people and how it is managed. Furthermore, a conflict between, say, two people will often be a reflection of deeper, underlying conflicts, such as different schools of thought about what should be done or even what the job is primarily all about (for example, two prison officers, one who stresses the importance of rehabilitation vs. one who prefers to focus on punishment aspects).

There can also be a problem-solving role at a wider or higher level—for example, organizational analysis or strategic "trouble shooting" can be invaluable to a company that is in danger of going bust.

Managing Change

But when problems arise is not the only time applied sociology can step up to the mark. Making sense of social or organizational change can be helped by a sociological perspective. Change management is complex and often difficult, and so the holistic, critical approach of sociology can be a useful basis for developing a fuller understanding of what changes are happening or what needs to be done to make desired changes happen.

One aspect of this is the ability to "tune in" to power dynamics and seek to ensure that discrimination does not arise as part of the change process. Change will, of course, affect different people in different ways, but it is essential to ensure that, for example, minority groups do not lose out disproportionately. This is, of course, bread and butter to a sociologist.

Social Amelioration

Improving society is no easy task, but there are steps that can be taken to move in that direction. Community development would be an example of this. This generally involves working alongside communities in a spirit of partnership to identify community strong points that can be built on and problems that can be addressed (Ledwith, 2011). Empowerment is a core theme. It takes little imagination to work out that sociology has the potential to make a huge contribution to such social amelioration efforts and initiatives—in fact, it would be difficult to imagine them succeeding without drawing on sociological knowledge.

Community development is just one example of social amelioration strategies that can benefit from what sociology has to offer.

Voice of Experience 11.2

I have always enjoyed my work in HR, but the last two years have been particularly good. That's because it is two years since I moved into a specialist "troubleshooter" role. In my time I have covered various aspects of HR work, the usual hiring and firing, health and safety and so on. But what is so good about my current role is that every situation is different, and yet I can see common themes. I did a joint honors degree in psychology and sociology, and, to be honest, I expected the psychology part to be more useful in my new job. But, to my surprise, I have found the sociology stuff useful too. It's all about people, I suppose.

Amanda, a specialist human resources officer in a
multinational company

WHAT Can Sociology Offer?

The answer to this question should be clear by now, but just to sum up briefly, I want to highlight four main things: social awareness; a critical perspective; sociological interventions; and research and statistical data.

Social Awareness

We have discussed how there is a dominant ideology of atomism that keeps bringing us back to a focus on the individual. While the individual is then in sharp, clear focus, the social background is blurred and thus obscured. What sociology does is to show us what is missing from such a picture. It shows us that atomism is giving us just a partial view that can be misleading; it is leaving out some important aspects of the social context, not least the six elements of our SPIDER model of the web of society.

A Critical Perspective

Taking things at face value and not questioning them can leave us open to exploitation. It can leave unequal power relations unchallenged and allow discrimination to go unchecked. It can therefore leave us ill-equipped to deal with various aspects of the challenges life can lay before us. Sociology's critical but constructive questioning is therefore an important tool in enabling us to see past the camouflage that masks social inequalities and their associated problems (Dorling, 2015; 2017).

Sociological Interventions

But it is not just understanding that sociology can offer, important and worthwhile though that is, it can also offer us direct ways of intervening in social situations, direct ways of problem solving, change management and social amelioration as mentioned earlier in this chapter plus organizational development as discussed in Chapter 10. These interventions, when managed well, can make a very positive and impressive difference. Consider, for example, the views of Steele, Scarisbrick-Hauser and Hauser:

> Individuals skilled in applied sociology have the ability to become excellent strategists and planners. After all, planning requires an understanding of social systems, social processes and social change. To construct a plan, you must have some knowledge of the social environment in which that plan will be carried out. This environment could range from a small group or task team on the microscopic level to a large global company or society at the macroscopic level. All of this requires taking a comprehensive view of the structure of the group, the roles that individuals play within the structure, and the possible outcomes of the strategies selected.
>
> *(1999, p. 73)*

Social Research and Statistical Data

Sociology already has an impressive array of potentially useful research studies and data that can be drawn upon as appropriate. In addition, specific research studies can be commissioned to inform policy and strategy in relation to particular problems, challenges or opportunities. In this respect, research can be a further form of applied sociology intervention. For example I have used workplace well-being surveys with organizations to help them identify what they are doing well in terms of the leadership challenge of workplace well-being, so that they can build on that success, and what they are not doing so well, so that they can make necessary changes to bring about improvements.

WHY Should We Use Sociology?

In very brief terms we should use sociology because not to do so would leave us with a partial and potentially misleading picture of the situations we are called upon to deal with. It would leave us prone to the unquestioned influences and constraints of discourses and ideologies that serve the interests of the power elite at the expense of less powerful groups of people. It would leave us far less well equipped to understand and tackle the major social challenges we face and it would lead to our missing major opportunities to make improvements and positive changes.

We should use sociology because it is a listening art; it amplifies voices that are silenced by dominant ideologies, by the power of hegemony, and it is a seeing art because it enables us to see the power structures, inequalities and injustices that are camouflaged and hidden by "the stories" that present the social order that can be changed as if it is the natural order that cannot be changed. It therefore plays a part in countering the disempowering effects of hegemony and thereby opens up new vistas, new possibilities for how we live our lives and how we treat one another.

Practice Focus 11.3

Julie was a sociology professor in a suburban university. She had been attracted to sociology from an early age. What made her even more enthusiastic, however, was the turning point at university where she came across Marx's idea that understanding society is not enough; the point is to change it. She totally rejected Marx's political ideas, but she was so glad she had come across his ideas, as this was what she wanted to do with her sociological understanding: to use it to make a positive difference. Yes, she thought, there is definitely a place for people who want to study pure sociology, to engage in understanding society without ever getting involved at a practical level. However, she felt it would be really sad and disappointing if that was all sociologists ever did. She therefore worked very hard indeed to enthuse her students about sociology not only as an important social science discipline, but also as an important applied discipline, one that could really make a positive difference.

Making It Happen

So, as we come towards the end of our journey together into the fascinating world of applied sociology, there are just three sets of issues I want to comment on before we reach our conclusion.

How Do I Make Use of This Knowledge?

You may be asking yourself: How do we fit all this knowledge in? How do we keep it all in mind? If you think about it, we have covered a huge amount of ground in one short book: following our foundation building in Part One about the nature of sociology and its value as a *pragmatic* tool (or set of tools), Part Two introduced us to the SPIDER model of the web of society, encompassing social:

Structures
Processes
Institutions
Discourses and ideologies
Expectations
Relations

And, as if that was not enough, you have been encouraged to think of these as six constantly interacting and evolving dimensions of a larger whole, rather than as separate entities to be considered in isolation. To cap it all, in Part Three, we have looked at: the centrality of the relationship between the individual and society (arguing for an "individual *in* society" model, rather than the more common "individual vs. society" one); the double importance of the organizational context (where applied sociology can be seen to work *in* the workplace and *on* the workplace); and finally, the importance of holistic practice.

Given that the focus of the book is on using sociological knowledge (and especially the sociological imagination) *in practice*, and not just for an essay or examination, how on earth can you be expected to remember it all? My answer to that is in two parts:

(i) We should recall our earlier idea of theorizing practice (Thompson, 2017b). That is, instead of following the traditional model of "applying theory to practice," we should think of it the other way round: begin with practice and then draw on your theoretical knowledge of sociology as and when required. This is the basis of critically reflective practice (Thompson and Thompson, 2008).

(ii) Practice makes perfect. The more you use sociological knowledge in practice, the easier it becomes. The more you engage with sociological insights in a practice context, the more links you will be able to see between the circumstances you are in and what sociology has to offer. Over time you will come to "own" the knowledge; it becomes *your* knowledge (your "practice wisdom," as some people would put it), rather than just something you read in a book. It comes to life, and that is a big, big part of the adventure of applied sociology.

The PATCH Model

One helpful way to conceptualize major aspects of the holistic practice that applied sociology can offer is through the mnemonic of the PATCH model:

P*ower sensitive* As we have noted, power relations can be very effective by becoming "invisible" through processes of ideological "camouflage." That is, if no one can see the power imbalances, no one will be in a position to challenge them. One of the roles applied sociology can play is in making power relations visible and cutting through the ideological camouflage. In this way, applied sociology can help people to be better informed about their circumstances and how to respond to them. This is partly achieved by critical analysis—asking revealing questions about who has what power, in what circumstances and what are they doing with it.

Power is a complex, multidimensional phenomenon, and so we should be wary of simplistic approaches to its operation. PCS analysis can be helpful in this regard (Thompson, 2007). We can use it to explore:

- Power at the *personal* level—the use of particular strategies to achieve authority and standing, for example.
- Power at the *cultural* level—the role of discourses, for example, and ways that these can be challenged.
- Power at the *structural* level—the various ways in which social divisions operate to retain relations of dominance and subordination.
- The *double dialectic* that binds the levels together in terms of the continuous interactions: (i) between the personal and cultural levels in which dominant taken-for-granted ideas influence individuals and the embracing of those ideas by individuals subsequently reflects and reinforces those ideas; and (ii) between the cultural and structural levels in which ideas that reflect and reinforce the imbalance of power within the social structure operate as core elements of the cultural level.

Clearly, these are not simple or straightforward matters, but a careful analysis using this framework as an analytical tool can help us to form a broader and more meaningful picture.

A*ttuned to dynamics* Much of the way in which society tends to be portrayed in "common sense" terms is fairly static; it is just there as the backdrop to what is happening to individuals. While social change is not denied, it tends to take a backseat much of the time. The reality, of course, is that society is constantly changing. So, when people ask the question: "How can we change society?" they are asking the wrong question, as it is changing anyway. A better question would be: "How do we change society in the direction we would like it to go?"

If we cast our minds back to our SPIDER model of the social web, we can see that social structures are constantly shifting, they are structures in motion, unlike static structures in the building sense of structure. Social processes are, by their very nature, dynamic, constantly in motion. Social institutions are relatively stable, but they too are none the less constantly changing over time, constantly evolving. Discourses and ideologies also have a core of stability, but they too are none the less, dynamic, constantly in interaction and evolving because of that. Social expectations are also dynamic, in the sense that etiquette, social conventions and notions of what is or is not acceptable are subject to change. And, of course, social relations are, by their very nature, interactive and dynamic.

This takes us back to my earlier point that, within change, there will be elements of continuity, and within continuity there will be elements of change. Recognizing the significance of this dynamic nature of social life puts us in a much stronger position to understand, and respond to, change. Indeed, it is fair to say that much of what counts as "applied sociology interventions" is, in effect, grounded in the management of change, whether responding to externally arising changes or seeking to bring about desirable changes of our own (or our client's).

Theoretically informed As we have seen, sociological theory places a wealth of potentially useful knowledge at our disposal. The sociological imagination as a holistic and critical "window on the world" is a powerful analytical tool for making sense of complex social issues. Beyond this, there is a rich treasury of theory and research that tells us so much about social life, many examples of which we have seen in this book. But that is not all, we have only really scratched the surface of the theoretical knowledge base and wealth of research that is out there for us to draw upon as we need it.

Of course, there are competing perspectives within that knowledge base, conflicting accounts and approaches, but this just goes to show what a vibrant and dynamic subject sociology is. Different perspectives can enrich our understanding and highlight new vistas that we might not otherwise have thought of.

Critical One unfortunate stereotype of sociology I have come across on more than one occasion is the idea that sociology is too negative, that its role is to "criticize" society and can therefore present us with an unduly negative picture without an appreciation of society's positives. Of course, this is based on a fundamental misunderstanding of how the term "critical" is used in sociology (and in the social sciences more broadly). As I explained earlier, to be critical, in a social science sense, is to *question*, to seek to go beyond what is presented at face value, to look beneath the surface and explore underlying dynamics, institutions, discourses and so on.

This is an invaluable skill in an academic context, as it is part of the established basis of intellectual inquiry (Cottrell, 2011). However, it is also an important foundation of sociology as an applied discipline. For example, an applied sociologist working in a health care context would not simply accept dominant models of health, illness, recovery and so on, but be prepared to question any such dominant assumptions and see what lies beneath them. In particular, there is now a significant body of literature that explores social determinants of health (see, for example, Davidson, 2014; Nettleton, 2013). This is a key part of *critically* reflective practice, practice that engages with the sociological imagination and sees past the camouflage of ideology.

Holistic This has, of course, been a recurring theme of the book and has been especially featured in this chapter. This is because:

(i) It is a key part of what makes applied sociology useful; it provides a helpful overview that is so often neglected when a sociological perspective is not included. Reading or hearing so many accounts of human experience, you could be forgiven for thinking that society does not exist, that we all just operate in relative isolation.

(ii) It suits the interests of the powers that be for us to adopt a narrow, individualistic focus, as this contributes to keeping the unequal power relations invisible and therefore beyond question. It prevents us from "speaking truth to power," to use, and extend, the Quaker expression.

This PATCH model mnemonic should prove helpful as a sort of mental checklist as you engage making your sociology an applied sociology:

- **P** Am I taking account of the (often submerged) power relations?
- **A** Am I remembering to see the situation as dynamic and thereby avoiding the pitfall of assuming the circumstances I am engaged in as static?
- **T** Am I drawing on the wealth of theory and research that can inform my practice?
- **C** Am I asking revealing questions? Am I looking beneath the surface or am I allowing myself to be taken in by ideological camouflage?
- **H** Am I looking at the big picture and seeing beyond the individual factors or am I allowing myself to be a victim of atomistic thinking?

This model will not guarantee that you will get everything right, but it will certainly give you a helpful starting point and a foundation on which to build.

Have We Covered Everything?

No is the short answer, and far from it is the slightly longer answer. There is just so much more to sociology and what it has to offer. I have been enchanted by sociology and its appeal and pragmatic value for over 40 years, but I am still learning, I am still finding new ground to explore, new ideas to interest and excite me, new territory to explore. The following are just some of the areas we have either barely touched on or not at all in this book that have the potential to be of value in an applied sociology context:

> • the sociology of religion • the sociology of health • the sociology of education • deviance theory • sexuality • the sociology of language • comparative sociology • political sociology • conflict, war and terrorism • the life course and aging • the sociology of death, grief and bereavement • child abuse and exploitation • the sociology of disability • economics and business strategy • parenting and family life • the sociology of sport • the media • leisure and recreation • the environment •

So, the moral of the story, as it were, is that it is a vast field, and so we need to keep on learning. That is all part of the adventure.

Conclusion

"Holistic practice" is, in reality, shorthand for putting into practice the key lessons to have emerged from our discussions throughout the book. The core message of this final chapter, therefore, is that we have been talking throughout of *applied* sociology, so it is crucial that we apply that knowledge however and wherever we can. The theoretical knowledge base should give us the foundation of knowledge that we can: (i) use to "theorize practice," as discussed earlier (that is, draw upon our knowledge base for practical purposes in ways that suit the particular circumstances); and (ii) build on over time in a spirit of continuous professional development.

This book will not tell you everything you need to know, but it should be of value none the less and, I hope, will spur you to find out more and, indeed, to keep on learning.

Points to Ponder

1. What would you see as the dangers of not adopting a holistic perspective—that is, of failing to look at the wider picture of any situation that you are called upon to deal with?
2. In what ways do you feel sociology can contribute to processes of empowerment? Why are these important?
3. Consider each of the five elements of the PATCH model. How might these help you in your efforts to develop expertise as an applied sociologist?

Exercise 11

This book has been written with two groups of people in mind: (i) people in, or preparing for, a career in the "people professions"—that is, those areas of work where success depends on having a good understanding of people; and (ii) students of sociology or related subjects (applied social studies, for example) wanting to explore how sociology can be of practical value in a variety of work settings. If you are in Group (i), this final exercise is for you to list, by way of summary, the various ways in which sociological insights in general and the sociological imagination can be of help to you. If you are in Group (ii) the exercise is for you to list the ways you feel sociology can be useful for one or more career options you are considering. In particular, please identify how you feel the sociological imagination will be of value to you.

Guide to Further Learning

General Sociology Texts

Gergen, K. J. (2009). *An invitation to social construction* (2nd Edn.). London: Sage.

Giddens, A. and Sutton, P. W. (2017). *Sociology* (8th Edn.). Cambridge: Polity Press.

Macionis, J. J. (2015). *Sociology* (15th Edn.). London: Pearson.

Matthewman, S., West-Newman, C. L. and Curtis, B. (Eds.) (2013). *Being sociological* (2nd Edn.). London: Palgrave.

Woodward, K. (2014). *Social sciences: The big issues* (3rd Edn.). London: Routledge.

Sociological Research

Bryman, A. (2016). *Social research methods* (5th Edn.). New York: Oxford University Press.

Cresswell, J. W. (2013). *Research design: Qualitative, quantitative, and mixed methods approaches* (4th Edn.). Thousand Oaks, CA: Sage.

Frankfort-Nachmias, C., Nachmias, D. and DeWaard, J. (2014). *Research methods in the social sciences* (8th Edn.). New York: Worth Publishers.

Classic Historical Texts

Comte, A. (1988). *Introduction to positive philosophy*. Cambridge, MA: Hackett.

Durkheim, E. (1997). *Suicide: A study in sociology*. New York: Free Press.

Marx, K. (1994). *Selected writings*. Cambridge, MA: Hackett Publishing.

Mills, C. W. (1959). *The sociological imagination*. Oxford: Oxford University Press.

Weber, M. (1930). *The Protestant ethic and the spirit of capitalism*. London: George Allen & Unwin.

Social Structures

Back, L. and Solomos, J. (Eds.) (2009). *Theories of race and racism: A reader* (2nd Edn.). London: Routledge.

Chomsky, N. (2012). *Power systems*. London: Penguin.

Connell, R. W. and Pearse, R. (2015). *Gender in world perspective* (3rd Edn.). Cambridge: Polity.

Jones, O. (2012). *Chavs: The demonization of the working class*. London: Verso.

May, V. M. (2015). *Pursuing intersectionality: Unsettling dominant imaginaries*. London: Routledge.

Witcher, S. (2015). *Inclusive equality: A vision for social justice*. Bristol: The Policy Press.

Social Processes

Grusec, J. E. and Hastings, P. D. (Eds.) (2016). *Handbook of socialization: Theory and practice* (2nd Edn.). New York: Guilford Press.

Marger, M. (2013). *Social inequality: Patterns and processes* (6th Edn.). New York: McGraw-Hill Education.

Thompson, N. (2017). *Social problems and social justice*. London: Palgrave.

Social Institutions

Chambers, D. (2012). *A sociology of family life*. Cambridge: Polity.

Curran, J. (2011). *Media and society* (5th Edn.). London: Bloomsbury Academic.

Social Discourses and Ideologies

Ball, T., Dagger, R. and O'Neil, D. I. (Eds.) (2016). *Ideals and ideologies: A reader* (10th Edn.). New York: Routledge.

Foucault, M. (1972). *The archaeology of knowledge*. London: Tavistock.

Foucault, M. (1975). *The birth of the clinic: An archaeology of medical perception*. New York: Vintage Books.

Foucault, M. (1977). *Discipline and punish: The birth of the prison*. London: Penguin.

Mooney, A. and Evans, B. (2015). *Language, society and power: An introduction* (4th Edn.). London: Routledge.

Social Expectations

Goffman, E. (1990). *Presentation of self in everyday life*. London: Penguin.

Goffman, E. (1990). *Stigma: Notes on the management of spoiled identity*. London: Penguin.

Mead, G. H. (1967). *Mind, self and society*. Chicago: University of Chicago Press.

Sandstrom, K. L., Lively, K. J., Martin, D. D. and Fine, G. A. (2013). *Symbols, selves, and social reality: A symbolic interactionist approach to social psychology and sociology* (4th Edn.). New York: Oxford University Press.

Social Relations

Coleman, P. T. and Ferguson, R. (2014). *Making conflict work*. London: Piatkus.

Healey, J. F. and O'Brien, E. (2016). *Race, ethnicity, gender, and class: The sociology of group conflict and change* (7th Edn.). Thousand Oaks, CA: Sage.

Illouz, E. (2012). *Why love hurts*. Cambridge: Polity.

May, V. (Ed.) (2011). *Sociology of personal life*. Basingstoke: Palgrave Macmillan.

Identity

Lawler, S. (2014). *Identity: Sociological perspectives* (2nd Edn.). Cambridge: Polity.

Scott, S. (2015). *Negotiating identity: Symbolic interactionist approaches to social identity*. Cambridge: Polity.

Thompson, N. (2017a). *Theorizing practice* (2nd Edn.). London: Palgrave, Chapter 4.

The Organizational Context

Linstead, S., Fulop, L. and Lilley, S. (2009). *Management and organization: A critical text* (2nd Edn.). Basingstoke, UK: Palgrave Macmillan.

Schnall, P. L., Dobson, M. and Rosskam, E. (Eds.) (2009). *Unhealthy work: Causes, consequences, cures*. Amityville, NY: Baywood.

Thompson, N. (2013). *People management*. Basingstoke: Palgrave Macmillan.

Thompson, N. (2016). *The authentic leader*. London: Palgrave.

Applied Sociology

Price, J., Straus, R. and Breese, J. (2009). *Doing sociology: Case studies in sociological practice*. Lanham, MD: Lexington Books.

Rogers, A. and Pilgrim, D. (2014). *A sociology of mental health and illness* (5th Edn.). Maidenhead: Open University Press.

Steele, S. F. and Price, J. (2007). *Applied sociology: Terms, topics, tools, and tasks* (2nd Edn.). Boston, MA: Cengage Learning.

Thompson, N. (2012). *The people solutions sourcebook* (2nd Edn.). Basingstoke, UK: Palgrave Macmillan.

Websites

Intute	www.intute.ac.uk/sociology
Sociosite	www.sociosite.net
International Sociological Association	www.isa-sociology.org
Public Sociologies	http://burawoy.berkeley.edu/PS.Webpage/ps.mainpage.htm
Earlham Sociology Pages	www.earlhamsociologypages.co.uk/
SocJourn	www.sociology.org/
Harvard Department of Sociology	http://sociology.fas.harvard.edu/pages/resources
The SocioWeb	www.socioweb.com/
Association for Applied and Clinical Sociology	www.aacsnet.net/
Sociology at Work	www.sociologyatwork.org/about/what-is-applied-sociology/
Understanding the World Today	http://gsociology.icaap.org/

References

Allan, J. (2017). Women's contributions to classical sociology. In N. Thompson and G. Cox (Eds.). *Handbook of the sociology of death, grief and bereavement*. New York: Routledge, pp. 85–100.

Althusser, L. (1971). *Lenin and philosophy, and other essays*. London: New Left Books.

Appignanesi, L. (2008). *Mad, bad and sad: A history of women and the mind doctors from 1800 to the present*. London: Virago.

Applewhite, A. (2016). *This chair rocks: A manifesto against ageism*. New York: Networked Books.

Armstrong, J. (2013). *Life lessons from Nietzsche*. London: Macmillan.

Back, L. (2007). *The art of listening*. Oxford: Berg.

Back, L. and Solomos, J. (Eds.) (2009). *Theories of race and racism: A reader* (2nd Edn.). London: Routledge.

Bauman, Z. (2010). *44 letters from the liquid modern world*. Cambridge, UK: Polity Press.

Bauman, Z. (2014). *What use is sociology?* Cambridge, UK: Polity Press.

Bauman, Z. and May, T. (2001). *Thinking sociologically* (2nd Edn.). Oxford: Blackwell.

Beauvoir, S. de (1972). *The second sex*. Harmondsworth, UK: Penguin.

Beck, U. (1999). *The brave new world of work*. Frankfurt/New York: Campus Verlag.

Beck, U. (2002). Beyond status and class? In U. Beck and E. Beck-Gernsheim, *Individualization*. London: Sage, pp. 30–41.

Bentall, R. P. (2010). *Doctoring the mind: Why psychiatric treatments fail*. London: Penguin.

Bentall, R. P., Corcoran, C., Howard, R., Blackwood, R. and Kinderman, P. (2001). Persecutory delusions: A review and theoretical integration. *Clinical Psychology Review*, 21, pp. 1143–92.

Berger, P. and Luckmann, T. (1967). *The social construction of reality*. Harmondsworth: Penguin.

Bernstein, W. J. (2013). *Masters of the word*. New York: Grove Press.

Birchwood, M., Meaden, A., Trower, P., Gilbert, P. and Plaistow, J. (2000). The power and omnipotence of voices: Subordination and entrapment by voices and significant others. *Psychological Medicine*, 30, pp. 337–44.

Bourdieu, P. (1977). *Outline of a theory of practice*. Cambridge: Cambridge University Press.

Bourdieu, P. (1986). *Distinction: A social critique of the judgement of taste*. London: Routledge & Kegan Paul.

Bourdieu, P. (1988). *Language and symbolic power*. Cambridge: Polity Press.

Bourdieu, P. and Wacquant, L. (1992a). *An invitation to reflexive sociology*. Cambridge: Polity.

Buroway, M. (2005). For public sociology: Presidential address. *American Sociological Review*, 70, pp. 4–28.

Bushman, B. J. (Ed.) (2016). *Aggression and violence: A social psychological perspective*. Hove, UK: Psychology Press.

Cann, P. and Dean, M. (Eds.) (2009). *Unequal ageing: The untold story of exclusion in old age*. Bristol: The Policy Press.

Cavanaugh, W. T. (2009). *The myth of religious violence: Secular ideology and the roots of modern conflict*. New York: Open University Press.

Chamberlin, J. (1997). A working definition of empowerment. *Psychiatric Rehabilitation Journal*, 20(4), pp. 43–6.

Chomsky, N. (2012). *Power systems*. London: Penguin.

Cockburn, P. (2015). *The rise of Islamic State: ISIS and the new Sunni revolution*. London: Verso.

Cohen, C. I. and Timini, S. (Eds.) (2008). *Liberatory psychiatry: Philosophy, politics and mental health*. Cambridge: Cambridge University Press.

Coleman, P. T. and Ferguson, R. (2014). *Making conflict work*. London: Piatkus.

Connell, R. W. and Pearse, R. (2015). *Gender in world perspective* (3rd Edn.). Cambridge: Polity.

Corby, B., Shemmings, D. and Wilkins, D. (2012). *Child abuse: An evidence base for confident practice* (4th Edn.). Maidenhead: Open University Press.

Cottrell, S. (2011). *Critical thinking skills: Developing effective analysis and argument*. Basingstoke, UK: Palgrave Macmillan.

Cox, G. R. (2017). George Herbert Mead. In N. Thompson and G. R. Cox (Eds.). *Handbook of the sociology of death, grief and bereavement*. New York: Routledge, pp. 60–72.

Crossley, N. (2006). *Contesting psychiatry: Social movements in mental health*. London: Routledge.

Cumming, E. and Henry, W. E. (1961). *Growing old*. New York: Basic Books.

Cupach, W. R. and Metts, S. (2008). Face theory: Goffman's dramatistic approach to interpersonal communication. In L. Baxter and D. Braithwaite (Eds.). *Engaging theories in interpersonal communication: Multiple perspectives*. Los Angeles, CA: Sage Publications, pp. 203–14.

Davidson, A. (2014). *Social determinants of health*. Oxford: Oxford University Press.

Davie, G. (2013). *The sociology of religion: A critical agenda* (2nd Edn.). Thousand Oaks, CA: Sage.

Davies, J. (2013). *Cracked: Why psychiatry is doing more harm than good*. London: Icon.

Dobratz, B. A. and Shanks-Meile, S. L. (2000). *The white separatist movement in the United States: "White power, white pride!"* Baltimore, MD: Johns Hopkins University Press.

Doel, M. and Kelly, T. B. (2014). *A-Z of groups and groupwork*. Basingstoke, UK: Palgrave Macmillan.

Doka, K. J. (Ed.) (1989). *Disenfranchised grief: Recognizing hidden sorrow*. San Francisco, CA: Jossey-Bass.

Doka, K. J. (Ed.) (2001). *Disenfranchised grief: New directions, challenges, and strategies for practice*. Champaign, IL: Research Press.

Doka, K. J. and Martin, T. L. (2010). *Grieving beyond gender: Understanding the ways men and women mourn* (2nd Edn.). New York: Routledge.

Dorling, D. (2011). *Injustice*. Bristol, UK: Policy Press.

Dorling, D. (2013). *Unequal health: The scandal of our times*. Bristol: The Policy Press.

Dorling, D. (2014). *Inequality and the 1%*. London: Verso.

Dorling, D. (2015). *Injustice: How social inequality still persists* (2nd Edn.). Bristol, UK: The Policy Press.

Dorling, D. (2017). *The equality effect: Improving life for everyone*. London: New Internationalist Publications.

Duncombe, S. (2002). *Cultural resistance*. London: Verso.

Durkheim, E. (2013). *The division of labour in society*. Basingstoke, UK: Palgrave Macmillan.

Edward, J., Ruskin, N. and Turrini, P. (2015). *Separation/individuation: Theory and application*. New York: Routledge.

Fine, C. (2011). *Delusions of gender: The real science behind sex differences*. London: Icon Books.

Foucault, M. (1972). *The archaeology of knowledge*. London: Tavistock.

Foucault, M. (1975). *The birth of the clinic: An archaeology of medical perception*. New York: Vintage Books.

Foucault, M. (1977). *Discipline and punish: The birth of the prison*. London: Allen Lane.

Foucault, M. (1988). Practicing criticism, or "Is it really important to think?" May 30–31, 1981. In L. Kritzman (Ed.). *Foucault, politics, philosophy, culture*. New York: Routledge, pp. 85–96.

Frenkel, E., Kugelmass, S., Nathan, M. and Ingraham, L. (1995). Locus of control and mental health in adolescence and adulthood. *Schizophrenia Bulletin*, 21, pp. 219–26.

Friedman, R. (2014). *The best place to work: The art and science of creating an extraordinary workplace*. New York: Perigee.

Furedi, F. (2004). *Therapy culture: Cultivating vulnerability in an uncertain age*. London: Routledge.

Gergen, K. J. (2009). *Invitation to social construction* (2nd Edn.). London: Sage.

Giddens, A. (1979). *Central problems in social theory: Action, structure and contradiction in social analysis*. London: Macmillan.

Giddens, A. and Sutton, P. W. (2014). *Essential concepts in sociology*. Cambridge: Polity.

Gilbert, P. and Allen, S. (1998). The role of defeat and entrapment (arrested flight) in depression: An exploration of an evolutionary view. *Psychological Medicine*, 28, pp. 585–98.

Goffman, E. (1990a). *Presentation of self in everyday life*. London: Penguin.

Goffman, E. (1990b). *Stigma: Notes on the management of spoiled identity*. London: Penguin.

Goldacre, B. (2013). *Bad pharma: Hoe medicine is broken and how we can fix it*. London: Fourth Estate.

Gorz, A. (1999). *Reclaiming work: Beyond the wage-based society*. Cambridge: Polity Press.

Hall, S. (1996). The problem of ideology: Marxism without guarantees. In D. Morley and K-H. Chen (Eds.). *Stuart Hall: Critical dialogues in cultural studies*. London: Routledge, pp. 25–46.

Hames, R. D. (2007). *The five literacies of leadership: What authentic leaders know and you need to find out*. Chichester, UK: John Wiley.

Hamilton, M. (2001). *The sociology of religion: Theoretical and comparative perspectives* (2nd Edn.). London: Routledge.

Harris, P. (2005). *Drug induced: Addiction and treatment in perspective*. Lyme Regis, UK: Russell House Publishing.

Harari, Y. N. (2011). *Sapiens: A brief history of humankind*. London: Vintage Books.

Hari, J. (2015). *Chasing the scream*. London: Bloomsbury.

Harms, L. (2018). Narrative approaches. In N. Thompson and P. Stepney (Eds.). *Social work theory and methods: The essentials*. New York: Routledge.

Harris, A. (2014). *Distributed leadership matters: Perspectives, practicalities, and potential*. Thousand Oaks, CA: Corwin.

Haworth, J. and Hart, G. (Eds.) (2012). *Well-being: Individual, community and social perspectives*. Basingstoke, UK: Palgrave Macmillan.

Hopkins, A. E. (2015). Face management theory: Modern conceptualizations and future directions. *Inquiries*, 7(4), pp. 1–6.

Hunt, S. (2016). *The life course: A sociological introduction* (2nd Edn.). London: Palgrave.

Hyde, B. (2008). *Children and spirituality: Searching for meaning and connectedness*. London: Jessica Kingsley Publishers.

Illouz, E. (2012). *Why love hurts*. Cambridge: Polity.

Jaeckel, M. (1991). Clinical sociology. *Teaching Sociology*, 19(1), pp. 96–102.

James, O. (2007). *Affluenza*. London: Vermillion.

James, O. (2008). *The selfish capitalist: Origins of affluenza*. London: Vermillion.

Jandt, F. E. (2015). *An introduction to intercultural communication: Identities in a global community* (8th Edn.). Thousand Oaks, CA: Sage.

Jones, O. (2015). *The Establishment and how they get away with it*. London: Penguin.

Kennedy-Pipe, C., Clubb, G., Mabon, S. and Schmid, A. P. (Eds.) (2015). *Terrorism and political violence*. Thousand Oaks, CA: Sage.

Langan, M. and Lee, P. (Eds.) (1989). *Radical social work today*. London: Unwin Hyman.

Law, J. (1994). *Organizing modernity: Social ordering and social theory*. Hoboken, NJ: Wiley-Blackwell.

Ledwith, M. (2011). *Community development: A critical approach* (2nd Edn.). Bristol: The Policy Press.

Leonard, E. (2015). *Crime, inequality, and power*. New York: Routledge.

Lin, N. (2002). *Social capital: A theory of social structure and action*. Cambridge: Cambridge University Press.

Lombard, N. and McMillan, L. (2013). *Violence against women: Current theory and practice in domestic abuse, sexual violence and exploitation*. London: Jessica Kingsley Publishers.

Lund, B. (2011). *Understanding housing policy*. Bristol, UK: Policy Press.

McKittrick, D. and McVea, D. (2012). *Making sense of the troubles: A history of the Northern Ireland conflict*. London: Penguin.

McNamee, S. (2016). *The social study of childhood*. London: Palgrave.

Marx, K. (1845). Theses on Feuerbach. In F. Marx and F. Engels (Eds.) (1968). *Selected works*. London: Lawrence & Wishart, pp. 28–30.

Marx, K. and Engels, F. (2011). *The German ideology*. Eastford, CT: Martino Fine Books.

Maton, K. (2012). Habitus. In M. Grenfell (Ed.). *Bourdieu: Key concepts* (2nd Edn.). Durham, UK: Acumen, pp. 48–64.

Matthewman, S. and West-Newman, C. L. (2013). Introduction: Being sociological. In S. Matthewman, C. L. West-Newman, and B. Curtisds (Eds.). *Being sociological* (2nd Edn.). London: Palgrave, pp. 1–20.

Matthewman, S., West-Newman, C. L. and Curtis, B. (Eds.) (2013). *Being sociological* (2nd Edn.). London: Palgrave.

Maturana, H. and Varela, F. J. (1980). *Autopoiesis and cognition: The realizations of the living.* London: Reidl.

May, V. M. (2015). *Pursuing intersectionality: Unsettling dominant imaginaries.* London: Routledge.

Mead, G. H. (1967). *Mind, self and society.* Chicago: University of Chicago Press.

Mendoza, K.-A. (2015). *Austerity: The demolition of the welfare state and the rise of the zombie economy.* London: New Internationalist.

Mills, C. W. (1959). *The sociological imagination.* New York: Oxford University Press.

Mitchell, P. R. and Schoeffel, J. (Eds.) (2002). *Understanding power: The indispensable Chomsky.* London: Vintage.

Mooney, A. and Evans, B. (2015). *Language, society and power: An introduction* (4th Edn.). London: Routledge.

Neimeyer, R. A., Harris, D. L. M., Winokuer, H. R. and Thornton, G. F. (Eds.) (2011). *Grief and bereavement in contemporary society.* New York: Routledge.

Nettleton, S. (2013). *The sociology of health and illness* (3rd Edn.). Cambridge: Polity.

Oliver, M. and Barnes, C. (2012). *The new politics of disablement* (2nd Edn.). Basingstoke, UK: Palgrave Macmillan.

Piketty, T. (2014). *Capital in the twenty-first century.* Cambridge, MA: Belknap, Harvard.

Pink, D. (2011). *Drive: The surprising truth about what motivates us.* London: Canongate Books.

Rice, J. S. (1996). *A disease of one's own: Psychotherapy, addiction and the emergence of co-dependency.* New Brunswick, NJ: Transaction.

Rogers, A. and Pilgrim, A. (2014). *A sociology of mental health and illness* (5th Edn.). Maidenhead, UK: Open University Press.

Ryan, W. (1988). *Blaming the victim: Ideology serves the establishment* (2nd Edn.). London: Pantheon.

Sartre, J-P. (1958). *Being and nothingness.* London: Methuen.

Sartre, J-P. (1969). *Being and nothingness: An essay on phenomenological ontology.* London: Methuen.

Sartre, J-P. (1973). *Search for a method.* New York: Vintage.

Sartre, J-P. (2004). *Critique of dialectical reason.* Volume 1. London: Verso.

Schnall, P. L., Dobson, M. and Rosskam, E. (Eds.) (2009). *Unhealthy work: Causes, consequences, cures.* Amityville, NY: Baywood.

Selten, J-P. and Cantor-Graae, R. (2007). Hypothesis: Social defeat as a risk factor for schizophrenia. *British Journal of Psychiatry*, 191(suppl. 51), pp. S9–12.

Shaw, R. (2013). Relating: Families. In S. Matthewman, C. L. West-Newman, and B. Curtis (Eds.). *Being sociological* (2nd Edn.). London: Palgrave, pp. 175–94.

Smart, C. (2011). Children's personal lives. In V. May (Ed.). *Sociology of personal life.* Basingstoke, UK: Palgrave Macmillan, pp. 98–108.

Smith, E. (2012). *Key issues in education and social justice.* Thousand Oaks, CA: Sage.

Sprintzen, D. (2009). *Critique of western philosophy and social theory.* Basingstoke, UK: Palgrave Macmillan.

Steele, S. F., Scarisbrick-Hauser, A. and Hauser, W. J. (1999). *Solution-centered sociology: Addressing problems through applied sociology.* Thousand Oaks, CA: Sage.

Stiglitz, J. E. (2013). *The price of inequality.* London: Penguin.

Stones, R. (2005). *Structuration theory.* Basingstoke, UK: Palgrave Macmillan.

Swain, J., French, S., Barnes, C. and Thomas, C. (Eds.) (2014). *Disabling barriers, enabling environments: An introduction to disability studies*. London: Sage.

Tew, J. (2011). *Social approaches to mental distress*. Basingstoke, UK: Palgrave Macmillan.

Thompson, N. (2007). *Power and empowerment*. Lyme Regis, UK: Russell House Publishing.

Thompson, N. (2009). *Loss, grief and trauma in the workplace*. Amityville, NY: Baywood.

Thompson, N. (2011a). *Effective communication: A guide for the people professions* (2nd Edn.). Basingstoke, UK: Palgrave Macmillan.

Thompson, N. (2011b). *Effective teamwork*. An e-book published by Avenue Media Solutions.

Thompson, N. (2012a). *Grief and its challenges*. London: Palgrave.

Thompson, N. (2012b). *The people solutions sourcebook* (2nd Edn.). Basingstoke, UK: Palgrave Macmillan.

Thompson, N. (2013). *People management*. Basingstoke, UK: Palgrave Macmillan.

Thompson, N. (2015a). *Stress matters*. An e-book published by Avenue Media Solutions.

Thompson, N. (2015b). *Tackling bullying and harassment in the workplace*. An e-book published by Avenue Media Solutions.

Thompson, N. (2015c). *Understanding social work: Preparing for practice* (4th Edn.). London: Palgrave.

Thompson, N. (2016a). *The authentic leader*. London: Palgrave.

Thompson, N. (2016b). *Anti-discriminatory practice: Equality, diversity and social justice* (6th Edn.). London: Palgrave.

Thompson, N. (2016c). Spirituality in a materialist world. In D. L. Harris and T. Bordere (Eds.). *Handbook of social justice in loss and grief: Exploring, equity, diversity and inclusion*. New York: Routledge, pp. 191–201.

Thompson, N. (2017a). *Social problems and social justice*. London: Palgrave.

Thompson, N. (2017b). *Theorizing practice* (2nd Edn.). London: Palgrave.

Thompson, N. (2017c). Religion and spirituality. In N. Thompson and G. R. Cox (Eds.). *Handbook of the sociology of death, grief and bereavement*. New York: Routledge, pp. 337–50.

Thompson, N. (2018). *Promoting equality: Working with diversity and difference* (4th Edn.). London: Palgrave.

Thompson, N. and Bates, J. (Eds.) (2009). *Promoting workplace well-being*. Basingstoke, UK: Palgrave Macmillan.

Thompson, N. and Bevan, D. (2015). Death in the workplace. *Illness, Crisis & Loss* 23(3): pp. 211–225.

Thompson, N. and Cox, G. R. (Eds.) (2017). *Handbook of the sociology of death, grief and bereavement*. New York: Routledge.

Thompson, S. (2015). *Reciprocity and dependency in old age: Indian and UK perspectives*. New York: Springer.

Thompson, S. (2016). Promoting reciprocity in old age: A social work challenge. *Practice: Social Work in Action*, 28(5), pp. 341–55.

Thompson, S. and Thompson, N. (2008). *The critically reflective practitioner*. Basingstoke, UK: Palgrave Macmillan.

Thomson, P. (2012). Field. In M. Grenfell (Ed.). *Bourdieu: Key concepts* (2nd Edn.). Durham, UK: Acumen, pp. 65–80.

Thornicroft, G. (2006). *Shunned: Discrimination against people with mental illness*. Oxford: Oxford University Press.

Tummey, R. and Turner, T. (Eds.) (2008). *Critical issues in mental health*. Basingstoke, UK: Palgrave Macmillan.

Turner, J. H. (2011). *The problem of emotions in society*. London: Routledge.

Ussher, J. M. (1991). *Women's madness: Misogyny or mental illness?* Amherst, MA: University of Massachusetts Press.

Walker, J. and Knauer, V. (2011). Humiliation, self-esteem and violence. *The Journal of Forensic Psychiatry and Psychology*, 22(5), pp. 724–41.

Weber, M. (1930). *The protestant ethic and the spirit of capitalism*. London: George Allen & Unwin.

West-Newman, C. L. (2013). Feeling: Emotions. In S. Matthewman, C. L. West-Newman, and B. Curtis (Eds.). *Being sociological* (2nd Edn.). London: Palgrave, pp. 195–212.

Wilkinson, R. G. and Pickett, K. (2009). *The spirit level: Why more equal societies almost always do better*. London: Allen Lane.

Witcher, S. (2015). *Inclusive equality: A vision for social justice*. Bristol: The Policy Press.

Wrong, D. H. (1961). The oversocialized conception of man in modern sociology. *American Sociological Review*, 26(2), pp. 183–93.

Index